D0903104

Hospitals and Health-Care Facilities

Butterworth Architecture Design and Development Guides

9 10

Hospitals and Health-Care Facilities

A Design and Development Guide

Anthony Cox
CBE, AADipl, FRIBA

Philip Groves
FRIBA, DL
Chairman, Architects' Co-Partnership

Butterworth Architecture
London Boston Sydney Singapore Wellington Toronto

O
RA
967
.C65
1990

Butterworth Architecture
is an imprint of Butterworth Scientific

 PART OF REED INTERNATIONAL P.L.C.

All rights reserved. No part of this publication may be reproduced in any
material form (including photocopying or storing it in any medium by electronic
means and whether or not transiently or incidentally to some other use of this
publication) without the written permission of the copyright owner except in
accordance with the provisions of the Copyright, Designs and Patents Act 1988 or
under the terms of a licence issued by the Copyright Licensing Agency Ltd,
33–34 Alfred Place, London, England WC1E 7DP. Applications for the copyright
owner's written permission to reproduce any part of this publication should be
addressed to the Publishers.

Warning: The doing of an unauthorised act in relation to a copyright work may
result in both a civil claim for damages and criminal prosecution.

This book is sold subject to the Standard Conditions of Sale of Net Books and may
not be re-sold in the UK below the net price given by the Publishers in their current
price list.

First edition published in 1981 as *Design for Health Care*

This edition first published 1990

© **Butterworth & Co. (Publishers) Ltd, 1990**

British Library Cataloguing in Publication Data

Cox, Anthony
    Hospitals and health care facilities: a design and
    development guide.—Rev. 2nd. ed.
    1. Health services. Buildings. Design
    I. Title   II. Groves, Philip   III. Cox, Anthony.
    Design for health care
    725.5

ISBN 0-408-03189-1

Library of Congress Cataloging in Publication Data

Cox, Anthony, CBE.
    Hospitals and health care facilities.

    Rev. ed. of: Design for health care. 1981.
    Includes bibliographical references.
    1. Health facilities—Design and construction.
I. Groves, Philip.   II. Cox, Anthony, CBE.   Design for
health care.   III. Title.   [DNLM: 1. Health facilities.
2. Hospital Design and Construction   WX 140 C877d]
RA967.C65   1990   725′.5   89-71262
ISBN 0-408-03189-1

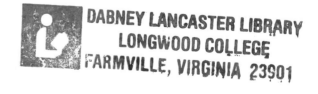
DABNEY LANCASTER LIBRARY
LONGWOOD COLLEGE
FARMVILLE, VIRGINIA 23901

Composition by Genesis Typesetting, Borough Green, Sevenoaks, Kent
Printed and bound in Great Britain by Courier International Ltd., Tiptree, Essex

Preface

Medical science and technology advance rapidly and there is little reason to suppose that the pace will slacken. In drugs, antibiotics, surgery and in the alleviation of nearly all forms of illness and infirmity there have been dramatic developments in the lifetime of many of us. Pioneered in what are known as the developed countries, the impact of these advances is reaching the whole of the inhabited globe, for communications and social attitudes have combined to bring the possibilities of health care to the consciousness of an ever increasing number of people. The process seems irreversible. Preventing sickness, alleviating it when it occurs and saving life when this is possible have long attracted individual effort; these aims are now becoming generally recognised as social imperatives. The potential expense of the acceleration of health care is incalculable; for those involved in its development it is a mountain to be scaled, but for the exchequer it is a bottomless pit.

Health care impels the provision of a wide variety of buildings, to serve many different functions and accommodate the whole life span of man. Shelter is needed for the promotion of health and the prevention of sickness, for assisting natural functions like childbirth, for curing disabilities and repairing malfunctions and for supporting the afflicted and incapacitated. This shelter may be said to fall into a number of generic types, but although medical knowledge is largely international the ways in which it is applied and in which care is delivered in one country and another are likely to differ, as are the forms of building appropriate to the particular circumstances. Although sharing similarities, the forms are likely to reflect the nature of the organisation, culture, economy and geography of their situation, and even the peculiarities of their social microclimate.

There are no simple universal solutions. All countries, and even differing areas of the same country, present their own problems and demand different answers; they range from the huge and highly automated hospital to the itinerant barefoot doctor who needs no premises. It is dangerous to generalise but it is probably reasonable to make a broad distinction between the developed and the developing world and to suggest that it is unwise to apply to the latter the solutions of the former without recognising fundamental dissimilarities. There are often great differences between them in religious belief, in social attitudes and in their physical and cultural infrastructure. The diseases to be mastered also differ, as do the imperatives of climate and the available manpower for staffing. Above all, in whatever part of the world health care is demanded the financial resources to initiate the facilities and to provide for their continuing operation are always limited.

It has been well said that the first task of a health service is to reach all the people all the time at the best level of care that a country can afford. This raises questions of political outlook and priority beyond the scope of this book, which is primarily about buildings. But it must be said that buildings are not the principal source of health care and that although shelter of various degrees of sophistication is usually necessary, and although the form that shelter takes can either help or hinder the tasks performed within it, it is the care itself

that matters. And this depends on people; on doctors and surgeons, nurses and auxiliaries, chemists, cooks and social workers, technicians and administrators, cleaners and maintenance staff organised in a system within which everyone can be encouraged to work in an interrelated way for the same human purpose. And all these must be supported by finance and supplies, and reinforced by a system of education and training that can assure continuous reinforcements to their numbers.

This book attempts to explain the functions of a wide range of buildings for health care but it does not cover them all. It is not a reference book; it is intended to be an introduction and assumes no special knowledge from the reader. Its context is those societies in which health care is deliberately organised, whether by state control, insurance arrangements or voluntary effort, or by some combination of these approaches. Although much of it is based on British practice it looks at both the developed and the developing world and examines the principal types of building needed at each level of care in relation to the whole system within which they operate. These range from those at the grass roots, nearest people's homes, through local surgeries and health centres to the small hospital, the general hospital, the teaching hospital, the private hospital, and the services for mental illness and mental handicap, the elderly and the dying. The function of each facility is outlined, together with the type of activity it houses and the physical arrangements likely to help the activity. The book can do no more than give an outline of the background against which more detailed publications, of which there are many and which often express divergent views, can be seen in perspective.

There is probably more detailed literature with a bearing on buildings for health care than on any other category of architecture. The briefing documents that architects have to assimilate, particularly if their buildings are part of a nationally funded programme, are often in such scrupulous detail that they can be intimidating. Not only that, but their projects are likely to be circumscribed by rigorous limits of space and cost. In Britain the guidance from the responsible Ministry, whether mandatory or advisory, is invaluable; but it is so extensive that it can be hard to see the wood for the trees.

Health services are rich in articulate and dedicated professionals with strong views, and on some matters there may be little consensus of opinion. To write about the design of buildings for health care is to walk through a minefield, with the danger not only of treading on explosive material but also the risk of setting off detonations in surrounding areas. Readers are warned not to seek any easy answers in this book and to appreciate that many of its generalisations may be open to challenge.

Much of this book is based on our earlier publication *Design for Health Care* but the text has been extended, amended and brought up to date where necessary. Most of the original illustrations are retained but many new examples have been added. There are new chapters on the private sector, the care of the elderly and on terminal care. At the time that the text was being completed the British Government issued its White Paper on the Health

DABNEY LANCASTER LIBRARY

1000145742

v

Services, 'Working for Patients'. It is too soon to predict the outcome but we have added a few references where it seems appropriate.

A book of this nature necessarily relies on the work, thought and experience of many people, and on their writings – or if they are architects more often on their designs. It is impossible to acknowledge them all, and if we have misinterpreted some of them the fault is ours. Besides the architects, health authorities and others who have supplied us with plans, photographs and descriptions, and the organisations that have given permission for reproduction, we are grateful for the help of people who have read parts of the text or who have volunteered information. Their advice may not always have been followed in the way they might have wished and none of them bears any responsibility for the result, but we could not have done without them.

We are particularly indebted to Frances Aitken of the Maudsley Hospital and to Gerald White, health planner with Architects Co-Partnership, for their help and to the architect Roger Dixon for valuable suggestions, to Brian Ellsmoor, of the architects Stewart Hendry and Smith, for his guidance on hospices, and to Oliver Rowell of Nuffield Hospitals for his help on Independent Hospitals. We are also grateful to the British Architectural Library at the RIBA for their searches. Finally, once again, we thank the Kings Fund Library, whose resources have been invaluable.

Anthony Cox
Philip Groves

Contents

1

The organisation of health care

Health care presents a different problem in every country, for the way it is organised is a response to geography, climate, historical development, economic situation and social, cultural and political conditions. In the 'advanced' or developed world there is an established and inherited machinery for medical support and a substantial proportion of national resources is devoted to health care.

The various ways in which this is done range from systems of predominantly private enterprise at one extreme to complete State provision at the other, with a variety of combinations in between. In the developing countries, on the other hand, there is usually little inherited machinery of a comparable scale and the provision of health care has to be built up on almost entirely fresh foundations. Appreciation of these differences is fundamental to an understanding of the situation which prevails in a country.

The developed and the developing world

In the USA there are voluntary hospitals and other establishments owned by philanthropic organisations both religious and secular, including many belonging to sickness insurance funds. There are also private establishments run on a commercial basis, and municipal, State and Federal establishments for those unable to afford other forms of care. Broadly, the middle classes have private insurance arrangements and use private sources of care based on fees; the poor and the racial minorities have little choice but to use the local county or city hospital.

Co-ordination is by mutual agreement between the various establishments and the maintenance of technical and medical standards is exercised by independent professional associations. This is not unlike the arrangements that prevailed in the UK prior to 1939.

At the other extreme, in the Socialist countries of Eastern Europe there are no private hospitals. All hospitals are part of the public service for preventive and curative health; they enjoy no autonomy and are virtually State controlled from the centre. In the USSR there are regional, town, district and sector hospitals, and a very large number of polyclinics of which the majority in urban areas are attached to hospitals.

In Western Europe the pattern is dominated by various insurance schemes to which employers and employees contribute. They are largely compulsory. In some countries medical practitioners receive standard fees from the schemes for consultation and treatment at no additional cost to the patient; in others the patient pays a fee and is later reimbursed in whole or in part. Hospital care is dealt with in a similar manner, as are medicines.

In Denmark the whole population has compulsory health insurance. All medical and hospital care is free, financed partly by the state and partly by a local income tax. Insurance schemes fall into two groups: in one (covering over 90% of the population) the patient has a free choice of general practitioner without charge; in the other the doctor can charge more than his standard reimbursable fee. Medicine in hospital is free; outside hospital the patient is reimbursed the cost on a scale of 75% for medicines treating certain defined diseases, 50% for those with a valuable therapeutic effect, and nil in other cases.

In Belgium there are compulsory insurance schemes for almost everyone through a large number of sick funds that levy contributions from employers and employees. These are co-ordinated by a national institute for sickness and invalidity insurance. The patient pays the general practitioner direct and is later reimbursed wholly or in part by his sick fund – the disabled, widows, orphans and pensioners receive 100%. Patients in hospital pay a standard fee for all services; they also pay the doctor and for medicines. The hospital fee is reimbursed in full for stays of up to 40 days, after which the patient pays the whole cost if he can afford it. The cost of medicines is reimbursed on a system similar to that in Denmark.

In France there are social security systems for everyone, with a levy on employers and employees, administered by a board representing employers and unions. General practitioners charge standard fees; specialists can charge more. Patients are reimbursed 80% of the standard fee for consultations, subject to a maximum, but many chronic or severe diseases are treated without charge to the patient. The cost of medicines is reimbursed on a system similar to that in Denmark. The patients nominally pay 20% of the cost of hospital care but maternity and psychiatric beds are free. However, because of the maximum charges mentioned above, almost all hospital care is virtually free.

The system in the Netherlands is similar to that in France but less comprehensive. Some two thirds of the population are insured under a state system through a levy on earnings paid in equal proportions by employers and employees. This provides for doctors, dentists, hospitals and medicines without further charges. The remainder of the population have private health insurance.

In West Germany, where much more is spent on health care than in the UK and there is a surplus of beds, health insurance through one of the many sickness funds is compulsory for all the employed and their dependents. These statutory schemes provide virtually free health care, with minor charges for medicine, dentistry and spectacles. Over 90% of the population belong to them. Hospitals are provided by local authorities and voluntary bodies. Patients attend specialist doctors of their choice at their surgeries; only university hospitals have out-patients departments. The sickness funds negotiate charges with doctors and hospitals according to the service provided, but treatment is free to the patient at the point of delivery.

In the UK there are private hospitals, some of them commercial and many run by insurance organisations, and there are opportunities for private health care from independent professionals. But since 1948 the National Health Service has established a comprehensive system of inter-related social and medical services that, apart from some minor charges, are available to everyone without fee, irrespective of their age, sex, religion, economic position or ailment.

These services are administered by the local municipal authorities and the hospital authorities, who enjoy a degree of autonomy within budgets, guidelines and legislation established by central government. About 86% of the cost of this National Health Service is met by taxation and the remainder by compulsory insurance contributions from all employers and employees, and by various minor charges.

In the developing areas of the world, where there are greater problems and usually slighter resources, the deliberate organisation of health care is expanding rapidly. It follows almost inevitably from economic and social progress, from the expectations generated by education and from the political pressures of the population. Indeed, it can be said that continuing progress can scarcely take place without it.

Governments are impelled to frame a policy for health care and to assume either an executive or advisory role in implementing it. The pattern is increasingly one of provision by the state, with varying degrees of control, frequently working alongside existing private or philanthropic institutions such as missionary organisations or relatively small commercial units patronised by patients who can afford them. The extent and sophistication of the service depends not only on the country's attitude to social welfare and its administrative structure, but more fundamentally on the level of its economic development – on what it can afford to spend.

Primary, secondary and tertiary care

Whatever their administrative organisation and however they are financed, all systems of health care delivery comprise a range of institutions which, at least in theory, are graded according to their degree of sophistication and specialisation and the level of care that they can provide.

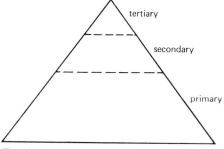

The Health Pyramid

Three main levels can be identified and are usually termed primary, secondary and tertiary. Primary care embraces all the general health practice services, educational, preventive and curative, that are offered to the population at the point of entry into the system. Secondary care comprises the care provided by more specialised services to which people are referred by the primary care services. Tertiary care includes highly specialised services not normally found at secondary level, including super-specialities such as plastic surgery, neurosurgery and heart surgery.

These are very broad divisions, within which there will be finer gradations depending on the appropriate methods of organisation in a particular country, but as

basic categorisations they are recognised and understood throughout the world.

The principle of referral of patients from a lower level of care to a higher level as a method of sorting them according to their need for specialist diagnosis or the nature or degree of their disabilities is also universally recognised. Less widely recognised perhaps, or at least less widely practised, is a referral system that aims to work in both directions, from lower to higher in the first instance and then in reverse, for example during convalescence.

Primary care

At the primary care level are all those health services which are based in the community and relatively accessible to patients and their families; they are at the periphery of the system. These services include preventative health measures such as immunisation programmes, antenatal and child care, and simple diagnosis and treatment. They are operated by doctors, nurses, medical auxiliaries and social workers based in aid posts, dispensaries, clinics and health centres that serve relatively small numbers of people and are situated as close as possible to their homes. This enables medical and other staff to be in contact with their patients' habitual environment.

In the more developed and urbanised countries much of this primary care is provided by the general medical practitioner, who deals with patients at a personal level. Often this doctor works with colleagues in a group practice which shares the services of at least a trained nurse and a secretary. However, in rural areas of the less developed regions of the world the simplest establishment for primary care may be an aid post manned or visited by one auxiliary worker.

Secondary care

At the secondary level there is the general hospital, to which patients from a wide surrounding area or district are referred when necessary by primary care units for more sophisticated diagnosis or treatment. Hospitals are an indispensable part of the provision that is made for health because there will always be a proportion of patients who need the particular skills and equipment that can be concentrated in them and because they are essential centres for medical and health education and research.

However, hospitals are inevitably a very expensive element in any health service, for they are costly to build and equip and the money necessary to staff and run them can be enormous. Indeed, their annual running costs may be as much as about a third of the initial capital cost of constructing and equipping them. The running costs of a hospital are particularly high if it needs to accept a large number of in-patients instead of treating them as out-patients. If the in-patients have to stay for a long time then the hospital's expenses are increased and its potential effectiveness reduced. Even in economically advanced countries there are newly constructed hospitals which cannot be brought fully or even partly into use because the funds to maintain them in action cannot be assured.

Apart from any other considerations, such as the pattern of population and the stage that a country has reached in its economic development, it must therefore clearly be the aim of health care to avoid the necessity of referring patients to a general hospital if this is medically practicable. When referral to hospital is essential it is desirable that patients should, if possible, receive their specialist diagnosis and treatment as out-patients and be admitted as in-patients only when that degree of care is essential for their recovery. Even in these cases, patients should not be kept in hospital for longer than is absolutely necessary. If these aims are to be achieved it is vital that there should be primary health care and support outside in the community.

No country can afford to concentrate disproportionately on secondary care. In any event the general hospital will, for most people, be a considerable distance from their homes and will present an alien environment. It is also unlikely to be a suitable centre for primary care even for the minority for whom it is within easy reach.

Community hospitals

At the level of hospital care there has, in the opinion of many people, been an unfortunate tendency in some of the developed countries to concentrate large and sophisticated hospitals of between 300 and 1000 or more beds at regional or district centres. This has often meant the neglect of small local units more acceptable to and more easily within reach of the community. This tendency can also be seen in some parts of the developing world. In addition to the relative simplicity of organising large units in urban areas, the prestige of the big establishment seems sometimes to have taken precedence over the fundamental provision of health care that can be available to the more dispersed elements of population. Even in the UK – a relatively close knit and urbanised community with good communications – there is some feeling that this tendency is undesirable. There has been relatively little provision of facilities somewhere between the immediately local and primary level of the general medical practitioner in the consulting room or health centre and the often rather remote District General Hospital.

There have been arguments in favour of the concept of the more accessible hospital with perhaps fifty beds and an emphasis on out-patient treatment and day care, which is closely in touch with local practitioners and health and social workers. A similar function was often performed in the UK before the advent of the National Health Service by the voluntary 'Cottage hospital', as it used to be called, where patients were attended by their own general practitioners. This is a function that is better regarded as an extension of primary care rather than as a lower level of secondary care. Rural hospitals in many of the African countries and in India play a similar role.

With primary care at the local level and secondary care at district level, tertiary care is at regional level in the more highly specialised hospital. This is usually larger than the general hospital and has a greater emphasis on

teaching, particularly of doctors. In most cases there is a close relationship with a medical school and with medical research.

A typical pattern of health care

Although for a variety of reasons it is by no means as simple and tidy as this, the pattern of organised health care at primary and secondary levels in a country such as the UK might theoretically take the following shape in outline. (It should be remembered that the UK has a comprehensive health service and a well-established tradition of local general medical practitioners.) At the primary level we should find the family doctor having, at the most, some 2300 patients on his list (the present average), many of whom he might of course see rarely if at all.

Family doctors, together with dentists, social workers and other health workers would be grouped in health centres or clinics to serve a population of some 15 000, although less in some rural situations and more in the denser urban areas. Some health centres would be linked with a community hospital which might serve a population of the order of 50 000. In these hospitals general medical practitioners could oversee the treatment of those of their patients who need more care than they can receive at home but do not need a higher level of hospitalisation.

At the secondary level, we should find the District General Hospital, with a catchment area of up to about 500 000 people. Although 'general' in name this might well include certain specialities not provided by other district general hospitals in the larger region.

Health care in developing countries

Whilst it may be generally agreed that the desirable theoretical basis for the promotion of health care is the primary, secondary and tertiary system, it is a pattern more easily described than achieved in practice. It implies a hierarchy of increasingly specialised establishments in which there are very many primary units, immediately available to the individual and the family, and relatively few tertiary units which are more remote.

It is the primary level, the foundation of the pyramid, that probably presents the greatest difficulties. Even in the economically advanced, geographically tight knit and demographically relatively stable communities of the UK the primary level is difficult enough to achieve; it is very much more difficult in some of the larger territories of the developing world. In most of these countries economic resources are slight, the population more dispersed, distances are a more formidable obstacle for want of adequate roads and lack of transport, or because of cultural resistance to travelling outside home ground. The relatively few towns with their greater facilities and varied opportunities act as formidable magnets to attract and retain the better educated medical and technical personnel.

Although many developing countries have embarked on programmes of nationally organised health care delivery, the problems of decentralisation of establishments and their administration are such that for many of the rural population the facilities remain out of reach. In some places there has been a tendency to develop relatively sophisticated hospital services at the centre with the intention of expanding the services outwards and downwards, but all too often the intention remains unfulfilled.

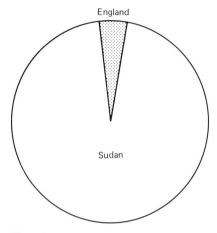

The relative areas of England (population 47.25 million) and the Sudan (population 19.5 million). In 1987 there were 1035 Health Centres in England. Under the 1978/84 National Health Programme for the Sudan 1247 Primary Health Care Units needed to be built during the seven year period

It would be misleading to generalise about the less developed countries of the world, for they have different characteristics and the degree of their development varies. But some measure of the problem of health service delivery can perhaps be appreciated if it is realised that in many regions about three-quarters of the population is scattered in rural areas and that, in spite of migration to the urban centres, the number is likely to rise. Many rural districts are widely dispersed, are isolated and difficult to reach.

Material resources for dealing with the problem are generally minimal. In some Asian and African countries, for example, it was estimated in the early 1970s that the average per capita income was rather less than one-fortieth of that in France and about one-fiftieth of that in the USA. It has been said that if growth stopped in the USA and the growth of Bangladesh doubled annually it would take 200 years for Bangladesh to overtake the wealth of the USA. In this context much of what the west understands by modern health facilities is largely irrelevant for the majority of the people.

The problems of designing buildings to accommodate the basic facilities are not very complicated. They do, however, demand a degree of understanding which is not always appreciated. They will not be solved by the export of sophisticated systems and equipment from the advanced countries, for these can at the best reach only a tiny minority of the population and may present staffing and maintenance obstacles which are insurmountable.

The difference in the scale of the problem between a developed and a developing country can perhaps be expressed diagrammatically, by comparing the areas of England and the Sudan, and the number of health

centres listed for England in the 1987 Hospitals' Year Book with the number of very much simpler, but nevertheless analogous, primary health care units that it was aimed to provide in the Sudan under its five year plan.

The Sudan had placed a high priority on primary health care delivery and had in hand an ambitiously comprehensive programme. Even so, this crude comparison dramatises the differences of population density and distance and demonstrates the irrelevance of applying western criteria to the problem which some of the less developed countries are trying to tackle. This is particularly so if it is appreciated that England possesses a tightly knit network of communications whereas the Sudan has only a few hundred miles of metalled road and in large areas of the country much of the population is nomadic.

Although the Sudan with its huge expanses of desert is not a typical country, either in size, nature or distribution of population, it should not be thought that other developing countries do not have similar difficulties. Frequently the executive strains of their civil authorities – regional, provincial and local – inhibit the decentralisation of the administration of health services and their correlation with other social services such as public health.

Most developing countries have problems arising from distance and lack of transport and telecommunications. They have widely dispersed settlements and relatively few urban centres, poor housing, lack of clean water or adequate drainage, or suitable building materials and labour in the places where they are most needed. Perhaps above all, they have problems of finance and appropriate medical and paramedical staffing, of health education, medical supplies and contact between staff and the patients' homes.

A working party of the Medical Committee of the Conference of Missionary Societies observed in 1975 that in reasonably open and reasonably flat country a high proportion of the population would travel 4.8 km (3 miles) to a health centre but that beyond five miles attendance was sporadic. They concluded that in these circumstances a centre was theoretically required at the middle of every 259 sq km (100 sq miles) of territory. They also noted that a bullock cart can travel for six hours at 3 m.p.h. without halt and that this is a reasonable practicable time between emergency referral at a health centre and reception at a hospital.

It followed, again theoretically, that if the centre was more than about 32 km (20 miles) from the hospital some other form of transport would be needed. These simple figures drive home the realities of the situation in many parts of the world, for the close network of services that might ideally follow from them will clearly be unattainable for a long time.

Grass roots care

National planning, organisation and finance are fundamental to any system of health delivery which can hope to reach all the people, but there is good reason to think that in much of the developing world the most effective results are obtained by building upwards from the grass roots with the involvement of the local community rather than by extending the existing and more sophisticated facilities in the urban centres outwards to the villages.

With the use of relatively simple medical techniques and personnel, and accommodation appropriate and acceptable to the community, priorities are more likely to be in the right order and the primary problems of health education, elementary hygiene, sanitation and nutrition can be tackled at the point where they really matter, and can be seen to matter, and where the improved results from simple medical care can help to breed confidence in the efficacy of new methods.

China probably provides the most vivid example of this approach to basic health care. A policy aimed at the prevention of disease and the enlistment of the population in mass health and sanitation campaigns produced remarkable results. Locally recruited rural youths, 'barefoot doctors' with three months' formal training (of whom in the mid 1970s there were said to be over a million) acted as educators, practiced preventative medicine, and treated minor illnesses. There were analogous worker doctors in the factories and the cities.

Of all countries China presents the clearest picture in recognising the impossibility of developing 'normal' traditional health services based on a doctor–patient relationship if the needs of a large rural population spread over a vast territory are to be met, and of the value of the participation of the community itself in tackling the problem.

Country	Health spending per head (US$)
United States	$1926
Canada	1370
Switzerland	1217
Sweden	1195
Iceland	1072
France	1039
Germany	1031
Norway	1021
Netherlands	984
Luxembourg	968
Austria	903
Finland	900
Australia	877
Japan	831
Belgium	826
Denmark	800
Italy	764
New Zealand	715
United Kingdom	711
Ireland	549
Spain	486
Portugal	310
Greece	247
Turkey	140

Health spending per head in 1986. Figures are in US dollars, using GDP PPPs. Source: OECD Health Data Bank. (PPPs are international price indices which compare the prices of the same set of commodities in different countries)

Health care in the UK

It may be of value to outline the organisational structure of health care in Britain. Here there is a concentrated inheritance of diverse medical and technical skills, of plant and of buildings, and of a complex web of social services related to health care.

The national per capita expenditure on health, great though it is, cannot be said to match some other developed countries, for Britain's expenditure per head in the late 1980s was considerably less than most European countries. But it provides a national service that has brought health care within the reach of everyone and whatever its shortcomings it must be said that it represents good value for money.

The British structure is not described here as a model applicable to all situations, but as an indication of an attempt to provide health care at all levels for the whole population as a single unified service in which the nationalised health authorities and the local government organisations play complementary roles.

Since 1912 there had been a National Health Insurance Scheme which entitled patients to free treatment by a general practitioner and to free medicine, but these benefits were limited to wage earners with relatively low incomes. Those people above this level and the self-employed, wives who did not go out to work, and children, did not qualify. These had either to pay medical fees (or apply for public assistance if they could not afford them) or they might attend the casualty

department of a voluntary charitable hospital. Anyone admitted to hospital, whether insured or not, usually had to pay what the hospital considered appropriate.

By coincidence the British National Health Act of 1948 was passed in the centenary year of the Public Health Act of 1848 that gave powers for the construction of water supply and sewerage to combat the killing infections of the nineteenth century. Thus a hundred years after the infrastructure of primary health care had been laid down a system of health care delivery was established for everyone.

It was a fundamental principle from the beginning of the National Health Service in 1948, and it remains so still, that it should be available to all people, should cover all necessary forms of health care, and should be provided free of charge to the patient at the time of use. (This is in contrast to some other Western European countries where patients pay a proportion of the charge when they avail themselves of the service.) Costs were to be met from taxation and compulsory insurance contributions by employers and employees.

When the National Health Service was introduced most general practitioners became 'independent contractors' to the service and most voluntary hospitals, including teaching hospitals and the hospitals previously run by the local authorities, were transferred to national ownership. Fundamentally it was a rationalisation of already highly but arbitrarily developed health care delivery services to make them available to all in accordance with medical need and by no other criteria.

As the Royal Commission on the service pointed out in 1979, one of the most significant achievements was to free people from the fear of being unable to afford treatment for acute or chronic illness. That patients often waited too long for treatment had to be seen in the light of disappointingly slow national economic growth and the mounting costs which were in no small part a consequence of developments in medical, nursing and therapeutic techniques to levels of sophistication and expense that were not originally foreseen. For example, medical interventions such as heart surgery, organ transplants and hip replacements were not feasible when the service was begun.

It may be added that as any health service develops so do people's expectations and demands increase: it has been said of the USA that if the demand for health care was to be fully met, the entire national budget would need to be devoted to this one social service.

At its inception the service was organised in three separate parts – the family practitioner services, the hospital and specialist services, and those health services which were provided by the local authorities. Because it was based on existing establishments, each of these three parts was organised within different geographical boundaries and was separately planned and financed.

However, the financial provision was soon found to be inadequate and supplementary funding became necessary. A committee of enquiry was appointed; it reported in 1956 that there was no evidence of extravagance or inefficiency but that more money should be allocated, and it highlighted the need to remedy the backlog in building work. This led in 1962 to a ten year Hospital Plan, in which the significant concept was the District General Hospital of between 600 and 800 beds, based on catchment areas of 100 000 to 150 000 population.

Because of the interdependence of the three parts the service was reorganised in the mid 1970s to improve their co-ordination and to bring them together under a single authority. The parts comprised the hospitals and specialised services (at the secondary and tertiary levels), the family practitioner services and school health service, and the personal health services together with environmental health (housing, sanitation, refuse disposal, etc). Personal health services include health centres, health visiting, home nursing and midwifery, maternity and child health care, family planning, medical and nursing arrangements for the prevention of illness, vaccination, immunisation and epidemiological work, and all the ambulance services.

The structure of the service was organised on three administrative levels: central, regional and area. Some areas were subdivided into districts. The central government Department of Health and Social Security was responsible to Parliament for the health services as a whole. This government department determined national policy, carried out the central strategic planning and monitored the operational results. It settled the nature and scale of the services provided throughout the country, allocated resources to regions, and carried out some types of research and purchasing.

Most Area Health Authorities were broken down into Health Districts. Outside London there were one hundred and fifty-four Districts, varying in number between one and five per area. A District usually served a population of between 200 000 and 500 000 and it was on the District that the day-to-day running of services was based.

In a consultative paper, *Patients First*, published at the end of 1979, the Government announced its intention of simplifying the structure in England. The aim was to encourage as many management decisions as possible to be taken at a local level, in the hospital and the community, with the minimum of interference from central authorities.

There had been widespread criticism that the reorganisation of the mid-1970's had produced too many tiers and too many administrators, resulting in a top heavy bureaucracy unable to take decisions quickly. Consequently the Area tier was eliminated and district health authorities had a much greater degree of autonomy; the regions co-ordinated strategic plans and allocated resources but could stand back from the operational activities of the districts.

The intention was that, ideally, the new district authorities should be responsible for a locality which was 'natural' in terms of social geography and health care and large enough to justify the range of specialities normally provided by a district general hospital. Its boundaries would coincide with those of the other authorities responsible for social services, housing and education. In the main the districts would have populations of between 200 000 and 500 000.

Thus from 1982 onwards the structure became simpler. Areas were eliminated, and in England new District Health Authorities, of which there were 190, combined the functions of the previous Areas and Districts and were directly responsible to the Regional Health Authorities, which in turn were responsible to the central DHSS.

There was one further change in the mid 1980s, although it did not affect the basic structure. The Griffiths Report of 1983 on the use of resources, manpower and management recommended the introduction of general managers to give leadership, seek improvements in efficiency and motivate staff. The appointment of General Managers at all levels followed.

Altogether National Health Service hospitals now provide nearly half a million beds in addition to outpatient and accident and emergency services. They range from the large psychiatric hospital to the local 'cottage' hospital with 50 beds or less. The District General Hospital normally provides between 400 and 1000 beds. Some hospitals have some 'pay beds', which offer a degree of additional privacy and the opportunity of supervision by a consultant of the patient's choice, on the basis of a fee. Until 1980 the number of pay beds fell steadily but has subsequently increased and there are now about 3000.

The cost of the National Health Service is met from three sources. Currently 86% comes from taxation, 11%

from National Insurance contributions by employers and employees, and 3% from prescription, dental and optical charges to patients. Medical attention and hospital care remains free. Apart from the costs of central administration and various minor items the allocation of finance is divided into about 15% to the personal social services through the Local Authorities, 15% to the fees of family practitioners, dentists, opticians and retail pharmacists, and 65% or more to the Health Authorities for the capital and revenue costs of hospital and community health facilities, apportioned between the regions.

In addition to the National Health Service hospitals there are a significant number of independent establishments which provide health care. Finance for private patients can be provided through medical insurance schemes entirely separate from government provisions. Rather than offering comprehensive care or emergency services, the independent hospitals usually cater for specific categories of patients. In the field of surgery they concentrate on 'cold surgery', which can be arranged well in advance.

Such hospitals currently provide about 10 500 beds, a figure that has increased by half in the past decade. Independent nursing homes also provide some 78 000 beds, the great majority of which are for the care of the elderly. Most of these hospitals and homes are relatively small, with well under 100 beds.

The Government White Paper of 1989 did not propose to change the Regional and District divisions of the National Health Service but to reform them 'on business lines'. Nor did it alter funding primarily through taxation or the principle that, except for minor prescription, optical and dental charges, the Service should be available free to everybody. However, the proposals claimed to be – and will be if they are implemented – the most far-reaching reforms since the Service began.

Put simply, they can be said to aim at greater delegation of management, greater efficiency and thus better value for money, by the introduction of competition between the different levels of the Service, between hospitals wherever located – irrespective of district and whether in the public or private sector – and to some extent between general practitioners. In order to create

these incentives for efficient performance it was proposed to establish an internal market for health care in which funds followed the patients according to the destinations to which they were referred. Hospitals attracting the most patients would consequently attract the most income from national resources, except that vital services which needed to be provided locally, notably accident and emergency and other immediate admissions, and many geriatric and psychiatric admissions, would remain available irrespective of where the money came from.

Although many of the details remain unclear two critical proposals need to be mentioned. One affects general practitioners and the other National Health Service hospitals. The White Paper proposed that the larger GP practices, with lists of 11 000 patients or more, should be able to apply for their own budgets which they could expend on their patients' treatment at either any National Health Service hospitals or in the private sector – cash following the customers. And it was also intended that for prescriptions all general practitioners should have 'indicative' drug budgets, allocated regionally and broken down and monitored by the Family Practitioner Committees.

It was also proposed that National Health Service acute hospitals of more than 250 beds, of which there are more than 320, and perhaps others, should be able to become self-governing, run by boards of directors as National Health Service Hospital Trusts. They would earn their revenue by their services, through contracts with health authorities, from GP practices with budgets and from private patients, insurers and private hospitals. It was claimed that this method of funding would stimulate better performance and so a bigger share of the financial resources for the successful ones, which would then be able to invest their surplus in better services.

After preparatory administrative changes the White Paper proposed to begin the establishment of National Health Service Hospital Trusts and budgets for general practitioners during 1991. By the time this book is in print there may have been changes. The proposals have not been universally welcomed, particularly by the medical profession.

2

Community health services

The previous chapter emphasised the differences in the scale and nature of health care in the developed and the less developed world. Attention was given to the impracticability, unless it was supported by an infrastructure of primary care, of relying upon the large hospital, which besides being extremely costly to run is necessarily relatively remote, even in an urbanised society, and can have few firm roots in the community.

Primary care in the community

This chapter deals with some examples of units designed for primary care in the community, to which people can have easy access. Whilst they can play a positive role in guidance and the encouragement of health as distinct from dealing with sickness, for most people such units are likely to be their first point of contact with a health service, where they can be treated so that reference to a more specialised establishment is unnecessary. In the UK these are principally the 'surgeries' of the general medical practitioners; they are often grouped together with accommodation for some of the social and public health services and are known as health centres. Associated with the health centre there may be a few beds to provide a small local or community hospital, although this development remains relatively rare.

By contrast, in the less developed areas of the world medical practitioners are generally few and far between and are frequently beyond the pockets of the majority of people. Communities are very much more widely dispersed. Thus the facilities for primary care, although aiming to fulfil a similar function and sometimes known as health centres, are usually of a simpler nature. These are the subject of Chapter 3.

Health centres as places for primary care may be purely preventive or purely curative, or may integrate both these aspects. Integrated health centres where organised preventive services were combined with the primary care of general medical practitioners first appeared in the USSR as part of national policy in the 1920s, when a network of such establishments began to be set up as elements in a regional framework, with polyclinics and hospitals at secondary level.

However, despite the recognition in the British Ministry of Health's Dawson report of 1920 that 'preventive and curative medicine cannot be separated on any sound principle' it was not until 1945 that the concept of organised community care based on the integrated health centre began to gain wide acceptance in the UK, or indeed in most other countries.

'Surgery' or 'health centre' can signify different things. Regrettably they are often used to designate something that might more accurately be described as a centre reluctantly visited by people with minor sickness in the hope that they can be restored to health without having to go to hospital. A unit that demonstrated a different and more positive approach, better fitted to its title, was an independent British project that first attracted some notice over fifty years ago. It is of interest both for the idea behind it and for the physical form into which the idea was translated.

The Pioneer Health Centre at Peckham in South London was a voluntary experiment, independent of government and the local authority. It began in a small way in 1926 and was finally established, much expanded, in purpose-built premises in 1935. Intended as a centre for the local community, where the emphasis was on the promotion and the monitoring of health, local families were invited to use it as a club and as a condition of membership were offered periodic health overhaul of the whole family. It also provided ancillary services for infants, children and adults.

The function of the Pioneer Health Centre was primarily preventive and did not extend to treatment, and its nature was deliberately that of a community centre. Intended for the leisure use of 2000 families it was planned around an indoor swimming pool and had a day nursery and playground, a gymnasium, lounge, cafeteria, library and lecture room, and a few rooms for medical and dental inspection. It was an individual and isolated experiment and was built at a period before a health service was accessible to everybody, when the fear of going to a doctor and of the possible expense and loss of earnings that sickness might involve was very real. The 1939–45 war interrupted its activities and it continued for only a few years afterwards.

An entirely different type of health centre was built by a local authority in Finsbury, London, at about the same time as the Peckham centre. It is perhaps best known because of the attention it attracted architecturally.

The purpose of the Finsbury Health Centre was to bring together under one roof all the health services for which the local authority was responsible, which had previously been dispersed in different parts of the borough. Thus it housed the offices of the departments of the Medical Officer of Health and the Sanitary Inspector, the public cleansing and disinfecting station and the mortuary. For public use it provided a lecture hall and suites of rooms for clinics and treatment, for chiropody, dentistry, tuberculosis and for electrical treatment. But unlike the later health centres in the UK it made no provision for the general medical practitioner, whose services were not a function of the local authority.

In the UK the term health centre is sometimes used to describe the accommodation that, although specially built for the purpose, houses only a group practice of general practitioners with some help from secretaries and a nurse and does not necessarily have the close links with the local authority's personal and social health services that are the characteristic feature of the integrated health centre.

Such accommodation is better called a medical centre or by its customary but rather misleading title of 'surgery'. It is little different in function from the converted domestic accommodation used by many private general practitioners, except that it may be designed to fulfil its purpose more conveniently. It does however share with the integrated health centre some fundamental planning principles, albeit in a simple form, particularly in the arrangements that are desirable for the reception of patients and for the relationship between reception desk, waiting spaces, patient's records and consulting and treatment rooms.

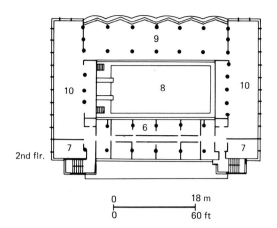

1st flr.

2nd flr.

The core of the Pioneer health Centre at Peckham was the swimming pool, visible through glazed screens from the social rooms flanking it. The Centre was a family club, providing the opportunity for the observation and monitoring of health; throughout the building a sense of community and flexibility of movement was encouraged by open planning and visibility from one area to another. Designer: Sir Owen Williams

```
0              18 m
├──────────────┤
0              60 ft
```

1	lounge and cafeteria	6	medical rooms
2	swimming pool	7	dental
3	lounge	8	upper part pool
4	upper part gym	9	library and rest room
5	upper part lecture hall	10	study and recreation

The Pioneer Health Centre. A day nursery and open-air play space, a gymnasium, lecture theatre and workshops were at ground level. The pool was on the floor above, flanked by lounges and cafeteria. (Photo: Pioneer Health Centre Ltd)

Today the family practitioner services of the National Health Service are administered by Family Practitioner Committees in their particular localities. The boundaries of these committees reflect those of the local authorities so that health and local authority services complement one another. The committees regulate the number of patients a practitioner has on his list – the average in England and Wales is about 2300. Few family doctors now work in single-handed practices; over 80% are in partnership or group practice teams, of which about a quarter work from health centres. Whether in independent group practices or health centres there has been an increasing tendency for practitioners to work in conjunction with nurses, midwives and health visitors and to constitute a primary care team.

1 office and reception
2 waiting
3 toilet
4 consulting
5 treatment

A small 'surgery' for two doctors. The reception office and waiting area are screened from the entrances to the two consulting rooms and the treatment room, which overlook a walled garden. There is a separate entrance for the doctors. Architects: Aldington and Craig

1 entrance hall
2 electrical treatment
3 public toilets
4 staff toilets etc
5 women's clinic
6 dental clinic
7 foot clinic
8 tubucular clinic
9 lecture theatre
10 health visitors
11 terrace
12 public health offices
13 reception wards and kitchen
14 caretaker's flat

Shortly before the 1939–45 War all the health services which were the responsibility of the borough of Finsbury and dispersed in different places were brought together in one building. Offices and clinics occupied the two wings. The borough disinfection and cleansing station and the mortuary were below part of the ground floor, entered from the rear. Architects: Tecton

A patients
B doctors
C treatment and ambulance
1 waiting
2 reception
3 general office
4 consulting
5 treatment/examination rooms
6 treatment
7 stores
8 staff garden
9 staff common room
10 practice manager
11 kitchen
12 doctors' common room
13 toilets
14 plant

A medical centre at Wellingborough, Northamptonshire. Five medical practices share a general office and a fully staffed treatment wing. Each doctor has his own consulting room overlooking a small screened courtyard which also serves as his private entrance. The waiting area can be divided by movable screens into sub-areas for the different practices. Each practice has its own reception desk and a sixth desk controls the treatment wing. The external entrance to the treatment wing is used by patients during clinical sessions and also by ambulances. There is no local authority accommodation. Architects: Aldington and Craig

1 waiting
2 reception
3 general office
4 test room
5 toilet
6 treatment
7 consulting room
8 health visitor
9 common room

0   10M
0   30Ft

A doctors' surgery in Peckham, London, with consulting rooms for four doctors on the ground floor and a common room and office for two health visitors upstairs. It is entered through a walled courtyard. Reception and general office allow discrete staff circulation from one end of the building to the other without interfering with the waiting area, which is arranged in two sections, the larger for the consulting rooms and the smaller near the treatment room. The consulting rooms overlook a small walled garden. Architect: Philip Wharmby

0   5   10M

1 reception	7 toilet
2 records	8 treatment
3 office	9 clinical room
4 common room	10 interview/examination
5 dispensary	11 nurse
6 waiting	

A single storey doctors' surgery at Heckington, Lincolnshire. The waiting area is separated slightly from the main entrance and reception desk, behind which are concentrated the records store, office, common room and dispensary, all intercommunicating independently of patients' circulation. Two consulting rooms flank a similar interview and examination room off a corridor that leads at one end to the treatment room and at the other to a nurses' room. Architects: Medical Architecture Research Unit, Polytechnic of North London

Health centres are owned by the District Health Authorities but practitioners may purchase or rent their own surgery premises. There are government schemes administered by the Family Practitioner Committees; these meet in large measure the costs involved. Except that the accommodation in a health centre may be more extensive than that of a group practice the procedures affecting the planning of the building are similar. Much that is written about health centres in the following pages applies also to group practices.

Health centres in the UK

With the introduction of the National Health Service in 1948 a network of integrated primary health centres was envisaged. It was intended that they should provide accommodation for rent by groups of general medical practitioners, nurses and administrative staff, where they could be housed together with the staff of the preventive services of the local authority.

At first progress was slow and few were built, probably partly because general practitioners, like dentists, chemists and opticians, were independent 'contractors' to the health service and responsible for the provision of their own premises. They were probably reluctant to participate in a nationally organised scheme, fearing that the proposal might be a first step towards becoming state employees and preferring to safeguard their independent position. But for largely practical reasons professional partnerships or group practices steadily increased in popularity during this period, and by the mid 1960s it was estimated that only about a quarter of all general practitioners were still running individual private practices.

By this time the Government had become seriously concerned about the escalating cost of hospital care; it was clear that if this was to be checked a much higher priority needed to be given to care in the community itself – in short, as far as possible to make it unnecessary for patients to be treated in hospital. Increased emphasis was placed on the importance of trying to integrate the work of general practitioners with the socially based services provided by local government. Thus although by the end of 1958 only ten new health centres had been completed in England, by 1968 the number had risen to

1 lobby
2 reception
3 records
4 waiting
5 consulting room
6 toilet
7 duty doctor
8 examination
9 nurse
10 isolation
11 social worker
12 secretaries
13 administrator
14 meeting room
15 terrace

0   10M

A group practice surgery in Highgate, London, for eight doctors. Constrained by a narrow site that slopes downwards from the road and is hemmed in by buildings on both sides, the plan is unorthodox but lucid. The reception counter is immediately apparent from the generous entrance, as is the volume of the top-lit waiting space beyond, which is approached by shallow stairways leading up and down to the two levels of consulting rooms. Consultation is by appointment; doctors leave their rooms and greet the next patient when ready. The arrangement of the consulting rooms is unusual but effective. Examination couch, sink and storage are in a recess which also serves as a screen from the waiting space. Clinical impedimenta do not obtrude into the room. Flanking a small sub-waiting space off the entrance lobby are the nurse's room and the duty doctor's room, accessible by wheelchair and linked by an examination room. Records are stored in bays behind the reception counter and can be deposited in cupboards accessible to the doctors at both lower and upper levels. Upstairs over the entrance are offices, a room for a social worker, and the practice meeting room. Architects: Douglas Stephen and Partners

one hundred and ten and has subsequently continued to increase, although partly for financial reasons the pace has not been as rapid as might have been hoped. Between 1972 and 1977 their number rose from 212 to 731 in England and Wales. There are now well over a thousand in England alone.

The number of patients a general practitioner has on his list in Britain ranges from about 1000 to 3500. On average, practices using health centres comprise four or five practitioners and a group of this size is likely to serve some 15 000 patients; but the size of health centres varies considerably, depending in part on their location, the extent of their catchment area, the policy of the local authority and the number and size of the local group practices that wish to be accommodated in the building.

Buildings range from a centre for a small practice of two or three doctors with a nurse, secretary and a minimum of local authority accommodation (perhaps an office for Home Help and some space for health education) to three or four practices with in addition dental surgeons, physiotherapists, chiropodists, mid-wives, district nurses, health visitors, school health services and, increasingly, provision for the education in community health of medical students, student nurses and student health visitors. From a rural catchment area of some 10 000 people or less at one end of the scale, the centre may cater for a population of 30 000 or more in an urban area.

The more comprehensive the centre's facilities the more difficult it is to provide a building that encourages the integration of a variety of personnel, and the more valuable it will be if it can succeed in doing so. It can, of course, do no more than facilitate and encourage integration, for a team approach to community care does not follow automatically from bringing together in the same building different people with different responsibilities.

Activities in health centres

Activities of health centres and most surgeries are of three types, arranged in sessions which may be daily, weekly or less frequent. Only one of these types of

1   GP reception
2   records and secretaries
3   waiting
4   consulting/examination
5   treatment
6   clean utility
7   dirty utility
8   toilet
9   community health reception
10 health education
11 kitchen
12 interview
13 community health consulting/
    examination
14 dental surgery
15 recovery
16 chiropody
17 health visitors
18 community nurse and district
    nurse
19 seminar and library
20 common room and kitchen
21 administration
22 nursing officers
23 spare
24 courtyard

Langthorne Health Centre, Leytonstone, London. Designed for a group of single independent general practitioners. A single storey building, it is arranged around two courtyards on each side of the central concourse. One courtyard adjoins the doctors' waiting spaces, consulting and treatment rooms, and the other the community health accommodation. Architect: Derek Stow

activity is likely to be taking place at any one time. Firstly, there is personal care, when the patient visits a general practitioner, a nurse or another individual worker, normally on his own initiative, to obtain help or treatment for a personal problem or ailment. Secondly, there are clinic sessions attended by numbers of people and organised for a particular purpose, such as antenatal supervision or immunisation. Thirdly, there are group activities conducted in classes, such as antenatal relaxation, keep-fit exercises, talks and demonstrations.

Although these divisions relate to British practice the function of a health centre anywhere in the world is likely to embrace these three principal types of activity.

In the UK the health centre is the general practitioners' base for home care when they are not engaged in 'surgery' sessions. It is also the base for the services of

home nurses, health visitors, midwives and social workers. Thus the health centre has the potential to reach out into the community rather than being merely a place to which the community comes for help, and it is also, increasingly, a base for teaching and research. In some communities it will become a social meeting point for mothers with young children, particularly if they attend regular sessions, and for some young mothers it may provide their easiest opportunity to meet other women in a new community. For these reasons alone a relaxed and pleasant environment is important.

Accommodation

The accommodation falls into five main categories: reception and waiting space; administration and storage

The main entrance to Langthorne Health Centre. Photo: Christine Ottewill

Spitalfields Health Centre, London, for a group practice of four general practitioners and accommodation for community health services and a dental clinic. On a confined and awkward site, the street entrance leads into a lofty space from which a stair rises to community health accommodation on the floor above and continues up to a smaller top floor of three dental surgeries with recovery room. Light floods down the stair well from the glazed roof. On the ground floor there is a clear route from the entrance, past reception and waiting to the consulting rooms, each of which adjoins an examination room. Architects: Shepheard Epstein and Hunter with J. S. Allan

1	lift	12	cleaners
2	prams	13	reception
3	reception	14	waiting
4	records	15	interview
5	waiting	16	district services consulting
6	toilet	17	health education
7	specimens/disabled toilet	18	staff room
8	consulting room	19	district nurse
9	examination room	20	school nurse
10	treatment	21	health visitor
11	preparation/storage		

of patients' records; rooms for consulting, interview and treatment (some of which, such as dentistry or chiropody, may contain special fixed equipment); space for class activities; and ancillary and communal rooms for use by the staff.

It has been argued that it is regrettable that the integrated health centres in Britain do not also provide a few beds where the general practitioner can have regular access to some of the patients. This would avoid the necessity of having to refer them to the more specialised services of a general hospital, which may not in fact be strictly necessary for the patient or even suitable. Indeed in 1968 the Royal Commission on Medical Education predicted that there would be a case for the provision of short-stay beds and facilities for minor surgery.

The concept of the small Community Hospital is relevant in this context, and there are examples of similarly extended health centres in some other countries.

Internal planning of health centres

Probably the most important factors to be taken into account in the overall plan form of a health centre, whatever its size, are simplicity and clarity in the circulation flow of patients, and the need to avoid this circulation becoming confused with that of the staff. It is also desirable to combine clarity with an atmosphere which is comfortable and human in scale. Some patients will be arriving at the centre for the first time, some will be

Health centre at Bethnal Green, London. Designed for three distinct elements – two separate doctors' practices and a team of community health workers – leading logically to the symmetrical plan in which the rooms for the two practices flank the entrance, each with its own reception and screened waiting space, and the health authority reception faces the entrance on the centre, with its accommodation ranged behind it. Offices and meeting rooms are upstairs, served by a gallery that overlooks the double height central space. Architects: Avanti Architects

1 reception (doctor 1)	8 consulting/examination/
2 waiting (doctor 1)	treatment
3 reception (doctor 2)	9 speech therapy
4 waiting (doctor 2)	10 chiropody
5 reception (Health Authority)	11 health education/child health
6 waiting (Health Authority)	12 health authority stores
7 toilet	

visiting a doctor for diagnosis, treatment or follow-up, others merely for a renewed prescription or the signature of a certificate. Some may be disabled or infirm, old or confused, or may be in wheelchairs; some will have children or will come with relatives.

The movement of patients may be considerable and as far as is practicable must be separated from the movement of staff and the transfer of records from central storage to consulting rooms. Each doctor may be seeing ten patients an hour, sometimes more, and a

group of six doctors may generate a patient flow, in and out, of sixty an hour, or one hundred and twenty journeys in one direction or another. It is important that those journeys should be short and simple and should not conflict with other journeys that staff are making about the building. The patient should arrive at the consulting room in as relaxed a mood as possible.

A main entrance		6 toilet
B staff		7 consulting
1 pram shelter		8 examination
2 reception/records		9 treatment
3 waiting		10 staff room
4 health education		11 public health nurse
5 dispensing		

A small health centre at Bishops Lydeard, Somerset, with three consulting rooms and separate examination rooms. There is a dispensary, and space for health education and for a local authority nurse. Architect: B. C. Adams, Somerset County Council

A main entrance	8 examination
B staff	9 general purpose room
C dental entrance	10 treatment
1 pram shelter	11 local authority nursing staff
2 home helps	12 staff common room
3 waiting/health education	13 dental waiting
4 reception/records	14 dental surgery
5 kitchen	15 recovery
6 toilet	16 office/lab
7 consulting	17 courtyard

A health centre at Glastonbury, Somerset, with a dental unit in a separate building. The four consulting rooms have separate examination rooms; there are combined waiting and health education spaces, and rooms for home helps and local authority nursing staff. All rooms overlook walled courtyards and are screened from the street and the car park behind the building. Boilers, stores and dark room are on a lower floor of the dental unit. Architect: B. C. Adams, Somerset County Council

Flow patterns

The normal pattern of flow of patients generated by general practitioners during a 'surgery' session is arrival at the centre and disposal of car, bicycle or push-chair. Bicycles and particularly push-chairs may need covered parking space, which in some communities should be sited so that the reception staff can keep an eye on them. Inside the building the pattern consists of: reporting at the reception point (which may be occupied with other patients on their way out or collecting prescriptions or making an enquiry); waiting until called (and perhaps ensuring that children are cared for); finding the way to the correct consulting room or group of consulting rooms and perhaps waiting again until the doctor is ready; during consultation perhaps moving to an examination room and after consultation perhaps receiving treatment in a different room; and finally, on the way out, perhaps visiting the reception point again or collecting children.

There may be other flows of patients, some of them at the same time (e.g. to dentists or chiropodists) but the movement generated by the general practitioners will be by far the largest. It is worth noting that people who are unfamiliar with a building like to leave it by the same route as that by which they entered and that staff, particularly general practitioners, need a way in and out independent of that used by patients.

The entrance to the Glastonbury health centre. The dental unit is on the left

A	main entrance and pram shelter	10	social worker
B	staff	11	administrator
1	reception/records	12	garden
2	waiting	13	chiropody
3	health education	14	consulting
4	speech therapy	15	examination
5	nurses	16	treatment
6	toilets	17	dental surgery
7	interview	18	recovery
8	rest room	19	dark room
9	typing	20	store

A health centre at Portishead, Somerset. A double corridor plan with two ranges of consulting rooms and separate examination rooms. Accommodation includes a dental surgery and rooms for chiropody, speech therapy, a social worker and local authority nurses. A large staff common room and small offices for a nurse and secretary are on an upper floor. Architect: B. C. Adams, Somerset County Council

A	patients	6	district services
B	staff	7	health education/child clinic
1	reception/records	8	staff room
2	waiting	9	health visitors
3	consulting/examination	10	district nurse services
4	treatment	11	store
5	kitchen	12	typists

A compact health centre in South Poplar, London, constructed from 16 modular units surrounding a central toplit waiting area that is screened on one side from the staff rooms and open on the other to the patients' corridor. Architects: Derek Stow and Partners

The reception area

The reception point needs to adjoin the store of patients' records and is sometimes combined with it; rapid retrieval of records is essential, and so is their confidentiality. The reception area should be immediately apparent and welcoming on entering the centre. It should be so arranged in relation to the waiting space that confidential conversations can take place between patient and receptionist, and it may be combined with the distribution point for welfare foods and medicines.

The size and the number of staff in attendance depend on the through-put. There is likely to be fairly busy telephone traffic. If there is an appointment system patients' records can be selected and delivered to the doctors before the session begins, but if not, it is essential to have particularly easy access from records to consulting rooms.

In some of the larger health centres the reception point is more akin to an enquiry counter. There may be separate receptionists and waiting spaces dispersed in the territory of each medical practice or dental suite. This will not eliminate the need for some general waiting space in the main reception area.

It is widely accepted that a large and impersonal waiting space is to be avoided, and that it should provide a sense of seclusion from other traffic. The space

A	main entrance and pram shelter	9	chiropody
B	staff	10	food sales
1	waiting	11	health education
2	reception/records	12	toddlers
3	consulting	13	local authority staff office
4	examination	14	staff common room
5	treatment	15	kitchen
6	toilet	16	nurses/health visitor
7	boiler	17	field work instructor
8	clinic	18	nursing officer
		19	car parking

A health centre at Mansfield Woodhouse, Nottinghamshire. Six consulting rooms with separate examination rooms are arranged in two practice groups with separate reception counters and waiting areas. The health education room and local authority services are on the upper floor. Architect: H. T. Swain, Nottinghamshire County Council

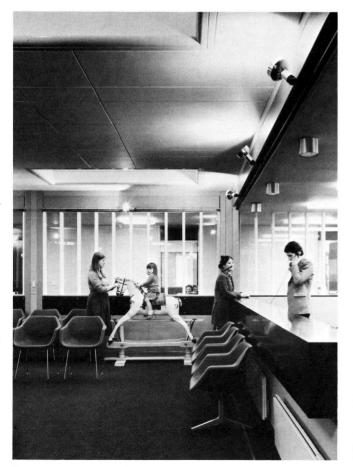

The waiting space and reception counter at South Poplar. (Photo: Henk Snoek/Fabienne de Backer)

Mansfield Woodhouse. The larger of the two waiting spaces, separated from the smaller by the stair and main entrance. (Photo: A. Hurst)

needed will depend on whether there is an appointment system, for this obviously reduces it considerably. But even with appointments waiting spaces tend to become overcrowded at times and the division of the space into separate wings or bays can be helpful in reducing the scale, particularly if more than about five consulting rooms are served from it. It is also more peaceful and can help reduce the risk of cross-infection.

The method of summoning patients from the waiting space to consulting rooms may have an important bearing on the relationship of these areas, and indeed on the relationship between doctors and patients. Public address systems and flashing lights are not conducive to a relaxed atmosphere. A lot can be said in favour of doctors leaving their rooms and greeting patients when they are ready for them.

It is important that all the main waiting space should be easily visible from the reception point and that the route from it to the consulting rooms should be easily identifiable, as short as possible, and should not involve crossing busy staff circulation routes such as those betwen reception, records and the consulting rooms. It is also an advantage for control purposes if the patient's route from main waiting space to consulting rooms can be observed from the reception point. Small subsidiary spaces close to the consulting rooms (not merely chairs in a corridor) where patients can wait briefly immediately before seeing the doctor, can be valuable; they are particularly important if in a large centre the consulting rooms have to be unduly far from the reception point and main waiting area.

Consulting rooms

Opinions differ about the best arrangements for the consulting rooms themselves, and whether separate examination rooms are desirable. Undressing, examination and minor treatment can all be done in the consulting room if it is large enough, but they can also take place in an adjacent examination room. The latter procedure can save some of the doctor's time, give greater flexibility and enable a nurse to deal with a patient in an adjacent

The chiropody room at Mansfield Woodhouse. (Photo: A. Hurst)

A main entrance and pram
   shelter
B doctors
C disabled
1 waiting
2 sub waiting
3 reception/records
4 food sales and kitchen
5 health education
6 toddlers
7 consulting
8 examination
9 chiropody
10 treatment
11 nurses' room
12 store
13 boilers

14 incinerator
15 director, social services
16 medical officer of health
17 clerk to MOH
18 health visitor
19 group adviser
20 administrator
21 clerks office
22 GP clerical staff
23 staff rest room
24 common room
25 dental waiting
26 dental surgery
27 recovery
28 dark room/lab.
29 telephone eqpt.
30 caretaker's house

0   15 m

A health centre at Pershore, Worcestershire, for two group practices. Consulting and examination rooms are arranged along two corridors flanking a central treatment room. There are two reception counters and sub-waiting spaces in addition to a general waiting area adjoining the health education room. The dental suite is entered separately and adjoins a caretaker's house. Accommodation upstairs includes offices for the Area Medical Officer of Health, the social services and health visitors and a common room. The building is near the town centre; the main entrance adjoins a covered court, where prams can be left in full view of the waiting space, and is approached either from the street or by a path across a garden linking it to a public library and a car park. Architects: Darbourne and Darke

Pershore. The entrance from the street, leading to the covered court. The caretaker's house is on the right, linked to the main building by the dental suite. (Photo: Martin Charles)

One of the sub-waiting spaces at Pershore, overlooking the covered court. (Photo: Martin Charles)

The top-lit treatment room at Pershore. (Photo: Martin Charles)

First floor

Ground floor

0 ——— 10 m
0 ——— 32 ft

A	main entrances
B	service
C	covered way/pram shelter
1	reception/records
2	GP waiting
3	LHA waiting
4	health education and kitchen
5	GP sub-waiting
6	GP consulting
7	examination
8	treatment
9	GP secretaries
10	lab.
11	clean and dirty utilities
12	interview
13	LHA consulting
14	chiropody
15	crèche
16	outdoor playspace
17	crèche cloaks and toilets
18	administrator
19	stores
20	disposal
21	canteen and kitchen
22	conference
23	library
24	audiology
25	superintendent
26	health visitors
27	geriatric visitors
28	GP social worker/health visitor
29	telephonist
30	typist
31	clinic nurses
32	district nurses
33	medical officers
34	social workers
35	LHA dental office
36	LHA dental surgery
37	recovery
38	GP dental office
39	GP dental surgery
40	lab and darkroom
41	store
42	staff cloaks
43	caretaker's flat
44	plant

Kentish Town health centre, London Borough of Camden. A large centre for two group practices and a wide range of local authority services. There are ten general practitioner consulting rooms; examination rooms are separate and communicate with a central treatment area behind the GP reception counters and records store. Consulting rooms and other offices are as far as possible of similar size to facilitate interchangeability. Accommodation on the ground floor includes reception and waiting space for the local health authority, health education, a crèche, chiropody and LHA consulting and treatment rooms for a family health clinic. Dental services are upstairs, with offices for social workers, health visitors and district nurses, a caretaker's flat, a medical library, conference and common room. The centre is also a base for undergraduates from the medical school of a London teaching hospital. Architect: S. A. G. Cook, London Borough of Camden examination room while the doctor continues with another patient in the consulting room.

However, there is much to be said for doing without examination rooms, partly from the patient's point of view and also in the interest of future uses. A series of standard units of consulting room size, suitable for most of the interview, examination, minor treatment or office functions, can offer a more flexible arrangement, particularly if the number of general practitioners or the balance of other staff changes in the future. Sometimes a suite of consulting rooms is provided with intercommunicating doors so that a doctor can, for example, make use of the next room whilst a patient he has finished examining is dressing.

If separate examination rooms are provided they should adjoin the consulting room and should not be on the opposite side of a corridor. There is sometimes a door between consulting and examination rooms, but unless they can be made adequately soundproof communicating doors can create problems when there are patients in adjoining rooms simultaneously. Some people consider it best to avoid communicating doors altogether.

Other rooms

Treatment rooms should be easily accessible from both the main waiting space and the consulting rooms. The extent and nature of the other accommodation, in addition to the basic consulting suites and the essential staff rooms, lavatories, cleaners' rooms and storage depend on the services provided but it will almost certainly include some class space for larger group activities or lectures. These activities do not usually occur at the same time as the major clinical sessions when many people are waiting and can generally be served by a room capable of use in conjunction with the main waiting space if the activity demands it. The minimum size of class space should be large enough for about twelve ante-natal patients to lie on the floor on mattresses during relaxation sessions. It should be near the main entrance so that people do not need to stray into the rest of the building when it is not in use.

Other accommodation may include a variety of offices, interview rooms or suites for specialised purposes. These may include offices for health visitors, midwives and social workers; treatment rooms for chiropodists; rooms for school health services (e.g. ophthalmology, speech therapy or audiology); dental suites comprising separate waiting rooms, dental surgeries, recovery rooms and perhaps a dental workshop.

Again there is much to be said in the interests of flexibility for planning these to a standard useful size where this is possible. People visiting any of these will usually arrive at the centre's reception point in the first instance and will be directed to subsidiary waiting spaces if appropriate. In large centres, dental patients, although coming in through the main entrance, are likely to go to a separate reception and records point under the control of the dental practice.

Whether the implications of the 1989 White Paper to which brief reference was made in Chapter 1 might result in the need for any additional accommodation is uncertain. But it seems possible that an increased

0   18 m
0   60 ft

1	reception/records	9	supply
2	dental waiting	10	utility
3	general waiting	11	ophthalmic
4	children's waiting	12	dental surgery
5	kitchen	13	dental consulting/recovery
6	health education	14	dental lab, dark room, office
7	multi-purpose consulting	15	common room
8	treatment		

Lakeside health centre, Thamesmead. A local centre built to serve the first completed area of the new town. Accommodation used by patients is on an upper floor and approached from a pedestrian deck where there is a pram shelter. A continuous band of dental rooms and multi-purpose rooms encloses a central core containing reception and records, treatment space and lavatories. One sub-divided reception and waiting area serves the whole building. The intention of the plan was to encourage the integration of general practitioners and local authority health workers by providing relatively undifferentiated areas, but separate territories are usually preferred. Architects: Derek Stow and Partners

Lakeside health centre. A combined consulting/examination room, with an intercommunicating door to the adjoining consulting room. The sloping window has light-diffusing glass. (Photo: Richard Einzig)

requirement for administrative space and equipment would result, because general practitioners would presumably not have time to shop around themselves for the best buy when referring their patients to a secondary level of care. Somebody else would have to watch the market and make the arrangements.

Siting of the building

A small health centre can often be arranged in a single storey building. Larger health centres will tend to be situated in urban areas where site space may be restricted and more than one floor is necessary. In these cases the parts of the building visited by patients should almost certainly not exceed two floors and a passenger lift large enough for a wheelchair is needed if patients have to reach rooms on an upper floor.

It would probably be generally agreed, however, that whenever possible not only should the rooms of each group practice be arranged as a suite to retain the team's identity, but different practices should not be too widely separated, particularly by a floor, if they are to be encouraged to work together. If some accommodation has to be less easily accessible it is preferable to separate functions like chiropody or dentistry rather than a part of the general medical practice. If there has to be a lift it is an advantage if it is situated where it can be easily supervised from the central reception point at the entrance to the building.

Some health centres have been sited in the grounds of a district general or a community hospital. This can encourage and facilitate closer liaison between consultants and general practitioners, although this benefit by no means follows automatically. It can move some of the consultant out-patient services from the hospital to the centre, and the centre can be supported by the special diagnostic and treatment services of the hospital.

Most health centres serve smaller catchment areas remote from a hospital and such proximity is relatively rare. The essential factor in their siting is that people should be able to reach them comparatively easily on foot or by public transport; a desirable feature is that the centre should be integrated with the local community, perhaps near the shopping centre, market or library. If there is no dispensary in the health centre it is helpful if there is one nearby (such as a chemist's shop in Britain). As to their architectural character, the most important thing is probably that they should be as welcoming and domestic in scale as possible, whatever their size, rather than imposing or unnecessarily clinical in atmosphere.

The community hospital

In Britain the first resort of most people is to their local doctor. With a well-established foundation of general practitioners and of para medical and other primary care workers, local co-ordination between them can be encouraged on a national basis. A network of fairly satisfactory health centres can be created, albeit gradually and with varying degrees of integration and usually in urban areas.

However, the gap between local doctor or health centre and the relatively large and remote district general hospital is a wide one. It can be a big step, both geographically and psychologically, for the patient who has to cross it and once across he is cut off from the

An area health centre for Thamesmead. Unlike the earlier Lakeside local centre the territories for the different units are clearly defined, but linked to one another. On the entrance floor two primary care units for group practices (sharing some central facilities) and the local authority's community health accommodation form three distinct entities with their own waiting areas. Upstairs one unit is for dental services and the other provides tutorial and research accommodation for a London teaching hospital. Architects: Derek Stow and Partners

1	reception/records	
2	manager	
3	pharmacy, waiting, dispense	
4	community health waiting	
5	food sales	
6	bed-sitting room	
7	kitchen	
8	toilet	
9	health education	
10	courtyard	
11	consulting	
12	nursing officer	
13	nurse	
14	clinical	
15	speech therapy	
16	store	
17	caretaker	
18	bins, disposal and plant	
19	pram shelter	
20	primary care waiting	
21	consulting/examination	
22	health visitor	
23	interview	
24	social worker	
25	seminar	
26	midwife	
27	psychiatric nurse	
28	secretaries	
29	fieldwork teacher	
30	specimens	
31	nurses service room	
32	treatment	
33	chiropody	
34	dental reception	
35	dental waiting	
36	void	
37	dental surgery	
38	recovery	
39	X-ray	
40	dark room	
41	office	
42	staff room	
43	dental lab.	
44	staff common room	
45	academic reception/ secretaries	
46	lockers	
47	tutorial staff	
48	research worker	
49	laboratory	
50	preparation	

A GP clinic entrance
B admissions and day patients
C maternity admissions
1 community hospital, first phase
2 later phases
3 service area

1 hairdressing/physiotherapy
2 occupational therapy
3 dayroom/dining
4 kitchen
5 toilets
6 bath
7 dirty utility
8 consulting/examination
9 office
10 sister
11 4 bed ward (semi-acute)
12 5 bed ward
13 single bed
14 treatment/clean utility
15 nurses station
16 general purpose
17 ward office
18 nursery
19 progress
20 sluice
21 fathers' waiting
22 staff room/dining
23 changing/lockers
24 store
25 day waiting space
26 cleaner

Wallingford Community Hospital, Oxfordshire. A medical centre in a converted building houses the consulting rooms for local general practitioners, X-ray and dental suites, nursing and administrative offices, and some bedsitting rooms for resident staff and students. It was linked to a new building containing a Day Care unit and seventeen medical and seventeen maternity beds, with provision for expansion. Architect: A. L. Arschavir, Oxford Regional Health Authority

support of his general practitioner and perhaps of family and friends until he returns to his local community after discharge.

This gap was previously bridged by the small 'cottage hospitals' as they were popularly known – otherwise 'general practitioner hospitals' – which were well established by the 1930s. Many had been built from the subscriptions of their local communities, for whom they provided a valued service and from whom they received much confidence, support and loyalty, not least from the medical profession. Indeed, in 1938 a British Medical Association report recognised a growing need for more such places where general practitioners could treat cases that were appropriate to their particular skills.

However, during the first two decades of the National Health Service the emphasis was on the establishment of District General Hospitals. The small local hospitals soon found themselves under pressure. The Ministry's 'Hospital Plan for England and Wales' in 1962 identified the strategy of District General Hospitals and made clear the intention of closing some of the smaller establishments. Inexorable economic pressures on the one hand and the fierce protagonism of practitioners and local people on the other led to a conflict of philosophies, and it was in this situation that the Oxford Regional Board initiated the concept of the Community Hospital and in 1973 began to operate the first phase of one in Wallingford, linked functionally and physically to a local health centre.

A year after Wallingford opened the Minister of Health issued a Circular recognising that smaller and more easily accessible establishments catering for local requirements were needed. He designated them by the name 'community hospitals', although it was clear that not all of them were intended to have exactly the same functions. Within certain guidelines the Regional Health Authorities were encouraged to plan the services and accommodation according to the requirements of the areas they served.

The Circular of 1974 recognised that this was a long term aim and that there were already small hospitals still receiving support locally. But the concept of the community hospital and the function it should perform was somewhat different. Whilst some of the existing small hospitals might be given a new role as community hospitals, perhaps altered or extended, others might have to close so that better use could be made of resources.

The Circular emphasised the importance of strengthening the roles of the family doctor and other community services. The district general hospital was too far away for many people, particularly those living in country areas and depending on public transport for visits to an outpatients' department or a day hospital, or for visiting an in-patient relative or friend. It envisaged that the community hospital would provide medical and nursing care for out-patients, day-patients and in-

Ground floor
1 reception
2 community health worker
3 evaluation office
4 female changing
5 male changing
6 cleaner
7 store
8 toilet
9 cloaks
10 dentist
11 social worker
12 consultant/speech therapist
13 staff office
14 consultant/chiropodist
15 hairdresser
16 treatment/clean utility
17 dirty utility
18 bath
19 workshop
20 sitting
21 dining
22 servery
23 occupational therapy
24 ADL kitchen
25 ADL bedroom
26 physiotherapy
27 passive physiotherapy
28 store
29 seminar room
30 conservatory

Upper floor
1 nurses station
2 single room
3 four-bed room
4 clean utility
5 sister
6 dirty utility
7 bath
8 toilet
9 shower
10 store
11 sitting/dining
12 servery
13 conservatory
14 boiler
15 staff room
16 terrace
17 raised walkway

The Community Care Centre in Lambeth, London, a pioneer
contribution to inner city health provision, neither conventional health
centre, day centre nor 'normal' community hospital. It has 20 in-patient
beds and a 35 place day centre for patients referred by the 28 general
practitioners who work with the centre. It provides a wide range of
remedial and educational services for the patients and to a lesser
extent for others who are not referred by their doctors, and aims to bring
together general practitioners, district health authority community
nurses and therapists, social workers and local volunteers and health
groups. The ranges of offices, clinical rooms and therapy rooms flank
the reception space at the entrance from the street. The greater part of
the other side of the ground floor is occupied by sitting room, dining
room and occupational therapy, all with access to the extensive
garden. They can be separated from one another by folding doors.
Upstairs four four-bed rooms and four single rooms are grouped
around the nurses station, all opening onto a terrace from which
projects a sun room linked to the ground floor by a two storey
conservatory. Between the ancillary rooms and toilets on this floor the
wide corridor, an ambulatory space, opens out into bays where patients
can sit and rest. Architect: Edward Cullinan

1 entrance foyer
2 reception and records
3 beverages
4 assisted shower
5 waiting
6 sister
7 staff cloaks
8 toilet
9 cleaner
10 store
11 eight-bed ward
12 single bed ward
13 dayroom
14 nurses base
15 treatment room
16 clean utility
17 dirty utility
18 linen
19 rest room
20 assisted bath
21 wheelchair bay
22 kitchen
23 staff dining and lounge
24 female staff cloaks
25 male staff cloaks

26 geriatric day hospital
27 day dining room/chapel
28 dirty utility
29 clean utility and treatment
30 occupational therapy
31 office
32 ADL bedroom
33 bathroom
34 kitchen
35 physiotherapy
36 wax treatment
37 common room
38 dental surgery
39 dental recovery
40 X-ray waiting
41 X-ray reception
42 X-ray
43 dark room
44 changing
45 consulting room
46 consulting and minor treatment
47 treatment room
48 courtyard

Mold Community Hospital for the Clwyd Health Authority, the first to be built in Wales, opened in 1984. It provides two 20-bed wards, one on an upper floor, for short-term and continuing care of patients under the charge of their own general practitioner. On the ground floor there are in addition rooms for consultants' clinics, a minor casualty service, a dental department, facilities for X-ray, physiotherapy, occupational and speech therapy, and a 15-place Day Hospital for those not needing in-patient treatment, principally the elderly. The echelon ward plan gives each bed a sense of identity and allows visual supervision from the nurses station of 16 of the 20 beds. The ward above it on the upper floor is similar, with the addition of a nursing officer's room, a hairdressing room, stores and plant. Architect: William H. Simpson, Chief Architect Welsh Health Common Services Authority

The Community Care Centre in Lambeth. The wards on the upper floor open on to a wide terrace, with the sun room and conservatory beyond. (Photo: Martin Charles)

A out-patients
B geriatric/EMI
C services
D day hospital
E GP ward
1 reception
2 office
3 cleaner
4 toilet
5 store
6 clean utility
7 sub-waiting
8 sister
9 consulting/examination
10 linen
11 dirty utility
12 clinette
13 changing

14 X-ray
15 radiologist
16 casualty treatment
17 nursing officer
18 conference
19 day/dining and quiet rooms
20 pantry
21 EMI
22 bath
23 one-bed ward
24 two-bed ward
25 three-bed ward
26 nurses base
27 doctor
28 linen
29 luggage
30 porter
31 interview
32 treatment
33 quiet room

34 shower
35 wheelchairs/trolleys
36 beverages
37 chiropody
38 hairdresser
39 physiotherapy
40 day room
41 occupational therapy
42 ADL
43 OT workshop
44 treatment/clean utility
45 HAO
46 launderette
47 staff changing
48 staff dining
49 kitchen
50 staff room
51 CSSD
52 linen
53 medical gases
54 plant
55 incinerator
56 viewing chapel
57 body store
58 chapel garden
59 substation
60 generator
61 mess
62 workshop

0 5 10 30M
0 100Ft

Ystradgynlais Community Hospital for Powys Health Authority was completed in 1986, following the Community hospital at Mold. Servicing a catchment area of about 16 000 people it has 52 beds, 30 for the elderly, 8 for the elderly mentally ill and 14 general practitioner beds, together with a 20-place day hospital, a psychiatric day hospital, provision for out-patients and X-ray, and a minor casualty department staffed by general practitioners on a round-the-clock basis. The desire for clear and easy communication between the various departments gave rise to wings radiating from a central hexagonal courtyard that allows space for the possible future extension of a sixth wing. It was a requirement that all patients should have a territory they could identify as their own; hence the high proportion of single rooms. For the same reason the multi-bed wards are subdivided by built-in wardrobes that partially screen each bed-head from its neighbour's. The building is wholly single storey. Wide overhanging eaves provide shade in summer but allow solar gain from low winter sun. Rooflights in the pitched roofs permit daylight to penetrate the high internal circulation spaces and reach the back of the deeper rooms through clerestorey windows. Architect: William H. Simpson, Chief Architect, Welsh Health Common Services Agency

Mold Community Hospital, seen from the entrance road

The approach to Ystradgynlais Community Hospital

patients who did not need the specialised facilities of the large hospital and who could not be properly cared for at home or in residential accommodation. It could also be a staging post on the way to the District General Hospital and on discharge from it.

It was recommended that the admission of in-patients should satisfy three criteria. Firstly, that the care they needed could not reasonably be provided in their homes; secondly, that the investigation or care they received should not be more specialised than that of the normal general practitioner; and thirdly, that they would benefit from care near their homes, where they could more easily be visited and continue their links with their local community.

Regional Health Authorities were given to understand that up to half the geriatric in-patient beds and half the day-patient places (including those for patients suffering from dementia) in any health district might be in community hospitals. In this respect the guidance differed from the Oxford concept. They could also receive patients with terminal illness who could not be cared for at home, and patients of all ages who needed temporary nursing care while the families who normally looked after them were ill or taking a holiday respite. The importance of active treatment, occupation and diversion was emphasised. General practitioners would normally be responsible for day to day care of all categories but it was intended that consultants should also hold clinics. It was recommended that where possible health centres and group practice premises should be closely associated with the community hospitals, which should be places where all branches of the health service could work together.

The Circular stated that community hospitals would normally be expected to provide between 50 and 150 beds, likely to serve a population of between 30 000 and 100 000. Only in Wales, where the relative isolation of some communities was exacerbated by the terrain, was it thought that less than 50 beds should be expected. As for accommodation, operating theatres were not envisaged. The surgical procedures should not extend beyond those which general practitioners would expect to perform in their own practice premises or a health centre, and facilities for general anaesthesia should be only for these minor procedures and for dentistry. Maternity beds were not expected, only ante-natal and post-natal clinics. Limited radiological services requiring only simple equipment were needed, but anything more complex should be done in the district general hospital. Pathology laboratories staffed by technicians and pathologists were not thought appropriate; and pharmaceutical services should be provided by visting staff from the district general hospital or by part-time local pharmacists.

Thirteen years after the publication of the Circular a King's Fund study showed that in 1987 there were in England 249 hospitals either designated by the Regional Health Authorities as Community Hospitals or considered to be fulfilling a similar function. It was clear that many of these were not officially categorised as Community Hospitals, being still known as General Practitioner Hospitals or Cottage Hospitals. They provided a total of 9050 beds and the majority were in the south of the country. Most of them were relatively small; 201 had less than 50 beds and only 48 had more. It was also clear that the functions they performed and the facilities they

1 entrance foyer
2 medical records
3 beverages
4 porter
5 toilet
6 waiting
7 overnight stay
8 doctor
9 sister
10 store
11 eight-bed ward
12 single-bed ward
13 day room
14 quiet room
15 nurses base
16 toilet/shower
17 cleaner
18 bathroom
19 clean utility
20 dirty utility
21 treatment room
22 linen
23 three-bed maternity ward
24 kitchen
25 secretary
26 nursing officer

Chirk, the latest of the Welsh community hospitals, is linked to a recently built day hospital. A 31-bed ward is on one side of the entrance hall. On the other side are out-patients, accident and emergency, staff and ancillary accommodation arranged around a courtyard. All rooms receive natural light and ventilation, either directly or, as at Ystradgynlais, through a high level clerestorey which also enables daylight to reach the rear of the deep plan ward. The ward is similar to the echelon arrangement at Mold but adjusted to give increased observation of the four single bedrooms from the nurses station. There is also a separate ward for three post-natal beds, with its own ancillary rooms. Architect: William H. Simpson, Chief Architect, Welsh Health Common Services Authority

27 female staff change
28 male staff change
29 seminar room
30 domestic supervisor
31 catering manager
32 kitchen and stores
33 dining
34 mortuary
35 viewing room
36 boiler
37 incinerator
38 courtyard

39 accident and emergency entrance
40 casualty waiting
41 interview
42 treatment room
43 clean utility
44 dirty utility
45 consultant
46 changing
47 office
48 dark room
49 X-ray

provided differed somewhat from those suggested in the Circular. Not only were they smaller but few of them had day hospitals, slightly over half of them – particularly the larger ones – had full operating theatres for more advanced procedures than the general practitioner would carry out on his own premises, and few had health centres physically attached. Many were, not unnaturally, in existing buildings little altered.

It is clear therefore that the nature of the community hospital varies. With the earlier cottage hospitals this may be for historical reasons; some of them remain under threat from the rationalisation of services and by continuing economic pressures. But for the patient the community hospital can perform an important function. For example, some admissions may be for uncompli-cated non-acute disabilities where home nursing is inappropriate or cannot be arranged; others may be post-operative cases from a district general hospital who would otherwise not be ready to leave and return home. In either case, besides providing local support at a scale appropriate to the patient's disability, the community hospital can help to make it possible for the expensive beds in the more specialised hospital to be released for those who are in greater need of them. It has been argued that as high a proportion as one quarter of all hospital beds could be provided in community hospitals.

Part of a community hospital may be reserved for elderly people who need constant nursing care and who might otherwise be taken to a hospital too far removed from their home environment and from relatives and friends, but this presents the obvious danger that it could lead to an immovable population of longstay patients. A few beds may also be available as short term 'rest beds' for acute psychiatric cases under the care of a local doctor, for instance for a nervous breakdown or when a patient cannot for some reason stay at home.

Besides providing beds a community hospital can fulfil the role of a day hospital, particularly in the field of non-specialist rehabilitation therapy. For day-patients it can reduce the burden of long travelling distances and for some of them the reluctance they may feel when faced with a larger and less personal establishment. Again it can reduce the load on the large hospital.

The nature and amount of accommodation that a community hospital provides will clearly vary from one locality to another and will depend upon local needs and policy. The accommodation is likely to be basically ward accommodation with a small proportion of single rooms supported by the normal ward ancillaries, with spaces for dayroom, dining, occupational therapy and physiother-apy, offices, kitchen, and rooms for staff, including dining and changing. Throughout the building it is probably

1 reception and food sales
2 pharmacy
3 administration
4 calorifiers
5 reception/records
6 waiting
7 health education
8 consulting
9 chiropody
10 speech therapy
11 nurses' station
12 treatment
13 dental reception
14 dental waiting
15 dental surgery
16 recovery
17 staff common room
18 clean utility
19 dirty utility
20 clinical
21 laboratory
22 radiodiagnostic
23 lavage
24 consultant
25 radiographer
26 gymnasium
27 occupational therapy
28 kitchen
29 dining room
30 store
31 linen

32 patients' launderette
33 progress
34 delivery
35 day space
36 single bed
37 five beds
38 nursery
39 four beds
40 doctor
41 courtyard
42 mortuary

The Community Hospital for Milton Keynes, Buckinghamshire. Three linked units comprise Health Centre, two 34-bed wards and 33 maternity beds, and a Day Hospital with relatively large out-patient, radiodiagnostic and rehabilitation departments. In the Health Centre there are separate examination rooms adjacent to the consulting rooms and a variety of offices for health visitors, social workers and home nurses etc. Architect: A. L. Arschavir, Oxford Regional Health Authority

Level 3
1 acute in-patients ward
2 geriatric in-patients ward
3 works
4 staff dining and kitchen

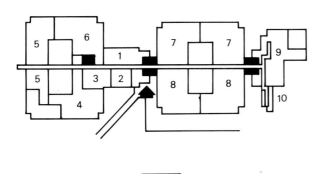

Level 2
1 primary care
2 dental
3 X-Ray
4 out-patients
5 psychiatric day hospital
6 community health
7 elderly and severely mentally
   infirm in-patients
8 geriatric in-patients
9 plant
10 staff entrance

Level 1
1 administration
2 rheumatology
3 geriatric day hospital
4 ESMI day hospital
5 rehabilitation

Cannock Community Hospital, Staffordshire, for the West Midlands Regional Health Authority, is on a narrow site sloping down from north to south. There is access at each of its three floor levels. Sheltered garden courtyards flank the central spine of the hospital street. The emphasis of the hospital is on rehabilitation of geriatric patients, the elderly mentally ill and on those with rheumatic disorders. It will provide 112 day places, and 224 beds of which 28 are for general practitioners' acute patients. There is an out-patients department but provision for accidents and emergencies is made at the Stafford District General Hospital. Architects: Denys Lasdun Peter Softley and Associates

even more important than it is in the normal hospital to recognise that many patients will be ambulant, or should be encouraged to be so, and that the design should facilitate this in any way it can. Day-patients will need a waiting or common room area of their own, together with separate lavatories, and may of course generate other needs according to the extent of the services it is decided to provide for them.

Work by the Oxford Regional Hospital Board has suggested that the day accommodation, principally for the elderly, physically handicapped or mentally ill, may best be run in small groups of not more than twenty (fifteen patients and five staff) each with its own day room as a social centre and its own room for occupational and physiotherapy, but sharing baths, toilets and dining space with other groups.

3

Primary care in developing countries

In the UK there has been an attempt to provide a centrally co-ordinated health service which is available to all. This has been built up within a complicated inherited structure of medical and social services and a developed and largely urban industrialised society. However, it is clear that although advances have been made in the last forty years or so there remain many difficulties and many differences of opinion about priorities, both theoretical and financial. There are also many different views about how best to design buildings that can help the people who work in them to do their jobs well and encourage the patients who visit them to find them agreeable.

In some others parts of the world the needs are more basic and the available resources of finance and manpower are very much smaller. Here problems of a different nature have to be overcome. Some countries are starting from almost nothing in their attempt to provide a health service for the community as a whole, and their problems have to be seen in a different context although the elements that will go towards their solution are perhaps not very different in principle from those in a developed country. The skeleton of the basic hierarchy of health care may well be similar but the organs and flesh are simpler, sometimes even rudimentary, and can only grow and develop with time.

In most developing countries health care must advance on a broad front towards an increased awareness in the community of some of the reasons for disease. These may include domestic causes such as contaminated water, lack of facilities for drainage, the disposal of waste, lack of care for personal hygiene and the storage, handling and preparation of food.

Preliminary model of the Tribal administrative Centre at Haima; an administrative, educational and health facility in the desert region of the Sultanate of Oman. The Centre is in the foreground and comprises, top left, the school; right, administration; bottom left, the medical centre. The three elements are separated by courtyards. Outlying buildings are residential villas and the guardhouse and prison. Architects: John R. Harris Associates (Photo: Sydney W. Newbery)

There is a need to improve the economy, to change social habits and to provide the material means to assist this change where possible. Nutrition, environmental health, family planning, maternity and child health and the control of communicable diseases are fundamental, and the provision of medical care can make little progress without a background of programmes of preventive care, housing and education.

Besides providing elementary medical attention a health service in a developing country, and particularly in a rural area, has thus to a much greater extent than in the developed world to perform the vital function of education and guidance in the community. But it is likely that the more effectively it can perform its medical and curative functions the more rapidly the community it serves will grow to trust it and co-operate in its longer term aims.

Grass roots care

Although officials may pronounce their national priorities to be sanitation, control of infections and primary care in their rural areas, much of the money too often seems to go into major urban hospitals and some into private care for the few who can afford it. Perhaps it is not surprising that tackling the fundamental problem moves slowly. Even if an adequate supply of drugs could be maintained, reliable health workers are necessary to administer them, and even if they can be trained they are likely to prefer the towns, reluctant to work in remote areas. Status is not a western phenomenon. In addition, many developing countries still lack middle level administrators capable of turning policies into practice.

Perhaps the most extraordinary advances in grass roots care have been made in China. It has by far the largest rural population in the world but between 1950 and 1982 public health measures are said to have increased life expectancy from 32 to 69 years. 'Barefoot doctors' played their part, but more fundamental were the mass campaigns to improve sanitation, eliminate the 'four pests' – rats, flies, mosquitoes and bedbugs – to vaccinate against infectious diseases and to control the vectors of major endemic disorders.

However, other countries provide evidence of attempting nationally organised but simplified methods of health care delivery, perhaps not so dramatic but nevertheless sharing the characteristics of the grass roots approach. The three examples taken range from the north to south of East Africa. In the Sudan, the largest in area, with the greatest difficulties of communication and having in part a nomadic desert population, the primary health care programme introduced in 1975 intended to make primary care of a socially and culturally acceptable nature as accessible as possible to the whole population. It aimed to encourage community development rather than direct itself mainly towards individuals. There was emphasis on local participation, on organisation and on the supply of materials and equipment, and on voluntary labour for construction and for transporting the sick.

In the settled areas of the Sudan a network of primary health care units was envisaged, each based on a population of some four thousand within a radius of attendance of about ten miles. It was proposed that five of these units should be supported by a dispensary for referral and the supply of drugs, each such complex serving a population of about 24 000, integrated by a referral system with health centres and secondary establishments. The aim was that there should be at least one community health worker for every 4000 people in the settled areas, and one nomadic worker, selected from amongst themselves by the nomad community, for every 1500 nomads.

Further south great efforts have been made in Tanzania to deploy community health workers, with the aim of making basic care accessible to everyone, alongside a substantial increase in the number of village health posts, dispensaries and health centres, linked to district, regional and consultant hospitals.

Similarly in Mozambique (independent for little more than a decade) the focus has been on prevention and participation. There are over a thousand health posts and health centres, embryonic though they might appear to western eyes, and a co-ordinated referral system to rural and district hospitals, provincial hospitals and three central hospitals that in spite of great obstacles aim to provide a comprehensive service to the whole community.

The 'aid post'

It has been argued that, in rural areas, the first unit of medical care should be an individual in every village with a little basic medical skill. This person may not necessarily be a full-time employee, but perhaps the indigenous midwife who might have a few drugs and dressings and whose primary purpose should be to spread an understanding of hygiene and elementary health care. The most simple actual establishment that needs a building, which would not be found in every village, is likely to be an 'aid post'. Probably this will not be staffed continuously but visited perhaps once a week by a para-medical assistant who might see about a hundred patients on each visit and might be assisted by a nurse.

Although it is potentially a good deal more than a first-aid post the requirements of such a building are likely to be very simple. Its construction will probably be in the vernacular, carried out by the local community, or perhaps in a mixture of indigenous and prefabricated 'imported' materials if resources, transport and skills are available.

In some communities it is likely to be an advantage if in character the building follows local tradition rather than introduces an alien atmosphere. But however simple the 'aid post' may be to begin with, if it is provided within a national or regional plan for health care it may well be conceived as the first element of a larger unit. In the future it may need to be expanded to provide additional facilities.

In the first instance the accommodation may consist of little more than a room for examination and treatment

1	female waiting	6	treatment	11	staff room
2	male waiting	7	dispensary	12	single bedroom
3	toilets	8	patients' preparation	13	covered way
4	reception/records	9	delivery	14	courtyard
5	lobby	10	recovery		

The medical centre at Haima. There is complete segregation of the sexes but the two treatment rooms intercommunicate. To deal with emergencies the female zone has a small delivery and recovery ward adjoining a single bedroom

1	waiting
2	examination
3	injections
4	dressings
5	equipment store
6	drug store
7	dispensing
8	store
9	drugs
10	laboratory
11	ante-natal clinic

A model plan (top) for a Primary Health Care Unit in the 78/84 National Health Programme for the Sudan. Staffed by one primary health care worker it is intended to serve a population of 4000 within a radius of attendance of about 16 km or 10 miles. It is capable of future extension into a dispensary (bottom) by the addition of a second building. A dispensary for referral, supervision and the supply of drugs should serve five Primary Health Care Units and a population of 24 000, staffed by a medical assistant, a nurse and a cleaner

A rural health centre to serve a community of less than 2500
inhabitants. It is staffed by one health worker visited about once a week
by a mobile team of doctor, nurse, sanitarian and health educator.
Architect: Abou Zeid Rageh, Cairo (with acknowledgement to WHO)

0   5 m
0   16 ft

1 waiting
2 registration and drugs
3 treatment
4 consulting
5 meetings and health
   education
6 microscope
7 sanitary inspector
8 staff toilet and shower
9 pantry
10 patients' toilet and cleaner

specific diseases, and also on its cultural acceptability.
For example, in most areas it is likely to be the out-patient
clinics and the distribution of medicines that have
priority. In other areas, where the rate of infant mortality is
high, the provision of wards for infants may come first; or
where living conditions and social habits particularly
endanger childbirth a maternity ward may be more
important. Elsewhere a few general beds for men and
women may be all that is possible.

Whatever the initial assessment of need it is likely that
with time the situation will change. The basic unit should
allow not only for expansion but should also permit some
flexibility for changes in use and for variations in the
relative numbers of beds for men and women. This is a
factor that can affect the plan fundamentally, particularly
in those parts of the world where strict segregation is
necessary.

Staffing and equipment

Whatever the size of the facility it is almost certain that,
compared with the western health centre or community
hospital, it will be run by a much smaller staff and that
there will be less specialisation of tasks. Equipment will
also be simpler and indeed it is important that it is of the
simplest, as skilled maintenance will not usually be
available. In the absence of country doctors it will
probably be the only centre within many miles to which
people can turn. Patients will not come by appointment
but are likely to arrive on foot or in bullock carts,
sometimes with their families and even with their
livestock. If their treatment involves a number of
consecutive visits, for example for dressings, injections

approached from an open waiting space in the form of a
sheltered verandah. Even in a facility such as this careful
provision for the security of drugs will be essential. This is
partly an administrative matter but the design of the
building and its equipment must recognise it, for security
of drugs can be a major problem in developing
countries, as indeed it has proved to be elsewhere.

The simple form of building to meet these needs is little
more than a hut. This can be seen in a slightly larger form
in the Sudanese proposals for primary health care units.
An extension might add more space for examination or
treatment, a dispensary, a small laboratory and an
expanded waiting area, or separate facilities for records
and space for health education and more staff. Later
extension might provide some beds. The nature of
growth depends on local needs but it is likely to be
important that growth should be foreseen. It should not
be inhibited by a nucleus from which it cannot easily
develop or which can only be adapted by alterations so
radical that, when change is needed, the facility is put
out of action. Throughout the world, education and an
increase in wealth, however slight, is always followed by
increasing public demand for better health care.

Development of the small unit

Growth will probably anticipate three roles: an increase
in the curative treatment of out-patients, the provision of
beds, and the co-ordination of public health services in
the improvement of general health and preventive action
against social diseases. The type of provision that is
made for the development of a basic unit into a small
hospital will depend largely on the nature of the
catchment area, on the living conditions of the community and their particular demands, on the prevalence of

0   10 m
0   32 ft

A patients
B visitors
1 waiting
2 reception/records
3 sub-waiting
4 examination/shower/
   toilet
5 treatment
6 lab and dispensary
7 drug store etc
8 staff toilet
9 delivery/sluice/
   shower/toilet
10 tea kitchen
11 duty station
12 men's beds
13 sluice/showers/toilets
14 women's beds

A health centre with eight beds and delivery room, with an out-patient
capacity of up to 100 patients a day. Staffed by two or three
nurses/midwives and an administrator, it is visited periodically by a
mobile health team. In-patients are cared for by their relatives.
Architects: Misereor, Aachen (with acknowledgement to WHO)

1 waiting and meeting room
2 medicines
3 injections and vaccinations
4 consulting
5 store
6 toilet
7 sitting/dining room
8 bedroom
9 kitchen and clothes yard
10 dentistry
11 information/records
12 health inspector
13 office
14 emergencies
15 obstetric beds
16 adult beds
17 children's beds
18 kitchen
19 laundry
20 delivery
21 labour
22 doctors' changing and toilet
23 clean utility/sterilisation
24 dirty utility
25 nurses' station
26 visitors
27 nurse's bedroom

Designs from Colombia for the National Hospital Fund, produced as an aid to the planning of health posts and health centres. The basic unit of the model health post (top), with separate staff living quarters, is first extended without significant alteration to provide for dentistry and offices (centre). Another building can subsequently be added (bottom) with labour and delivery rooms, pairs of beds for adults, children and obstetric patients, and a self-contained nurse's bedroom. Architect: Jorge de los Rios Mazure, Bogota (with acknowledgement to WHO)

or follow-up after diagnostic tests, they are unlikely to return home between treatments if the journey takes several days but may camp in the vicinity.

Even in areas where the facility is a short distance from patients' homes, and even in a town where there may possibly be an appointment system, patients are likely to arrive very early in the morning although it may involve them in waiting in large numbers for many hours in uncomfortable climatic conditions. Out-patient clinics will thus be dealing with a situation very different from that which is usual in an urbanised western society. In the wards, admission may mean that other members of the family will stay nearby and will play an important part in cooking for and generally looking after the patient. The admission of a small child to a bed will be likely to involve admitting the mother as well.

There are examples, notably in Africa, where provision is made for this influx of patients' families by the construction nearby of a hospital village or of simple hostels. Besides sheltering the relatives of the sick this accommodation can be used by non-infectious patients who are capable of looking after themselves. Such self-care patients may constitute a substantial proportion and deliberately organised residential shelter of this kind can considerably reduce the number who might otherwise be occupying hospital beds that require nursing attendance.

The larger health centres or out-patient departments in rural areas are likely to be manned by several auxiliaries but by only one doctor. In these circumstances a method of sorting patients into those who need only routine treatment or medicines and those who should be seen by the doctor may be necessary.

A GP entrance
B public health entrance
1 reception
2 male waiting
3 female waiting
4 mothercraft/health education
5 female toilet
6 male toilet
7 vaccination
8 doctor
9 director and secretary
10 health statistician
11 sanitary inspector
12 office
13 shop
14 staff toilet
15 doctors' sitting room
16 store
17 cleaner
18 male corridor
19 female corridor
20 consulting/examination
21 preparation/treatment
22 disposal
23 clinette
24 test
25 radiodiagnostic
26 dental surgery
27 recovery
28 treatment
29 dispensary

A general practitioners' clinic for use in association with a new hospital in the Middle East where there are as yet relatively few primary health care facilities. To avoid pressure and overcrowding in the out-patient department it is intended to act as a filter for referral. The strict segregation of the sexes produces an interlocking finger arrangement of independent corridors, but all consulting rooms communicate with both men's and women's corridors so that clinics can respond to variations in numbers. Architects: Architects' Co-Partnership

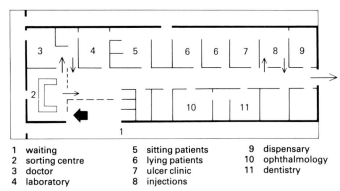

1 waiting	5 sitting patients	9 dispensary
2 sorting centre	6 lying patients	10 ophthalmology
3 doctor	7 ulcer clinic	11 dentistry
4 laboratory	8 injections	

Diagrammatic plan (after G. Ferrand) for an out-patients' department. Patients are filtered at the sorting centre and proceed either to the doctor's room or along the corridor to the various clinics, leaving the building at the other end after passing the dispensary

A simple arrangement based on a sorting method and one-way traffic, derived from French experience in West Africa, is for patients to wait on a covered verandah and to enter a long hut-like building at one end, where they are seen by a medical assistant at a sorting and records point. Those who need to visit the doctor are directed to an immediately adjoining doctor's room, but the majority are passed into a corridor that runs the length of the building, from which they distribute themselves into the various clinics and wait for treatment. All patients leave the building by way of the same corridor at the end remote from the entrance, passing a dispensary on their way out. Between the clinics there is access for staff, independent of the patients' corridor, from the doctor's room at one end to the dispensary at the other.

Wards and service rooms

If there are wards they are likely to be of the open type, particularly if nursing staff is limited in number. In addition there should be two or three rooms for isolation. In a small facility with only one nursing unit of perhaps twenty-five to thirty beds it may be sensible to place the service rooms at the centre so that the ward is divided into separate sections for men and women, or for other purposes for which segregation is desirable, whilst maintaining in principle one nursing unit. Smaller multi-bed bays may give greater flexibility in use but their adoption needs to be balanced against the degree of supervision that is desirable.

Service rooms will probably be reduced to essentials – a treatment room, a workroom for cleaning instruments, sterilisation and preparation, a ward kitchen or pantry, some storage space and offices for a nurse and doctor. Separate lavatories will be necessary for each sex, but unlike the dispersed and individual facilities that are favoured in the West, these are probably best concentrated together so that they are easy to supervise and keep clean. Also, in some climates, a degree of separation from the ward may be desirable for reasons of hygiene.

Lavatories may be combined with simple slop sink facilities for emptying bedpans. Day space may best be provided in the form of covered verandahs opening directly off the ward. This arrangement, in single-storey buildings, may be particularly suitable in giving easy access for visitors and patients' families without interfering with the work centre of the ward.

A theoretical example which by stages extends a simple health post by the addition, first of further clinics and supporting facilities and subsequently of in-patient beds, was produced in 1975 by the Medical Committee of the Conference of Missionary Societies in Great Britain and Ireland. It is not, nor is it intended to be, a model for all situations, but in addition to the practicality of its suggestions about the way growth might be guided, it demonstrates a design approach that pays regard to the rural culture and social habits of many tropical countries in the developing world. This approach is more relevant, sympathetic, and far simpler to implement than some of the sophisticated solutions, often entirely inappropriate, that are based on the experience of the western world and misapplied to totally different situations.

This does not mean that there are no situations where more sophisticated answers are appropriate. The World Health Organisation has published examples from contributors which, although simple in conception, assume a less primitive technology and different social habits. However, these usually share an approach that anticipates growth and provides for it by the simple addition of linked units or 'huts' in structures of one storey.

Prefabricated and mobile services

Some attempts have been made to explore the possibilities of prefabricated units. These may have uses where local materials are not readily available or suitable local labour is for one reason or another difficult to obtain, or speed of implementation is of particular importance. However, this is a relatively costly approach and in most situations is likely to be out of scale with the essential needs. But given, for instance, a large programme and reasonable facilities for transport, together with the necessary finance, there seems little to be said against it except that by its very nature it imports an entirely alien artefact into the community. Yet since any community that can be easily reached by the sort of vehicle necessary to transport prefabricated buildings will probably already be familiar with alien artefacts and may, indeed, place a higher social value upon them than upon its own vernacular, this may be no argument against their use.

In countries which can afford them (e.g. Qatar), fully prefabricated imported buildings which can be erected rapidly by a few skilled expatriates, who then return home, are preferred to traditional methods of construction which require large numbers of imported unskilled labourers who stay in the country for a long time and disturb its culture.

In other situations an approach more relevant than the completely prefabricated building may be the importation of simple structural members which can then be enclosed by local labour with an adaptation of the materials and methods that are normally available in the locality. This may also prove to be more flexible and more

1 waiting
2 consulting
3 examination/ante-natal
4 future extension
5 weighing
6 clean treatment
7 dirty treatment
8 laboratory
9 dispensary
10 reception/information
11 staff/conference
12 store
13 examination
14 dirty linen
15 laundry
16 linen
17 sterilising
18 clean-up/disposal
19 staff latrines
20 labour
21 delivery
22 children's and women's ward
23 men's ward
24 male latrines
25 female and hostel latrines
26 kitchens
27 in-patients' washing

1 stores/garage
2 shaded social area
3 out-patient and social area latrines
4 hostel
5 hostel and social area latrines/washing
6 women's and hostel latrines
7 in-patients' kitchens and washing
8 ward
9 reception/information and central facilities
10 out-patients
11 tree-shaded central area

A theoretical model showing the staged development from a small clinic into a well supported health centre to serve a population of up to 20 000 within a radius of ten to twenty miles. Within the context of an overall development there can be many variations on the theme to suit local needs and conditions. The example shows (top) an under-fives' general clinic. It is enlarged (centre) into a bigger clinic with ancillary rooms and more space for staff and storage. It is further extended (bottom) to provide maternity facilities and a few beds for men. Later extensions might enlarge it by increments of 25 beds into a 125-bed District Hospital. There is provision for hostels or dormitories for relatives and self-care patients, and for places where they can do their cooking and laundry. The plans assume that there is unlikely to be waterborne sewage. Architect: Mark Wells, with the Medical Committee of the Conference of Missionary Societies of Great Britain and Ireland

The treatment room in one of the containerised units at Thamesmead, delivered complete except for the loose equipment. Photo: Richard Einzig

1 reception/records
2 waiting
3 consulting/examination
4 treatment
5 toilets
6 dental surgery
7 dental store
8 store

A temporary and transportable health centre designed for use in different locations during the growth of the new community at Thamesmead. Four units of container size suitable for loading on vehicles, complete with all their internal fittings, were linked together on site by pre-fabricated roofs and floors forming the waiting space and corridors. Architects: Derek Stow and Partners suitable for subsequent adaptations and additions than some of the more fully prefabricated products which are difficult to modify.

An example of the fully prefabricated approach in an entirely different context, but which may be of relevance elsewhere, was the transportable health centre used in Britain at Thamesmead in South London when the new community was in the early years of construction. A temporary health facility was needed in various locations as construction advanced, which would be superseded by a permanent and larger building when the town had reached a more developed stage.

The building consisted of four units of approximately container size, each capable of being loaded on a vehicle. The units were structurally self-sufficient and complete with doors, windows and all services and fitted installations. They were linked together on site by prefabricated flooring, cladding and roofing which formed the waiting and circulation areas, where there were no requirements for servicing. Given the availability of incoming and outgoing services site preparation was minimal, as was the internal work necessary to bring the building into use.

In some parts of the world 'mobile homes' have been used for housing construction staff on major projects where no existing accommodation is available. It is possible that there may be something to be learnt from them for the smaller types of health buildings, or at least for those elements of them that justify relatively sophisticated accommodation. They have the benefits of convenience and comfort, and are relatively easily transported. Although high in cost, complete factory finished units which can be easily linked together, as an alternative to prefabricated elements that have to be assembled piece by piece and fitted out by procedures similar to normal building, may sometimes be more relevant in the developing world than they have generally been found to be elsewhere.

However, since adequate staffing for a health service is usually a greater problem than suitable buildings and can take a good deal longer to provide, it may be that in most situations instant availability is not really the first priority. Where there are adequate roads mobile units are probably more relevant in the context of a mobile health service. These can travel from one district to another and give support, with more sophisticated equipment and a higher degree of scarce medical skill, to the work of isolated rural health posts far distant from the nearest hospital. In Britain mobile transfusion units collecting blood from donors and X-ray scanning units for preventive medicine perform in their different ways an analogous function.

If communication by road is practicable it may be better to rotate a relatively high degree of service around the skeleton of a more elementary one than to attempt to build up permanent and more elaborate establishments everywhere. A service of this nature need not depend upon the use of large mobile trailers or lorries. The important thing is that the scarce and more highly skilled worker, based perhaps in the district hospital, should be available to visit and support the auxiliaries in the more remote outposts.

1 shaded waiting area
2 general treatment/office
3 examination
4 store
5 bath/toilet
6 sister's bedroom
7 nurses
8 clean utility
9 dirty utility
10 laundry
11 pantry
12 kitchen
13 general ward
14 sluice
15 observation ward
16 ward
17 labour room
18 health education
19 staff

Medical centre for the Aboriginal community of Ernabella in Australia, with provision for out-patient examination and treatment, seven short stay beds and a labour room. A separate multi-purpose building is used for health education, staff meetings and training. There is a shaded open-air waiting area between the two buildings. The beds are intended as overnight accommodation or for patients awaiting transport to the base hospital. The centre is staffed by two registered nurses and two or three Aboriginal women health workers. An aerial medical service supplies a fortnightly medical clinic. The centre was constructed in Adelaide, some 900 hundred miles away, and the parts transported by road for erection on the site. Architects: Public Buildings Department, South Australian Government

In Britain an example of such 'outreach' clinic facilities at a sophisticated level can be seen in Scotland, where the population of the Borders is about 100 000 and is spread in small centres over a wide area. In the more remote places there are roads but public transport is limited, making it extremely difficult for people to attend hospital as out-patients. Consultants in all specialties, based at the Borders General Hospital, therefore travel out regularly to local Health Centres, where they are able both to see patients and to discuss their medical history with their local general practitioner.

Where communications are difficult or long distances are involved a mobile health service that uses aircraft may be relevant. If China's 'barefoot doctor' is at one end of the scale the 'flying doctor' is at the other. Flying services have been used in Australia and in the Scottish Highlands but in developing countries their most significant application has probably been in connection with epidemiological surveys and mass immunisation campaigns and similar one-off projects funded with external aid.

Flying services are expensive, and are unlikely to justify themselves as a permanent element in the health facilities of a poor country, particularly if they are seen only as a means of transporting emergency patients over long distances to a centre which is equipped to deal with them or in bringing a doctor to an emergency. Where a country can afford a flying service of any sort it is more likely to be of value in carrying medical teams on regular scheduled visits to remote and isolated outposts that would take unreasonably long to reach by motor transport.

4

The general hospital

A general hospital is one that is organised to deal with a variety of conditions of illness needing specialised skills or equipment that cannot economically be provided in the patient's home or in small medical centres in the community. It brings together in a concentrated form most of the specialist services otherwise performed by a number of separate hospitals with more limited functions – hospitals for children, for women, for accidents, for orthopaedic work or for mental illness – and it provides care for both inpatients and outpatients.

Patients normally stay in a general hospital for a relatively short time, and the building is sometimes known as a general *acute* hospital. This implies illness of rapid onset and usually of short duration, to distinguish it from a hospital whose patients are, for example, chronically ill and who are for this reason likely to be of longer stay.

Within the National Health Service in Britain, the general hospital usually supports a school of nursing, and is known as a District General Hospital because it is based on a particular catchment area.

The size of hospitals

General hospitals are often categorised by the number of beds they contain but this gives little indication of their true extent and complexity. The ancillary departments, necessary to support the beds and to deal with outpatients, have greatly increased in size and sophistication in the last thirty-five years.

Hospitals contain three basic categories of accommodation, all different in function and physical requirements. Firstly there are the beds themselves, organised in wards of a size appropriate to their speciality and the nursing teams that look after them; to each ward is attached the accommodation necessary for its day-to-day clinical and domestic servicing. Secondly, there are the departments which provide the diagnostic, surgical, medical and therapeutic services needed to support the wards and minister to out-patients. Thirdly, there are the departments that look after the establishment as a whole, providing it with medical and domestic supplies, food and energy, and maintaining the physical fabric and equipment. The relative space occupied by these categories of accommodation varies somewhat with the type of hospital and the country in which it is situated but in a typical general hospital in a western country the total area of all the other departments may well be about equal to that of all the wards.

The size of general hospitals varies considerably, depending principally on the population of the area served. In the UK the preferred size is nowadays thought to be about 600 or 700 beds. It is difficult, and can be misleading, to make international comparisons but although there are many instances of much smaller general hospitals (and even 300 beds constitutes quite a large establishment) a range of between 600 and 1000 beds seems to be fairly widely accepted, with a tendency to avoid the upper figure.

From the patient's point of view and in its public impact a hospital of a thousand or more beds can be a formidable establishment and there may be persuasive arguments on human and environmental grounds for avoiding such a size unless there are compelling reasons to justify it. Much depends upon the manner in which a complex of this magnitude is designed, and in this respect there is by no means only one type of solution. It will be appreciated that below a certain number of beds, the supporting facilities that can be economically provided will be reduced and the specialist treatment that can be readily available will be limited.

Space and standards

Although techniques for diagnosis and treatment are largely international, the space standards for individual parts of a hospital can vary widely from one country to another. Besides cultural factors and different methods of working they reflect the funds allocated for construction and equipment and the money that will be available for the recurrent costs of staff and supplies and for keeping the facility operational.

In the UK during the last thirty five years there has been a substantial programme of hospital building, providing new facilities and replacing or extending old ones, in an attempt to keep pace with the demands of a health service available to everybody. Accompanying this programme there has been considerable operational research. Much ingenuity has been exercised in trying to eliminate 'wasteful' space in order to keep capital costs within budgets and at the same time to meet clinical needs and to provide good working conditions and an improved environment for patients.

Some of the resulting space standards should be regarded as absolute minima and would not necessarily be appropriate in many parts of the world, nor indeed would some of them be acceptable. For example, in some Moslem countries the need to separate the accommodation for men and women to a much greater degree than elsewhere, and the spaces in which they circulate, can add greatly to the area of some parts of a hospital. In other countries spaces that in Britain are considered essential may be almost irrelevant. Social customs such as hospital visiting by whole families at all hours of the day, or the supply of food to patients by relatives encamped nearby, can also have a profound influence on the type of space that is needed.

The space that is genuinely appropriate for the various components of a hospital is not always easy to determine. Sometimes it is related to the dimensions of machines or pieces of equipment, static or mobile, and to the activities performed by people around such equipment. For many such areas there are almost universal guidelines because the techniques employed are international and reasonable dimensions can be determined with some certainty if the scope of the facility and the methods of operation can be predicted. However, there are dangers in tailoring the space too precisely to fit a particular function that may alter after a few years, even before a building is occupied.

Appropriate space is also related to estimations of minimum distances for the avoidance of cross-infection, combined with social acceptability, as in the spacing of beds. Standards in western countries may be very different from those which the customs of another country permit or which are sometimes forced upon an overloaded establishment. In some circumstances it may be both unnecessary and unrealistic to plan for the arrangement of beds with curtains round each bed to give privacy during examinations or when the patient is using a bedpan. It may also be unnecessary for every patient to have both a locker and a bedside chair. People accustomed to living with their families and animals in the open air and retiring to one or two small rooms or to the roof are not likely to react in the same way as an urban western European or Northern American to what the latter might regard as a crowded ward. In a hot climate there may be a need for 'dayroom' facilities that would be entirely inappropriate elsewhere.

'Normal' solutions based on the experience of western countries can tend to become enshrined as absolutes for reasons of convenience. These solutions can come to be accepted all too readily by designers if they do not question them and enquire into the roots of the requirements and seek an appropriate answer.

Some countries are reaching a stage of development where they can build major new hospitals, perhaps for the first time in their history. Understandably they wish to provide the best available, but may be prone to the belief that standards of excellence are only to be found in models based on western patterns. They may not recognise that these standards have been produced in response to western demands and a dissimilar background.

In some countries of the developing world hospitals have been built whose relevance to the real needs of the population is doubtful in the extreme. The countries acquiring these hospitals may have no infrastructure of primary health care with which to underpin them and no adequate pool of professional and technical staff who can be recruited to run them. The installation may be an inappropriately sophisticated importation, conceived elsewhere with medical enthusiasm and commercial opportunism, and bought blindly for political reasons.

More than any other building for health care a hospital is an expensive and complicated installation and costs a great deal to keep in operation, particularly in its staffing overheads. In Britain about three-quarters of the running cost of a hospital is staffing cost, and the total running cost can exceed the original capital cost of building and equipping it in about three years. Its design should spring, in the first instance, not from a convenient schedule of customary accommodation but from a realistic analysis of the functions it is intended to fulfil and the manner in which it can perform them.

Variously known as a 'philosophy of service' or an 'operational policy' this analysis extends to a detailed appraisal of the proposed methods of working and the procedures that are to be adopted throughout the organisation. It must anticipate the activities in every part of the establishment, both in strategic terms and in considerable tactical detail. Unless the strategy is determined at the outset no amount of subsequent adjustment in the physical planning is likely to satisfy the actual requirements.

How are patients to reach the hospital and how are

they to be handled and deployed when they have got there? How are the many different categories of staff to reach it? Where are they going to change their clothes and leave their belongings and what amenities do they need during their working hours? How are the wards to be run and how are patients to be taken to the theatre or to other vital ancillary services? What are the procedures for handling specimens from their point of origin to the laboratories? How are medical and domestic supplies to be received, stored and distributed and how is food to be prepared, cooked and delivered to patients and staff? What arrangements are to be made for visitors? How is cleaning and maintenance to be performed, and refuse and infected matter to be disposed of? What actions will be necessary if there is a fire in the building?

These and many other procedures need to be thought through and determined in principle as a part of the designer's brief. Some of them may be irreconcilable in the context of the total problem and the planning solution that is possible in the particular instance; they may have to be changed or modified accordingly. It is important that these procedures should not be derived afterwards from the constraints of a building design that has been conceived in ignorance of them.

An understanding of primary requirements analogous to these is, of course, vital for the design of any building for health care, or indeed of any building for a special purpose. In the case of a hospital, the determination of the primary requirements is of particular importance because of the size, complexity and interdependence of the different parts and the universal acceptance that it should function with the maximum ease, efficiency and economy in saving human life.

In countries with a well established hospital service and a long tradition of experience and precedent the answers to some of the above questions of operational policy may be fairly conventional, in the sense that there is general agreement about a way of doing things. Much may even be codified in broad terms as a matter of national policy, not least because only then can expenditure be controlled, lengthy discussion between the various interests avoided and reasonably rapid design and construction achieved.

Even so there will from time to time be a breakthrough in one area or another demanding a reassessment of policy, altering relationships and affecting accommodation in detail. The provision of sterile supplies from a central source is a relatively recent example of this. In countries without such an established tradition a much more fundamental analysis of all aspects of operational policy is necessary if inappropriate and supposedly 'universal' assumptions are to be guarded against and strategic mistakes avoided.

General arrangement

Wherever a hospital is situated, whatever the culture and whatever its size and detailed operational policies, it will contain both wards and supporting departments. The wards may be categorised by speciality, by the sex or age of patients, and to some degree each will be run as a self-contained unit. These are considered in Chapter 5.

The supporting departments will be categorised by their speciality and the particular services they perform; each discharges a different function with its own staff and a certain amount of its own administration but many of them are closely related functionally to others. Not all departments are medical, surgical or therapeutic. Separate departments will be necessary for central administration, for the receipt and distribution of stores, for the preparation, cooking and distribution of food, for the physical maintenance of the building and its services and equipment, for heating, ventilation and other mechanical plant. The basic nature of some of the principal departments is the subject of Chapter 6.

The last half century has seen important changes in attitude towards the form that the planning of wards should take. Although opinions continue to vary and change on this matter and the solution for one society may be different from that for another, the spaces occupied by beds and their ancillary rooms are relatively finite units in a hospital. There may be fluctuations in the numbers of patients occupying beds of different specialities which may be due to seasonal changes or a reduction in the incidence of particular diseases by preventive advances or the introduction of new methods of treatment. For this reason it may be an advantage if there is some physical continuity between one ward unit and another so that one can expand by a few beds at the expense of its next door neighbour. Yet despite such minor modifications, it is improbable that wards will need to be altered in nature or size in any fundamental way during the useful life of the building. If the bed capacity of the hospital has to be increased further separate wards will be added; they are unlikely to affect the existing units.

In some of the central departments that support the wards, on the other hand, considerable changes may need to be anticipated. The relative importance of the functions they perform may alter and in some departments the space required for efficient operation may shrink or expand. In addition, the nature of the equipment and servicing may change and entirely new departments may need to be added.

The form and arrangement of the wards is fundamental and will have a major effect on the form of the whole building. However, the major strategic decisions in hospital planning will have to be taken in the relationship of the central departments to one another and to the wards. Future changes in the nature and size of the departments will have to be anticipated, as well as the logistic arrangements for communications and supplies. The problems are complex, particularly when the initial capital cost of the building is geared to the specific accommodation that can be justified at the time it is conceived. A loose fit, which probably implies the provision of more than the minimum efficient space, cannot usually be reconciled with the budget, even though the capital cost of the building is relatively small compared with the running cost over its useful life.

The complexities are usually intensified when the building has to be designed for a restricted site and the room for manoeuvre is very limited. But even on large open sites where there is plenty of space to spread, and

particularly in hospitals with more than about 500 beds, there may well be a conflict between planning in a form loose enough to provide for future change and expansion and the distances that staff and patients need to travel to get from one place to another.

Frequently there is the further complication that the hospital has to be built in stages, or is a phased extension of older buildings that are already in use. Usually the first stage and each subsequent enlargement must constitute a viable operational unit. The progressive work of construction (and perhaps modification of what has already been built) must interfere as little as possible with the function and amenity of the accommodation already occupied. Unlike many buildings a hospital is in use twenty-four hours a day on every day of the year; there are no week-end or holiday breaks during which alterations can be organised.

Form and ventilation

The total form of a hospital building and the relationships of its different parts will be influenced by many factors; one that is likely to be fundamental is the policy to be adopted for its ventilation.

Air conditioning is generally recognised as of the highest priority in the operating theatre suite. Air conditioning in this context means the ability to control the air temperature both above and below the ambient temperature and also to control the humidity, with sterile filtration in addition. In temperate climates, in most other departments, although for medical reasons air conditioning may be desirable, particularly in noisy and polluted urban situations, it cannot by any means be regarded as essential. It is, of course, more important in tropical countries and in hot desert areas where dust storms blow for half the year. In the wards there may be strong arguments against air conditioning, particularly when it is

1	services	4	beds	7	ambulances
2	blood centre	5	diagnostic/treatment	8	relatives' compound
3	teaching	6	entrances		

Health Services Centre at Khon Kaen, Thailand; a 580 bed teaching hospital capable of expansion to 700 beds. Designed to rely as little as possible on high technology, the buildings are naturally ventilated except in those few areas where medical needs call for air conditioning. A central hospital street in which patient, visitor and service traffics are segregated runs through the whole complex and most departments are independently extendable. Architects: Llewelyn-Davies Weeks

The first completed ward at Khon Kaen. Wide overhangs, sunscreens and natural through-ventilation

efficient maintenance cannot be relied upon. Total dependence upon it can quickly render a building uninhabitable in such circumstances.

Whether in a temperate or tropical climate total air conditioning makes possible a high ratio of internal space to external wall and permits a compact building form that would be entirely impracticable without it. Air conditioning may thus reduce the site area that is necessary and will tend to lead to economy in the cost of the actual fabric of the building, but not to that of its artificial lighting and other services or of its maintenance. Conversely, reliance on natural ventilation will impose inescapable constraints on the shape that the plan can take. Because natural ventilation will produce a relatively high ratio of external wall to floor area it will be likely to increase the cost of the building fabric although reducing that of its services and running costs.

Whatever the policy regarding ventilation, however, it is well to recognise that some forms of planning, particularly in multi-storey buildings, may make air conditioning essential. Even in temperate climates any block of accommodation with a depth of more than about 15 m which contains internal rooms is unlikely to be able to rely satisfactorily on natural ventilation, even when supplemented artificially. This is particularly true of internal rooms which generate heat from equipment. The building will need to be air conditioned if the temperature in the core of the block is to be prevented from rising above the ambient and a healthy and acceptable working environment is to be maintained.

entirely strange to the normal habitat, customs and expectations of the patients.

An artificial environment of 'pure' air throughout the building, however well filtered and tempered, is also no guarantee against infection. Air movement can have an important bearing on the incidence of infection, especially if air removed from an infected area is blown or sucked into another part of the building through ventilation or duct systems. Unfortunately, the installation of full air treatment does not always achieve a reduction of the incidence of outbreaks of infection. Indeed, many hospitals which are dependent for their ventilation on throwing open windows and doors (the method that was understandably so vigorously recommended by Florence Nightingale) have less frequent outbreaks than those with full air conditioning. Whether what has become known as Sick Building Syndrome, whose symptoms include headaches, lethargy and irritation of nose, eyes, throat and skin, can be attributed to air conditioned buildings has not been established, but it is certainly experienced most frequently in such buildings. However, not only is air conditioning expensive but it is a constant consumer of energy and an extremely demanding servant. And vigorous maintenance is essential, as recent outbreaks of Legionnaires' Disease have emphasised.

Unnecessary dependence on wholly artificial means of air control can impose intolerable difficulties when sophisticated systems break down and prompt and

1 power house
2 engineering/ maintenance
3 general supply
4 CSSD
5 linen supply/laundry
6 staff change
7 catering
8 laboratories
9 mortuary
10 pharmacy
11 prayer room
12 administration/ records/library
13 main entrance
14 specialist clinics

15 accident and emergency
16 diagnostic radiology
17 operating
18 delivery
19 male general acute ward
20 female/obstetric/ children's ward (future male ward)
21 GP clinic
22 future wards

Diagrammatic plan of a single storey 50-bed fully air-conditioned hospital for Saudi Arabia, capable of expansion to 100 beds by the addition of two ward units. All daylight to the wards is from shaded internal courtyards. Ward circulation is separated from the main L-shaped hospital street. Architects: Architects Co-Partnership

Model of an internal courtyard for Saudi Arabian hospitals, with eggcrate louvres for the control of sunlight. Archtects: Architects Co-Partnership

Salmaniya Medical Centre, Bahrain; a 550-bed air-conditioned hospital. Patients' rooms face north and south to minimise solar heat gain and the relatively small window openings are deeply shaded. East and west flank walls are blank. Architects: Llewelyn-Davies Weeks. (Photo: Henk Snoek Photography and Associates)

Preliminary model of Maiduguri Teaching Hospital in NE Nigeria, a hot dry region bordering on the Sahara. Separate fingers of accommodation face north and south and the ward areas are naturally ventilated and deeply shaded. Architect: John R. Harris. (Photo: Henk Snoek Photography and Associates)

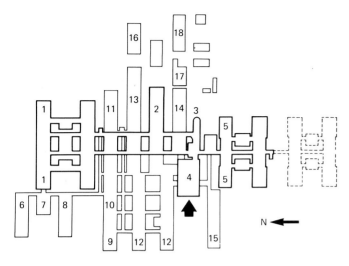

1 women's wards
2 operating
3 ramp
4 administration
5 men's wards
6 labour/delivery
7 obstetric theatre
8 maternity admissions
9 ENT/ophthalmic
10 accident and emergency
11 X-ray
12 clinics
13 pathology
14 kitchen and dining
15 physiotherapy
16 mortuary
17 laundry
18 engineering and maintenance

The 517 bed Maiduguri Teaching Hospital in the hot dry region of NE Nigeria, a Moslem area. Men's and women's wards are at opposite ends of the two storey spine, from which long fingers enclosing courtyards are developed outwards on the lower floor. A possible future extension to the south could provide a further 256 beds. Wards are naturally ventilated, theatres and ITU fully air conditioned, certain other areas such as offices are air conditioned with local window mounted units, and some rooms such as clean and dirty utilities are mechanically ventilated. Teaching accommodation is distributed in blocks throughout the building, mostly on the upper floor. Architect: John R. Harris

The form that a naturally ventilated hospital can take will be affected by the climate, but in tropical countries it will be dominated by it. In the warm humid regions, about 15° north and south of the Equator, free air movement through relatively shallow ranges of building is vital for comfort. In these locations it is desirable to plan for the maximum exposure of occupied spaces to the prevailing wind that is compatible with shading from the sun, and also to separate parallel blocks of building sufficiently widely not to shelter one another from the breeze. In hot dry or desert regions, on the other hand, the orientation of the building to minimise the exposure of external wall surface to the sun is paramount. Thus an orientation for inhabited spaces as near north/south as possible is important, as is the reduction to the minimum of those surfaces facing east and west which cannot be shaded from low altitude sunlight and which should have as few openings in them as possible.

As can so often be seen in vernacular buildings in desert regions, thick walls, small shaded openings, courtyards and protection from glare result in forms entirely different from the more open configurations of Central Africa or South East Asia where air movement is at a premium.

Contrasting examples

A characteristic mid-twentieth century form that expresses the relationship between ward accommodation and the supporting departments in an extremely direct way is the multi-storey ward block rising above a spreading base of specialist accommodation. Simple and compact, the structure is fairly economical; it lends itself well to the vertical stacking of communications and services and can occupy relatively little space on the site. Such an arrangement, or a similar tall ward block with supporting departments in an adjacent wing, may sometimes be the only practicable type of solution where ground space is at a premium. However, if the building is of any considerable height and cannot reasonably be served by stairs or ramps in an emergency it relies entirely on an adequate lift installation for its efficient functioning.

The ward block may be naturally ventilated if it is narrow enough, as may be the base if it spreads widely around courtyards. But if the former is compactly planned, with beds around the perimeter and a central core of service rooms and communications, as is often the case, and the base is similarly condensed (implying full air conditioning) the building is almost totally dependent on its mechanical equipment. It shares many characteristics with the international hotel building type but it may be doubted whether the functions a hospital has to fulfil are similar. Further, it tends to be a form that cannot readily be altered or extended in any organic manner.

In some developing countries, and particularly the oil-rich ones where air conditioning of major new buildings is taken for granted, this compact multi-storey arrangement, imported from elsewhere, could almost be said to have become a stereotype.

In the UK the image of the huge impersonal medical machine that this type of building all too easily presents has tended to become increasingly unacceptable to the public, and particularly to the potential patients. For this reason, quite independently of the economic consequence of running such a building and its longer term energy implications, the pendulum of preference has for some time been swinging strongly away towards a search for simpler technical methods, a more humane and domestic character, and more flexible solutions.

In some other countries, on the other hand, where health care is an emerging social facility, the imposing symbolism of a big building, and preferably a tall one, seems to catch the imagination of those politically responsible for its provision, even though there may be ample ground space for other types of solution. Whether it is a form really suitable for the culture and the technological resources of some areas of the world is highly questionable.

A relatively early British example of the opposite approach from the multi-storey ward block with the low base (or the matchbox on a muffin, as it has been called) can be seen at Wexham Park, Buckinghamshire, which was built during the first half of the 1960s. Here the multi-storey block contains only administration, secretarial services and residential accommodation for medical staff, none of whom are entirely dependent upon lifts but are only inconvenienced if they fail (see page 51).

1 main entrance
2 kitchen and staff dining
3 CSSD
4 dressings and drugs store
5 linen store
6 mortuary
7 administration
8 nurses' training school
9 pathology
10 physiotherapy
11 accident and emergency
12 X-ray
13 pharmacy
14 out-patients
15 39-bed ward
16 private wards
17 20 bed ENT/eye ward
A nurses' station
B day space
C toilets and baths
D disposal
E sister
F pantry
G treatment

1 specialist referral clinic
2 extension to out-patients and accident and emergency
3 special baby care and laboratory
4 engineering services
5 infectious diseases unit
6 second X-ray department
7 in-patient psychiatric unit
8 psychiatric out-patients
9 new physiotherapy department
10 open access clinic, preventive medicine and dental unit

Ground floor of the Rashid Hospital, Dubai; a fully air-conditioned building with 393 beds. It has a simple and direct organisation of hospital streets relieved by internal courtyards. Men's wards are on the ground floor, women's and children's on the upper together with the operating department and ITU, which adjoins the central lifts. Architect: John R. Harris

Extensions to the Rashid Hospital (shown in outline) add more beds, further diagnostic and treatment accommodation, a psychiatric unit and an open access outpatient clinic

Model of the Rashid Hospital. Out-patients, accidents, pharmacy and X-ray are in the single storey wing on the left; stores, CSSD and kitchen entrance on the right. (Photo: Henk Snoek Photography and Associates)

The Rashid Hospital, Dubai; air conditioned, with small window openings and balconies for the recessed day spaces in the wards. Kitchen, stores, CSSD and mortuary are in the unit on the right; out-patients, accident and emergency and X-ray are in the complementary wing on the other side of the main building. Architect: John R. Harris

Model for a 400 bed hospital on an urban island site in Khartoum, a hot dry climate. Out-patient, maternity, operating, diagnostic and service departments are at ground floor level, penetrated by small courtyards and air-conditioned only where medical needs justify it. Above this base there are four wards to each floor, facing north and south, deeply shaded and naturally ventilated, approached from a visitors' concourse served by ramp and lifts. In the foreground (right) there are shaded waiting and car parking areas. Architects: Architects' Co-partnership

1 reception/administration
2 pharmacy
3 pathology
4 out-patients clinic
5 doctors
6 operating
7 X-ray
8 casualties
9 five-bed bays
10 ancillary rooms
11 day spaces

0 — 61 m
0 — 200 ft

One of several standard 'Turnkey' hospitals for the Ministry of Health in Saudi Arabia, with up to 450 beds, constructed complete with all services, equipment, furniture, accessories and stores, including medical instruments and laboratory installations. They are fully air-conditioned. A lower floor of the two storey base contains kitchen, laundry, central sterilisation, physiotherapy, administration, lecture rooms and stores; the main entrance is on the floor above (left). The five storey ward block (above) has a racetrack plan with a central core of service rooms and vertical communications. The power house, transformers, switch rooms, workshops and mortuary are in a separate single storey building. Design/construction: Philipp Holzmann AG, Frankfurt

One of the standard 'Turnkey' hospitals in Saudi Arabia

At Wexham Park wards with 300 beds, and the diagnostic, treatment and other servicing departments, are all of only one storey in height and are spread out in fingers around the taller block, enclosing courtyards and gardens of domestic scale. The hospital occupies a relatively large site area and from the point of view of journey times from one part of the building to another probably stretches to near the limit of acceptability for a horizontal layout of one storey.

These two ways of solving the problem of the physical form of the hospital epitomise two fundamentally different approaches. One results in a sophisticated instrument, dependent on its supporting machinery, and is highly efficient provided the machinery works continuously. The other, although it may need more space, may be just as satisfactory clinically and although aided by machinery in certain parts, the function of the building is not entirely dependent upon it.

The simpler and non-mechanical solution may also offer a psychological advantage for staff and patients, particularly for patients who suddenly find themselves in an alien and disturbing world of medical procedures and unnatural intervention. Patients may obtain reassurance and perhaps a quicker recovery through relationships and symbols with which they can connect and which have some associations with their habitual lifestyle. To be fairly close to the ground, to open a window, to smell the world outside and hear its sounds may reassure the patient that he is still connected with the outside world. There is no straightforward answer to the question of which approach is the better.

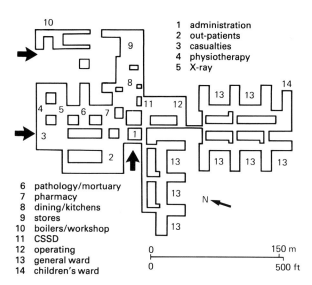

1 administration
2 out-patients
3 casualties
4 physiotherapy
5 X-ray
6 pathology/mortuary
7 pharmacy
8 dining/kitchens
9 stores
10 boilers/workshop
11 CSSD
12 operating
13 general ward
14 children's ward

Wexham Park Hospital. Single storey wards extend in fingers to the south and west from the sterilising and operating departments at the centre. Out-patients, pharmacy, casualties, X-ray and diagnostic departments extend at ground level around courtyards to the north; dining rooms, kitchen and stores to the east. Over the centre a higher building houses essentially non-clinical uses – administration and residential accommodation for medical staff. Architects: Powell and Moya. Consultants: Llewelyn-Davies Weeks

Superb multi-storey hospitals of the mechanically dependent type have been built during recent decades, notably in the USA and Canada. Here the complexity of distributing services such as conveyors, liquids, gases and air, and maintaining these without conflicting with clinical work or putting it at risk, has prompted designs of great sophistication. The accommodation is supported by an armature of service zones which occupies almost as much space as the area it serves.

Instead of being stacked directly one upon another clinical and research floors have been separated like a sandwich by independent interstitial spaces high enough for maintenance engineers to walk about in, in which services can be distributed to any part of the floor area. These spaces have been fed vertically by major communication ducts or towers, thus separating entirely the servicing zones from those which are dependent upon them.

The advantages of configurations of this sort are not limited to the ease of maintenance they confer on the hospital when it is in use or has to be altered. By providing separate territories in which construction workers and service engineers can operate independently and simultaneously these structures simplify and accelerate the process of building and commissioning. At a strategic level they also provide a carcase within which considerable flexibility of internal planning is possible, as the need to group heavily serviced areas together, or to superimpose them floor by floor to simplify the routes of services, is partly eliminated. They are mentioned in more detail in Chapter 7.

Thus for the most complicated and sophisticated buildings, such as large teaching hospitals in which clinical and research facilities may need to be integrated,

Model of Al-Karama hospital, Baghdad, a 1000-bed air-conditioned building on an island site. The hospital street runs round four sides of the central courtyard, with lifts and stairs at the corners, where the L-shaped wards are approached. There are two floors of wards, separated from the ground floor accommodation by an interstitial space for the distribution of services. On the ground floor of the rectangle are the specialist referral clinics, diagnostic and accident and emergency departments, education and administration. In the central courtyard are (left) the lecture theatre, (centre) the senior staff dining room and (right) the on-call suite. The wings on the right contain the operating theatre, sterilising room, supplies and laundry, with ramps connecting all floors. Staff residences are in the separate building. Architects: Architects Co-Partnership

Wexham Park. The central administrative and residential building rises
above the spreading single storey hospital. Architects, Powell and
Moya. Consultants: Llewelyn-Davies Weeks. (Photo: Colin Westwood)

The two arms of each ward unit at Wexham Park enclose a sheltered
garden. (Photo: Colin Westwood)

1 psychiatric in-patients
2 psychiatric out-patients
3 paediatric in-patients
4 paediatric out-patients
5 on-duty suite
6 medical in-patients
7 medical out-patients
8 metabolic in-patients
9 cardiac care in-patients
10 cardiovascular
11 multi-discipline labs.
12 electron microscopy

Diagram of the arrangement of one of the upper floors at McMaster. Vertical towers house either services or stairs and support the trussed floors. A continuous hospital street binds the assembly together and is lit at intervals from courtyards

The Health Service Centre under construction at McMaster University, Hamilton, Ontario. A large and sophisticated complex embracing hospital, medical school, school of nursing, and research, it aims to provide a simple envelope within which integration of departments, highly developed services and opportunities for change are possible. Mechanical services are distributed to the usable floors through the long-span spaces within the deep trusses, fed from service towers arranged on a rectangular grid. Architects: The Zeidler Partnership

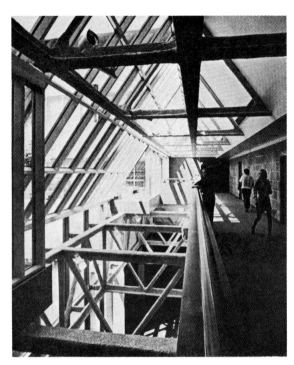

The McMaster hospital street where it passes alongside one of the courtyards

there may be good arguments to recommend them. However, although such arrangements may be lucid they can be costly to build, and are probably out of scale with the needs of the general hospital in many countries

Growth and change

Some of the apparently rational and coherent hospital forms adopted by designers display more abstract architectural logic than sense of historical reality. They tend towards a finite notion of a hospital building, for implicit in them is the assumption that the operational policies and the balance of the various types of accommodation will continue relatively unchanged during the life of the structure.

This assumption is not always well founded. One has only to look at some of the older hospitals in Britain to recognise the extensions to the earlier core that have come about over the last century. These are usually without any strategic planning armature to hold them together but have been added largely *ad hoc* as new needs and opportunities have presented themselves.

There seems little reason to suppose that medicine will cease to produce unforeseen demands and it is arguable that new hospitals will be subject to similar pressures. This is particularly so in developing countries where, although the initial accommodation may have to be relatively simple, the provision of facilities is likely to be rapidly extended in the future.

As the inevitability of growth and change has come to be recognised views have been expressed during the last few decades which maintain that, wherever it is situated, a hospital is never likely to be complete. As the building will inevitably require alterations and additions

during its working life, from the outset its physical organisation should be conceived with this in mind.

The classic demonstration of this as a generating approach to planning is to be seen in the UK at Northwick Park, Harrow, a district general hospital and clinical research centre designed early in the 1960s. It is probably the most uncompromising and theoretically 'pure' evidence of this philosophy, and remains a seminal example that in one form or another has probably had as profound an influence as any on hospital planning strategy ever since.

Three plans showing the development method at Northwick Park Hospital and Clinical Research Centre. A linear hospital street forms the backbone to which ribs can be attached with relative freedom. It is the earliest example of deliberate indeterminacy in post-war hospital planning. Most of the hospital and research departments may be constructed, and later altered or expanded, independently of one another. Construction was carried out in phases over a period of nine years and during this time extensions and alterations to the original brief were made without disturbing the basic design. Architects: Llewelyn-Davies Weeks

Fundamental to the 'indeterminate' approach of Northwick Park is the concept of a linear and enclosed hospital street which provides a strategic backbone. Independent buildings for various functions can be attached to this with relative freedom, each building having one end connected to the street and the other unobstructed so that it can be extended laterally at some future date if this is necessary.

Although it is much more flexible, and at a higher level of sophistication, the basic pattern has similarities with the early military hutted hospital of the Crimean War, the old 'Fever hospitals' or the long 'Nightingale' wards. All of these (no doubt for quite different reasons) were characterised by accommodation placed at intervals and at right angles to a main access corridor or walkway.

With a planning strategy such as this the initial design, construction and commissioning of the building by stages is greatly facilitated. This is because the units are physically independent and not closely integrated with one another in a way that causes a change in one to have a ripple effect in contiguous departments. In addition, the growth of different parts is likely to be possible in large or small increments without interfering with others, as also is internal alteration to any individual part.

At Northwick Park no attempt is made to construct a finite architectural object. The indeterminacy is pursued with a logic that permeates the whole design, almost to the extent of seeming to avoid any extraneous imposition of visual order except in the employment of dimensionally related components of construction. Indeed the total result might not unreasonably be likened to the loose appearance of the large nineteenth century hospital to which frequent extensions and annexes have been added in the surrounding grounds when they were needed. There is, however, the important difference, logistic rather than visual, that at Northwick each element adjoins a deliberate and predetermined pattern of communications and is arranged from the outset with the possibility of alteration and extension in mind.

The hospital street

The principle of a line of communication or 'hospital street' to which fingers or nodules of accommodation are attached can be seen in an elementary and more rigid form in a study for a 300 bed hospital at St. Albans in Hertfordshire, undertaken in the late 1940s. As at Northwick Park the hospital street was arranged on two levels, one for services and supplies and the other for all other purposes. This ran as a spine below a long ward block which was capable of horizontal growth by the addition of further ward units.

Diagnostic and treatment departments, extendable at their free ends, were plugged into the street at ground level on the pattern of a fishbone. Much the same principle can be seen again in a later, larger and more developed form at the 800 bed York General Hospital, where the basic relationship of wards, hospital street and specialist departments is very similar.

The line of communication to which the various elements relate is not by any means invariably linear. It sometimes takes the form of either a loop, a figure of eight, a cross, or a combination of these patterns. In most hospitals it is not practicable, however desirable, to provide strict segregation between the streets for

Northwick Park. The hospital street is on the right, used by patient staff and visitors. Supply services occupy a separate street underneath. Dining rooms and lecture theatre are linked to the street on the left. In the background is a ward and research building. (Photo: Henk-Snoek Photography and Associates)

A late 1940's study for a hospital at St Albans. A two level hospital street for people and supplies runs below an extendable ward block, with vertical communication at intervals. Diagnostic and treatment departments and a separate maternity unit are plugged into the street, and are also extendable. Operating theatres are on the top floor. Architects: Architects' Co-Partnership

1   diagnostic and treatment
2   service and supply
3   in-patient wards
4   area for future development

York District General Hospital. This provides 812 beds with the possibility of extension to over 1000. Most of the accommodation is between one and four storeys in height. Extendable diagnostic and treatment departments communicate at ground level with a simple linear hospital street for people and supplies which runs below a double-banked ward block that has cross links enclosing courtyards. Architects: Llewelyn-Davies Weeks

supplies or other goods and those for people, although by the disposition of departments it may be possible to avoid serious conflict between the major categories of traffic, both from the point of view of its density and of the potential risk of cross-infection.

It is an advantage to avoid the routes for visitors being combined to any great extent with other internal circulation, for instance, and to arrange that potential traffic past critical areas such as operating suites is minimised. It is also desirable that infected and dirty material which is being removed for processing or disposal passes along routes which neither cross those constantly in use by patients and staff nor pass sensitive clinical areas. The latter include theatres and surgical wards, maternity departments, and places occupied by patients with reduced protection or immunity from infection.

The source of infection is not confined to clinical areas. The origin of infection, and its results, can be in any part of a hospital including, for example, kitchens and laundries. Control of infection depends largely upon the behaviour and disciplines of people but it can be greatly assisted by the physical planning of the building.

The arrangement of the elements of accommodation along a linear hospital street can demand a lot of space on the site and in a large hospital may result in travel

York District General Hospital

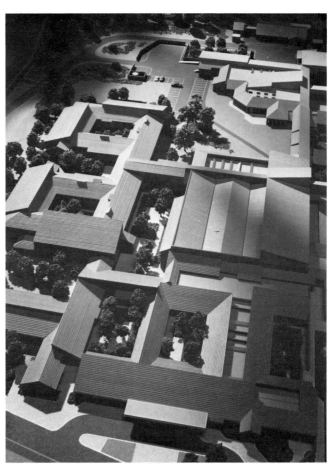

Model of the first stage of the North Tyneside District General hospital, providing 324 beds. The site falls from right to left of the picture and the buildings nowhere exceed two storeys. The operating and sterile supply departments are in the centre, linked on the left to a quadrangular ward building of two storeys. On the right they are linked to accident and emergency, intensive therapy and X-ray, which are single storey. The maternity department on the side nearest the main road is also single storey. Single storey children's wards adjoin, on the right, the spine that runs up to kitchen, dining room, stores and boiler house. The hospital streets incorporate ramps and stairs, and lifts are only necessary for transporting beds, trolleys, wheelchairs and heavy loads. Expansion to 600 beds is possible by the addition of further quadrangular ward blocks, day hospital, physiotherapy and out-patients to the right of the picture. Architects: George Trew Dunn Beckles Willson Bowes. (Photo: Henk Snoek/Crispin Boyle)

North Tyneside hospital is planned around intimate garden courtyards of varied scale and character. Services are distributed in enclosed and accessible routes within the pitched roofs. (Photo: Henk Snoek/Crispin Boyle)

distances that are unacceptably extended. It can also be argued that, in some forms, this arrangement encourages the isolation of specialities in separate units and may create physical and psychological obstacles that inhibit intercommunication.

The tendency of individual medical disciplines to merge with one another or to become interdependent suggests the need for a form that provides close relationships. There is a conflict between integrated planning and patterns which are looser. The former tends to encourage the search for the perfect answer at a particular moment in history. The looser forms permit not only an ebb and flow between disciplines but can also respond to pressures which it is difficult and sometimes impossible to anticipate.

A British sequence

An outline of four examples of the trend of design thinking in Britain as represented by the Ministry of Health (subsequently the Department of Health and Social Security) and the Regional Hospital Boards is given below. These demonstrate, over a period of years, a sequence of different types of solution to the problem of the general hospital in the context of a large, continuous and centrally financed national hospital building programme in which there has been development work, feedback and redevelopment, in parallel with an increasing need for economy. In addition to setting standards, controlling costs and publishing guidance notes the Ministry has sponsored research and design and development work, some of which it has carried out itself.

Greenwich

The first major example was the Greenwich District General hospital in South London which has 800 beds to serve a population of some 165 000. Built at about the same time as Northwick Park it exemplifies a very different approach. Greenwich was, of course, a response to a different problem, at a different scale and on a relatively urban site. Whilst it attempted to make provision for future change, to allow for growth was not

1 boilers
2 laundry
3 mortuary
4 kitchen
5 restaurant
6 pathology
7 ward block
8 haemodialysis
9 main entrance/administration
10 radiotherapy
11 out-patients
12 X-ray
13 central store
14 pharmacy
15 ward block
16 education
17 maternity
18 operating
19 ITU/burns etc.
20 physical medicine
21 geriatric day ward
22 accidents

South Teesside General Hospital. A low rise design similar to the North Tyneside example. Three storey quadrangular ward blocks of 360 beds are connected by short links to the central complex of supporting facilities, through which runs a rectangular system of hospital streets. Supply and service departments are attached to a linear tail. The first stage of construction (heavy outline) provides one ward block, haemodialysis, X-ray, radiotherapy, operating and a small out-patient department, in addition to boiler house, laundry, mortuary, kitchen and restaurant. Later stages add further ward blocks and a maternity unit, bringing the total number of beds up to about 1200, and enlarge the operating and out-patients' departments and intensive therapy, physical medicine, day wards, accidents, pathology, pharmacy and central stores. These enlargements can be made without interference to the completed stages and in most cases can be phased independently of the addition of ward blocks. Architects: George Trew Dunn Beckles Wilson Bowes

part of its objective and it is thus considerably more compact.

Greenwich has three clinical floors, all 2.75 m clear height, superimposed in a simple rectangular shape and separated from one another by interstitial service floors. Instead of being linear, the hospital street is rectangular and within it are enclosed all the specialist departments except out-patients.

All wards are arranged on the perimeter of the building in a continuous band around the hospital street, separated from it by their ancillary rooms. Within the rectangle of the street the diagnostic, treatment and supply departments form the core of each floor, divided by corridors into four quarters. This core is perforated by three courtyards, as the building is not so high as to render relatively small courtyards unacceptable. The whole building is air-conditioned.

Although a large hospital, the form of the building facilitates rapid horizontal movement between departments which need to have close relationships. For example surgical beds, gynaecology, the maternity suite, theatres and intensive therapy are all grouped on the same floor. Vertical communication by lifts and the irritating waiting time that can result is cut to a minimum.

Model of first stage of South Teesside hospital. Later stages enlarge the building by additions to the foreground and to the right of the picture. (Photo: Henk Snoek Photography and Associates)

Upper floor
1 out-patients/ENT/paediatric
2 theatres
3 anaesthetic service/
   administration
4 ITU
5 kitchen/dining
6 medical management
7 acute ward
8 two psychiatric wards
9 two acute wards
10 acute ward and day ward

Ground floor
1 entrance/records/chapel
2 out-patients/orthopaedic
   clinic
3 X-ray
4 administration/body store
5 pathology/medical records
6 stores/works/pharmacy
7 works/plant/disposal
8 acute ward
9 geriatric and psychogeriatric
   wards
10 rehabilitation
11 psychiatric day activities

*Edith Cavell District General Hospital, Peterborough. Block plans of the
first phase of a two storey hospital providing 180 acute and 96
psychiatric/psychogeriatric beds, showing disposition of departments
off the main hospital street and potential future expansion. The hospital
street is repeated in the roof space for access to plant rooms and boiler
houses. Architect: A. A. Crampin, Regional Architect, East Anglian
Regional Health Authority*

In addition to lifts there is some inter-floor communication
by escalator, which in a low rise building is quick and
easy for many purposes.

The opportunity for horizontal travel also facilitates the
movement of bedfast patients in case of fire. They can
readily be wheeled in their beds into a separate and
remote fire compartment with little risk of having to be
evacuated by stair or lift.

The location of the diagnostic and treatment departments in the central core of the building enables them to
be planned where they are most convenient functionally.
But, on the other hand, they cannot easily expand, for
they are imprisoned on all four sides by the wards. The
continuous peripheral banding of the wards offers
opportunities for minor changes in the extent of one
nursing unit at the expense of its neighbour without major
alteration. However, this banding tends to make for
relatively extended walking distances along straight
corridors within each unit.

Although Greenwich was not designed with major
expansion in mind it makes provision for alterations to its
internal planning and servicing. Long spans of 19.5 m
leave the floors relatively unencumbered by structural
columns or walls. The clinical floors are separated by
interstitial spaces for the distribution, maintenance and
alteration of services (whose 1.7 m height is less
generous than desirable).

But in spite of its potential internal flexibility, and
although it was in fact constructed in stages, it is
fundamentally a finite solution. In some respects the
building is easier to extend than a tower and podium but,
nevertheless, this type of arrangement does not lend
itself naturally to being built in instalments nor to organic
growth beyond its original form.

With its interstitial spaces and the dependence on
air-conditioning the building is relatively costly and,
irrespective of merit, is unlikely to be applicable where
economy is an overriding restraint. This has indeed

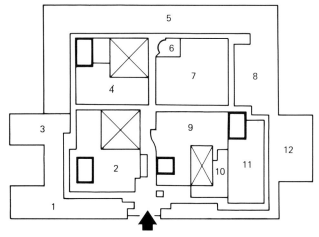

1 out-patients' clinic
2 ante-natal
3 day theatres/ward
4 geriatric day hospital
5 geriatric wards
6 chapel
7 X-ray
8 psychiatric unit
9 kitchen/dining

10 dispensary
11 accident and emergency
12 physical medicine
13 maternity wards
14 delivery/special care babies
15 gynaecological wards
16 surgical wards
17 orthopaedic wards
18 administration

19 operating
20 intensive therapy
21 medical wards
22 paediatric wards
23 isolation
24 training centre
25 pathology/mortuary

Diagrams of the general arrangement of the three principal floors of Greenwich District General Hospital; 800 beds in a fully air-conditioned, compact, low-rise format. A rectangular hospital street surrounds the core of specialist departments, relieved by three courtyards. The clinical floors are separated by interstitial service floors, connected by four vertical shafts (heavy outline). The beds are banded continuously around the perimeter. Below the main entrance floor (above) a semi-basement contains principally food preparation for the three floor kitchens above, car parking and boiler house. Architect: W. E. Tatton Brown, Department of Health and Social Security, with the S.E. Metropolitan Regional Health Board

1 out-patients
2 gynaecological/ante-natal
3 physical medicine
4 gymnasium
5 accident and emergency
6 orthopaedic/fracture
7 records
8 administration
9 psychiatric ward
10 central supply/disposal etc.
11 isolation ward
12 geriatric ward
13 mortuary
14 education/library
15 X-ray
16 pathology
17 pharmacy
18 general acute ward
19 gynaecological ward
20 maternity ward
21 special baby unit
22 labour suite
23 maternity admissions
24 children's ward
25 ENT/eye ward
26 TSSU
27 operating
28 recovery
29 intensive care
30 central treatment
31 shortstay/day unit
32 staff dining
33 kitchen
34 ramps

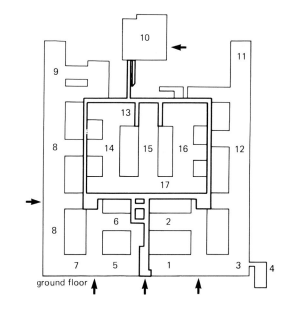

upper floor

ground floor

The 'Best Buy' hospital provides 550 beds on two storeys. The format has some similarity to Greenwich but the plan is perforated with courtyards, permitting a large measure of natural ventilation and lighting throughout the building. Beds occupy only three sides of the rectangle; on the fourth a separate works and supplies unit is linked to the hospital street by ramps.

proved to be the case. It is in its characteristically horizontal rather than vertical deployment of space that its approach is most obviously echoed in later general hospital design in Britain.

Best Buy

This simpler and less costly solution was initiated by the Ministry of Health in the 1960s and has subsequently been further developed. In general conception it has affinities with Greenwich but is less solidly packed and relies almost entirely on natural light and ventilation.

The building is arranged on only two storeys and has no interstitial service spaces. Because of its economy (some of which was sought by omitting departments customarily found in District General Hospitals, such as central sterilisation and laundry, that could reasonably be shared with other hospitals in the vicinity) the design was called 'Best Buy' – a persuasive title that is indicative of the desire of a central government department to encourage semi-autonomous outlying executive authorities to adopt its suggestions.

The 'Best Buy' hospitals such as Frimley, Surrey, and Bury St. Edmonds, Suffolk, are smaller than Greenwich, each providing about 550 beds. Although in essence they have the same rectangular hospital street enclosing the central diagnostic and treatment departments they are less compact and are lit and ventilated by internal courtyards, as if fresh air had been injected into the solid form of Greenwich.

The accommodation around three sides of the perimeter is mostly wards, approached from three lengths of the rectangular hospital street, from which it is separated by further courtyards. On the fourth side of the rectangle an independent works and supply unit, from which material can be moved by trains of tugs pulling trolleys, is connected by ramps to both floors of the street.

Harness

Both Greenwich and 'Best Buy' were in a sense model hospitals. They were based on a ring of circulation and conceived as a whole. They offered little opportunity for future growth, or for construction and taking into use by stages.

The development that followed, known as 'Harness', was conceived in terms of a more open-ended aggregation of units of accommodation along a linear spine of circulation. It may be regarded not only as a system of hospital planning but also as an administrative method. 'Harness' attempted to embody the results of research and experience in the formulation both of standardised plans for the various departments, and of a method by which these could be fitted together in a variety of ways. This was done in anticipation that there would be an acceleration of hospital building in the 1970s which would inevitably involve many designers and 'clients' who were inexperienced in the overall complexities of hospital planning. Whilst 'Harness' offered scope for different arrangements, not the least of its objectives was to reduce the lengthy process of individual design and to simplify questions of functional acceptability and the control of building cost.

'Harness' was intended for general hospitals of from 500 to 1100 beds. It was based on standard operational policies, for which plans for units of accommodation for most of the departments were designed. The units were

Air view of the 'Best Buy' hospital at Frimley Park, Surrey. Architects: Hospital Design Partnership, with the Department of Health and Social Security Hospital Design Unit. (Photo: Handford Photography, by courtesy of Holland, Hannen and Cubitts Ltd)

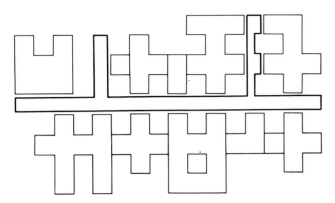

The basic 'Harness' concept is a linear hospital street to which standard and non-standard units of accommodation with different configurations, planned on a 15 m square grid, are attached with relative freedom but geometric consistency and enclose courtyards that provide natural light and ventilation

of different sizes but dimensionally related to a 15 m clear span square grid. These units were capable of arrangement in a variety of combinations and of superimposition up to a height of four storeys, 'harnessed' together by a linear hospital street from which further spurs of communication could run at a right angle. The resulting assembly produced a pattern of accommodation enclosing courtyards which provided natural light and ventilation to the perimeter of all the units.

The conception extended beyond unit plans for the various departments. It was combined with a standardised precast structural system with which the units could be constructed. Natural ventilation virtually eliminated the need for large air-handling ducts. Unlike the relatively costly self-contained interstitial service zones of Greenwich, services were distributed from the hospital street within the structural spans, threaded through lattice beams and accessible from the ceiling of the floor below.

Nucleus

A neater and geometrically more lucid system of planning known as 'Nucleus' was developed from 'Harness'. It was conceived so that it offered the opportunity of the construction of a hospital in stages from a first phase of about 300 beds with the potential of expansion to about 900. The system could also be used for extending existing hospitals by the addition of various combinations of individual units. Since its inception in 1975 some 65 Nucleus projects have been completed or are under construction and about the same number are being planned.

Like 'Harness' it is based on standardised operational policies and the aggregation of preplanned units along a linear hospital street, but it differs from 'Harness' in that each unit is a star shaped cluster or 'template' of identical overall dimensions.

When set beside one another the templates produce a consistent geometry that results in a true chequerboard of squares on a 16.2 m grid. This grid is further divided into sub-grids of 8.1 m on one axis and 5.4 m on the other, and in general the detail relates to a 100 mm

planning grid. Floor to ceiling heights are 2700 mm, with a 1200 mm zone between floor and ceiling for structure and services. The system is intended for buildings of a maximum of three storeys but preferably two, with natural lighting and ventilation to the majority of the accommodation.

Each cruciform template or cluster contains either wards or supporting departments. Typical accommodation within any one cluster comprises a pair of adult acute wards with a total of 56 beds; childrens' wards with 40

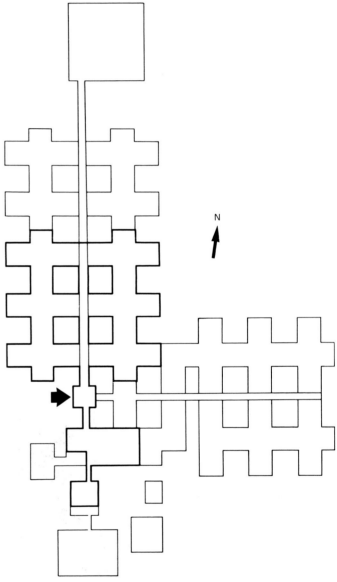

Plan showing the first stage (heavy outline) and subsequent stages of Maidstone District General Hospital, a two storey 'Nucleus' arrangement. Wards, operating, accidents, X-ray, pharmacy, rehabilitation and administration are in the northern clusters; on the southern extension to the hospital street are the main entrance and education, then pathology, mortuary, medical records, stores and sterile supplies, and lastly the boiler house. Plant rooms rise above the general level of the roofs at the intersections with the hospital street. The first stage provides 300 beds and later extensions northwards and eastwards can increase this to 800, including accommodation for geriatric and radiotherapy to the north and psychiatric day patients to the east. Architects: Powell, Moya and Partners

Sectional perspective of part of the 'Nucleus' District General Hospital at Maidstone, Kent, showing roof lighting and the distribution of services. Architects: Powell, Moya and Partners

beds; operating theatres and postoperative recovery; accident and emergency and fracture clinic; adult day care, intensive therapy unit and central treatment; X-Ray and administration; out-patients, medical records and dispensary; rehabilitation, pharmacy, snack bar and staff change.

The 'industrial' accommodation for catering, stores, boiler house and works is not necessarily standardised but designed for the specific requirements of the particular hospital and linked to the hospital street at an appropriate point. Alternatively, there are standard 'templates' available, not cruciform in plan, for support services departments such as catering and pharmacy. There are also cruciform 'templates' in which the 'free'

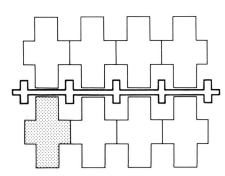

The basic 'template' is a cluster which contains wards, departments, or combinations of smaller departments. Placed side by side and connected to a linear hospital street the clusters produce a chequerboard of squares. All vertical circulation is related to the street.

Model of the first stage of Maidstone District General Hospital. (Photo: Sydney W. Newbery)

Upper floor

1 library/meeting
2 adult acute ward
3 intensive care unit
4 on call
5 treatment
6 adult day care
7 theatres
8 HSDU
9 catering
10 canteen

Ground floor

Southport and Formby District General Hospital. Block plans of the first phase of a two storey Nucleus hospital providing 304 beds, 67 of them geriatric. The disposition of the main entrance and boiler house etc. departs from preferred Nucleus arrangements to allow for futher expansion on this particular site. Architects: Regional Design Group, Mersey Regional Health Authority

1 administration
2 out-patients
3 X-ray
4 accident and emergency
5 dental
6 administration
7 staff change
8 children's ward
9 adult acute ward
10 pharmacy
11 rehabilitation
12 ophthalmics
13 pathology
14 services
15 supply distribution (linen)
16 works
17 mortuary

end is elongated by two 5.4 m bays to suit wards for the elderly, or by three such bays for an eight-room X-Ray department.

Unlike its predecessor, 'Nucleus' is not integrated with a specific structural system. It provides a zoning strategy for the distribution of services from the hospital street and from roof plant rooms. The basic dimensions of the clusters permit a variety of methods of construction, a choice of materials and differences of architectural treatment. The system provides the potential for a low-key, domestic and humane atmosphere, the antithesis of the monumental and intimidating, particularly where it is restricted largely to two storeys.

Although producing a pattern that occupies a relatively large site area 'Nucleus' is not so demanding of space as the independent pavilion type of development along a linear street. It also offers better opportunities for the contiguity of departments. At the junction of one 'nucleus' with another this advantage is combined with a natural form of fire compartmentation and the opportunity of escape from one compartment into another.

Although restricting the potential growth of an individual department, unless it be at the expense of its neighbour or by the addition of a further template or extension at the periphery, it is in principle a remarkably flexible approach. It gives the opportunity for the superimposition of various combinations of accommodation upon one another and for the addition of wards or servicing departments in two directions along extensions of the hospital street or along other streets developed at right angles to it.

The rationalisation of all ward units and various combinations of supporting departments into cruciforms of precisely the same dimension may however be regarded with some degree of scepticism. It places restrictions on internal planning that can result in unsatisfactory relationships and sometimes in rooms too small for their purpose. The horizontal travel distances that are likely to be involved in larger hospitals can also be questioned, especially if such distances are aggravated by economies that result in an inadequate provision of lifts, although it is true that the most critical traffic is likely to be between departments that are functionally related and are thus close together.

Nevertheless it is a simple and ingenious arrangement and in sensitive hands is likely to result in buildings with a refreshingly human scale. In addition it is an approach that offers substantial advances as a flexible strategy for development in phases, and for the rapid planning and implementation of a programme of new hospitals or of extending old ones.

Whilst the engineering and architectural solution is left to the designers (and the examples already built show that there is scope for very different results) the material published on 'Nucleus' by the professionals in the government department responsible covers such an unusually careful range of detail that anyone concerned with the design of a hospital, or part of a hospital, can ill-afford to ignore it. Comprehensive notes on the use of 'Nucleus', together with technical guidance documents on a wide range of components such as partitions, doorsets, windows, ceilings, sanitary assemblies and storage and benching arrangements are available. They are valuable information for anyone concerned with the exacting detail of hospital design.

Encapsulating in a variable but readily usable form much previous experience of functional performance and operational economy 'Nucleus' provides a basic discipline that can eliminate much of the time so often spent in argument, briefing and the search for perfection and unique solutions. Although there will always be situations to which the method cannot be applied, particularly on complicated rebuilds and infills on restricted urban sites and where there is no alternative but to build high, even in these cases the published planning data that 'Nucleus' provides may give valuable criteria and guidelines.

However, whatever form a hospital is to take, whether the approach is to be unique or based on a system such as 'Nucleus', there are some general principles it is wise to keep in mind. Demographic factors and developments in medical technology, to give but two reasons, are likely to lead to the need for change, to contraction in one place and alteration or expansion in another. Too finite a building form is likely to inhibit it.

For reasons of engineering services it is desirable to arrange heavily serviced departments close to one another, or one above another, and since these are the departments in which change seems most likely it may be prudent to place them next to 'soft' departments which are less criticial in this respect and which are easier to modify or move elsewhere if expansion of the 'hard' departments is necessary. In vertical stacking it is unwise to place areas such as wards over areas where there is a relatively high risk of fire, and both vertically and horizontally the whole hospital must be divided into fire compartments in which fire and smoke can be isolated, each compartment having a way of escape to the next and also to a main escape route. The reconciliation of these relationships with the operational requirements of the hospital is not a simple matter.

5

Wards

In-patient wards are classified by their speciality. In the General Hospital the usual ones are:

  the adult general acute
  the adult surgical
  the children's or paediatric
  the old people's or geriatric
  the maternity
  the orthopaedic
  the psychiatric.

Sometimes there are isolation wards for patients carrying an infection or who for some reason have suppressed immunity and need to be nursed in a bacteria-free environment. Adult wards are also likely to be differentiated by sex, depending on the way in which they are planned and the customs of the country.

Number of beds

Over a hundred years ago Florence Nightingale held that thirty-two was the maximum desirable number of patients in a ward unit. Although there have been revolutionary developments in medicine and surgery since then, and many changes in the way the ward has been planned, the number of patients that can be cared for by the ward sister and her team has remained remarkably similar.

Today the preferred number of patients in the general acute and surgical wards may be some four beds less than Florence Nightingale's thirty-two but it seems to be universally recognised that one team should not deal with more. Medical and surgical skill, centralised supplies and specialist facilities have not extended the range of what is sometimes known as 'tender loving care'.

The number of beds under one sister is likely to vary from about 28 to 30 in general wards, or about 20 to 24 for children. These numbers may be affected by nursing team arrangements, but in the interests of flexibility and possible future changes, and also for structural and servicing reasons (particularly in multi-storey buildings) ward units are usually about the same overall size, varying only in their internal planning. Wards with fewer beds tend to be those needing additional ancillary accommodation particular to their speciality and the sizes even out reasonably.

Location

The location of wards in relation to other departments of the hospital is rarely critical, except that surgical wards and those for intensive care are best in close proximity to the operating theatres. It is an advantage if this connection does not depend on the use of lifts, although this cannot always be achieved.

However, all wards need to be easily accessible from the hospital's main supply and disposal routes and to have convenient communication with the diagnostic and treatment departments, particularly such departments as physiotherapy which are visited by ambulant in-patients. In addition all wards should be capable of being reached by visitors along simple and coherent routes from which they are unlikely to stray into other parts of the building from which they should be excluded, or to pass sensitive areas where there are high risks of cross infection.

If the ward is to provide a sense of repose and be protected from excessive distractions and extraneous traffic it is important that it should be separated from the hospital's main communication routes. However, some modification of this may be desirable for the geriatric wards, where patients are not necessarily ill in the accepted sense and like to 'see the world go by'. No ward should be used as the principal means of access to another. Even though it may not be entirely on a cul-de-sac, the entrance to every ward should be capable of strict control.

Accommodation

The ward combines clinical and housekeeping facilities with the psychologically important function of providing the patient with a reassuring home in which he can be encouraged and supported towards an early recovery. The housekeeping element used to represent a much larger part of the work of the ward staff than it does today. This is now much reduced by centralisation of the supply of food, linen, drugs and sterilised articles, so that the ward no longer carries large local stocks of linen, crockery and medicines.

Local sterilisation of syringes, bowls and surgical instruments for minor procedures is usually superseded by the central supply of these items in packaged form. This has altered the nature of the work of the ward staff and has reduced the ancillary accommodation which is needed as part of the unit.

Apart from bathing, washing, toilet facilities and day spaces for ambulant patients, the ancillaries in the general ward normally consist of:

  a treatment room where surgical dressings can be attended to and minor operative procedures carried out with the minimum risk of cross-infection and without distressing other patients,
  a clean utility room principally for the preparation of equipment used in the treatment room,
  a dirty utility room for emptying and cleaning bedpans and urine bottles, cleaning other soiled items and disposing of materials such as dressings,
  a pantry for the preparation of beverages and for washing and drying crockery,
  a small equipment store,
  one or more nurses' stations,
  an office,
  provision for the storage of patients' clothes,
  a staff cloakroom,
  a cleaner's base,
  a disposal room.

The treatment room is sometimes placed between the clean and dirty utility rooms so that sterilised equipment from the Central Sterile Supply Department (CSSD) can be received and prepared in the clean utility, passed through a hatch into the treatment room, and after use passed through another hatch to the dirty utility, where it is washed before return to the CSSD.

In some hospitals the clinical facility of the treatment room has been removed from the ward unit and has been centralised. From the patients' point of view this has the disadvantage that by specialising treatment and taking it away from the familiar ward staff it becomes impersonalised. It also affects training, because the student nurses' opportunities for experience are much reduced.

Development of form

The classic Nightingale ward is long and narrow. It is approached from one end, lit and ventilated from both sides, and has two rows of beds arranged to face one another, their heads against the window walls. At one or both ends of the ward are the ancillary rooms and lavatories. The nurses' station from which the ward is controlled and the day space for patients who can get out of bed are islands in the central passage between the feet of the beds.

Florence Nightingale did not invent this form, for it is a plan with a long history and appears, in 13th century French religious foundations, as a nave of beds with an altar at one end. In its 19th century form Florence Nightingale gave it her seal of approval as the recommended way of achieving cross-ventilation and nursing efficiency. Some of the wards at St. Thomas' hospital in London are an example from the 1870s.

An interesting and remarkably successful cruciform variant from the end of the century, and still in use, is to be found in another London hospital at University College. Here the long nave of the ward is intersected by transepts that contain about a third of the beds and thus reduce its overall length. These transepts humanise its scale and provide some opportunity (whether or not it was originally intended) for the location of patients according to the nature or degree of the care they need.

1 sister
2 linen
3 kitchen
4 single ward
5 toilets/dirty utility
6 balcony
7 baths/washroom
8 fire escape

A 30-bed Nightingale ward at St Thomas' Hospital, London, little altered since it was built in 1871 except for the addition of some sanitary fittings and the substitution of radiators for the original open fires. The nurses' base is about half-way along the ward and the central a isle beyond it is used as a day space. The width of the ward is about 8 m and the length 35.5 m

1 linen
2 scullery
3 sluice
4 nurses' toilet
5 patients' toilet
6 bath
7 portable bath

A variation on the Nightingale ward, built at University College Hospital, London, at the beginning of the twentieth century. The width of the main 'nave' of the ward is about 7.6 m and the length 25.3 m. Sinks and washbasins were provided at the centre. It originally contained 24 beds but the capacity has subsequently been increased to 28 by the addition of four beds backing onto short screen walls which spring from the central shafts and continue the line of the 'nave' at the crossing. The narrow access link has also been enlarged on both sides to form a ward pantry and linen room, and at the far end the bathrooms have been extended and the ward scullery converted into a treatment room

An important change of direction in the planning of wards was introduced at the Rigs Hospital in Copenhagen in 1910. The 'nave' was wider and on both sides was subdivided by screens into bays. Each bay contained three or four beds arranged two deep and parallel to the external walls; patients no longer faced the light from the windows opposite.

Two such units of thirteen beds were set out symmetrically about a central nurses' room and a single bedded special care room, and other ancillary rooms and stairs were placed at the two extremities of the block. With the increasing desire for greater privacy than the Nightingale ward could offer this type of arrangement in multi-bed bays became common, although by no means universal, in the 1920s and 1930s. Sometimes the subdivision into bays was minimal, as at Rigs, but sometimes the bays were developed into partially or fully enclosed rooms, with various degrees of glazing to the central corridor. Except for a few single rooms the bays usually contained four beds.

In the USA the economics of personal health insurance arrangements led to three or two bed patterns with a higher degree of privacy from the corridor and influenced planning fundamentally. Elsewhere the larger multi-bed bay pattern combined with a proportion of single rooms has continued to find favour, with the important variation that beds are frequently planned three instead of two deep. This expedient shortens the walking distance along the adjacent corridor and is usually made acceptable for the beds furthest from the windows by the use of supplementary artificial lighting.

In the period immediately after 1945 hospitals in the UK and elsewhere were planned with bays of beds and ancillary rooms arranged on both sides of a central corridor, cross-ventilated naturally through the windows. Mechanical ventilation made possible the compression of this form into a double corridor plan in which the ancillary rooms occupied the centre of the building (lit and ventilated artificially) and the beds occupied the two external faces. This enabled the whole frontage of the block to be used for beds and shortened its length.

0   60 ft
0   18 m

A typical ward plan at the McMaster Health Science Centre, Hamilton, Ontario. The 36 beds are divided into two 18-bed units on a racetrack plan, each unit grouped around a nurses' station and work area that overlooks the single rooms for patients requiring intensive nursing care. The other bays are convertible into either two-bed or four-bed units. All rooms have immediate access to lavatories. The central core contains a treatment room, storage room, offices and conference rooms, and a visitors' waiting room. Architects: The Zeidler Partnership

The logical development of this approach was what became known as the 'racetrack' or 'deep' plan. With this arrangement all four faces of the block were occupied by beds and dayrooms, served by a continuous 'racetrack' corridor which enclosed a central core of ancillary rooms and services. The precedent for this came from North America, where on account of the extremes of climate and the acceptance of mechanisation, air-conditioning was regarded as a normal facility like drainage or electricity. Both 'racetrack' and double corridor plans have the advantage of concentrating the accommodation and reducing the length of journeys for the nursing staff. The ward units can be relatively compact instead of being strung out along corridors, and the external faces of the block can be occupied only by rooms which really need natural light and prospect.

In the early days of post-1945 hospital building there were some notable examples in the UK of this type of highly condensed ward plan. However, its virtues have not generally been thought to justify the high capital and running costs of the air-conditioning which it necessitates but which the climate does not always demand. There has consequently been little British development along these lines apart from exceptional cases, such as some of the major teaching hospitals or where buildings are situated in particularly polluted or noisy urban areas. Instead, the tendency has been towards solutions that place less reliance upon technology but still aim to achieve compactness.

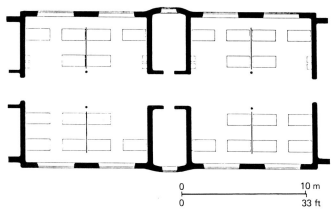

0   10 m
0   33 ft

A ward at the Rigs hospital, Copenhagen, 1910. The width is 11.3 m. The freestanding screens at the bedheads were not full height. The enclosure at the centre accommodated a single bedded special care room and nurses' room. Ancillary rooms were at the extremities

Influences on form

A primary requirement for the planning of the ward unit is that its form should facilitate the care and attention given by the nursing team to the patients. Nurses are on their feet most of the time and the work is demanding and tiring. The number of journeys they have to undertake in the course of their spell of duty and the length of those journeys need to be reduced to a minimum if the care of the patients is to be maximised.

For this reason alone compactness is important; but it can also be valuable in helping patients to be aware of the nursing staff and not feel isolated. A compact form can facilitate easy communication between patients and nurses without recourse to elaborate and impersonal electrical aids. As many beds as possible should be capable of being observed not only from the nurses' station or 'staff base' but also by nurses as they go about the ward on their routine duties. In this way not only do the nursing staff know what is happening in the ward but patients are reassured by their presence. When strung out along a corridor the subdivision of the ward into multi-bed bays or separate rooms can tend to work against contact of this nature:

It must be said, however, that the importance of this involuntary contact between nursing staff and patients seems to be a particularly British concern and is rarely much reflected in the planning of sophisticated wards elsewhere. Why this should be so is by no means clear. What does seem clear is that easy 'observability' simplifies the task of the nurses and should help a small team to give patients better attention than might otherwise be possible.

Probably the most significant influence on the design of wards was the Nuffield study on aspects of the hospital, begun in 1949 and published in 1955. Also, the experimental prototype wards that the Nuffield team built to test their conclusions. Their work on wards was based on a functional investigation of what the nursing methods were, what actually took place in the ward, the number of journeys undertaken daily and their length, the relative number of patients who were either bedfast or ambulant (or potentially ambulant) and the actual space necessary for the staff to perform certain functions without inconvenience.

Amongst other considerations the study examined the constraints and opportunities of daylight, sunlight, ventilation and acoustics. The method of approach was remarkably fresh at the time it was undertaken and the resulting publication was clearly expressed and easily understandable. Its influence on ward planning in the UK and elsewhere has been considerable. If some 35 years later some of its conclusions do not seem to be so inevitable many of the questions into which it attempted to probe need to be kept prominently in mind when designing wards today.

The traditional method of staffing a ward is to have one ward sister responsible for a team of nurses of various degrees of experience, some of them students, who are overseeing the welfare of some twenty-eight to thirty-two patients. But it is important to appreciate that the planning of the Nuffield prototype wards was based on

1	single bed	6 kitchen
2	nurses' station	7 treatment
3	day space	8 utility
4	four-bed ward	9 sister
5	bath	

The Nuffield experimental ward at Larkfield Hospital, Greenock; a 'bi-nuclear' arrangement in which two 16-bed nursing units, each with its own nursing station, share ancillary rooms and day space and are supervised by one sister. The bed bays and some of the single rooms have a lavatory immediately adjacent. The ward has natural cross-ventilation. Architects: Llewelyn-Davies Weeks

the sister supervising two nursing teams, each of which had about twenty patients in its care. Thus there were two nurses' stations instead of one. The size of the whole unit was bigger than normal, but each nursing team's knowledge of the people it was looking after was increased because it had fewer patients. There were also economies in the amount of ancillary accommodation needed because it could serve a larger number of patients than was determined by a ward unit of conventional size.

The Nuffield ward plans at Musgrave Park in Belfast, Northern Ireland, and Larkfield in Greenock, Scotland, which were designed in the early 1950s, reflect this organisational difference and demonstrate the importance of understanding operational policy as a basis for design. Conversely, they indicate how a pre-determined layout could dictate the nature of an operational policy.

Comparative examples

The wards of two general hospitals designed in the late 1950s, at Slough and at High Wycombe, about 30 miles from London, also demonstrate this bi-nuclear subdivision into two areas of nursing responsibility. Both are based on two units of twenty beds; they contain identical accommodation but are arranged in very different ways. The Slough building follows the linear form of Larkfield. At High Wycombe the site was too restricted in extent and the wards were therefore planned in a more concentrated 'racetrack' form; it was the first hospital in Britain to adopt this format.

Soon after High Wycombe had been taken into use it became clear that it was functioning particularly well in terms of patient care. An evaluation and comparison of the two hospitals was undertaken to try to identify the extent to which its success might be attributable to design.

The most significant conclusion was the superiority of High Wycombe on account of the way in which the majority of beds were closely grouped in an almost semi-circular arrangement around the ends of the block, enclosing the working area and nurses' station. Subdivided into single rooms and relatively open multi-bed bays the beds were nevertheless easily observed from the nurses' station and there was a degree of visual contact between beds on opposite sides of the building.

The evaluation noted that in contrast to the linear form full use could be made of the available nursing staff, which was of great importance when nursing skills were scarce. Indeed some consultants, junior doctors and nursing staff felt that if staff was short they would prefer a Nightingale ward to the linear pattern.

High Wycombe possesses much of the physical unity and ease of visual communication that has been remarked upon as the virtue of the Nightingale ward, but it must be noted that it provides only twenty beds to each nursing unit. It is harder to achieve this close grouping when the beds approach thirty in number.

An arrangement that has some of the characteristics of High Wycombe but does not depend on a 'racetrack' plan can be seen in one of the layouts for wards in the

1 single bed	10 clean utility
2 nurses' station	11 day space
3 sluice	12 spare
4 four-bed ward	13 interview/relatives
5 toilets	14 doctor
6 six-bed ward	15 sister
7 bath	16 kitchen
8 dirty utility	17 equipment
9 treatment	18 balcony

A general surgical ward floor at High Wycombe Hospital. There are 40 beds in two units with two nurses' stations and one sister's room. The bed areas at each end are separated by doors from the central facilities. Each 20-bed unit is grouped around the nurses' working area and patients' lavatories. There is a notably good view of the beds from the nurses' station and across the building from one multi-bed bay to another. Architects: Powell and Moya. Consultants: Llewelyn-Davies Weeks

1 lift lobby	11 cleaners
2 staff change	12 dirty utility
3 nursing officer	13 equipment
4 ward office	14 pantry
5 doctors' office	15 assisted bath
6 seminar	16 treatment
7 toilet/shower	17 nurses station/clean utility
8 toilet/bath	18 six-bed bay
9 toilet	19 single room
10 linen	20 day/dining

Ward layout at St Mary's Hospital, Paddington. Half the floor plan is shown. The complete floor contains four wards, each of 28 beds closely grouped around a nurses' station, with a seminar room and doctors' office to each pair of wards. Day spaces intercommunicate between the two halves of the floor. The design aims to combine some of the qualities of the open Nightingale Ward with additional privacy, and to provide the opportunity of nursing men and women in the same unit and to allocate beds according to the patient's dependence on nursing supervision. Architects: Llewelyn-Davies Weeks

1 single bed	7 treatment
2 nurses' station	8 clean utility
3 day space	9 dirty utility
4 four-bed ward	10 sluice
5 bath	11 sister
6 kitchen	12 hospital street

A 'bi-nuclear' ward in the single storey hospital at Wexham Park. Two 16-bed nursing units, each with its nursing station, are entered from the hospital street at the centre of gravity and not at one end as at Larkfield. All the bed spaces and the shared day space overlook small scale garden courts. Architects: Powell and Moya

Six-bed bays at St Mary's, Paddington, seen from the nurses' station.
(Photo: Crispin Boyle Photography and Associates)

rebuilt St. Mary's Hospital at Paddington. In this case four wards of twenty-eight beds are approached from a central vertical access lobby. Each ward contains four multi-bed bays of six beds and four single rooms grouped around one nurses' station which backs on to the ancillary rooms.

A ward plan that departs from the Nightingale, the linear and the racetrack formats can be seen in the

1 single bed	8 dirty utility	15 doctor/relative
2 nurses' station	9 clean utility	16 pantry
3 treatment/bathroom	10 shower	17 day/dining room
4 four-bed ward	11 staff cloaks	18 quiet room
5 toilet	12 cleaner	19 laundry
6 six-bed ward	13 equipment	20 linen/clothing
7 bathroom	14 office	

A 24-bed geriatric ward unit with good visibility from the nurses' station, and with space around it for patients to be exercised and to practice mobility. Lavatories are within easy reach of all beds. Architects: R. G. Brown, North Western Regional Health Authority

The nurses' station at High Wycombe, looking towards a six-bed bay.
(Photo: Bill Toomey/Architects Journal)

'Harness' layout. But in the 'Nucleus' design the form provides a closer relationship between beds and the nurses' station. In 'Nucleus' two ward units, each of twenty-eight beds, are placed back-to-back with a common approach from the hospital street. Most of the ancillary rooms are in the core (there is no treatment room because this facility is centralised).

This layout, although condensed, allows two of the single rooms and half the beds in the multi-bed bays to be grouped around the staff base and the hub of the nurses' working area. The core is ventilated artificially and the bed areas are naturally lit and ventilated from the windows and the roof.

The geometrical ultimate of the Nightingale ward in terms of observability, ease of internal access, contact between patients and nurses, and a sense of community is a circle. In this the nurses' station is at the centre and the beds are disposed inside the circumference. Whether the degree of communication this arrangement provides is more valuable than the sense of relative privacy it destroys is open to argument; it probably depends on the attitudes of the community for whom it is intended. Like many other things in hospital planning it is not a matter likely to be entirely susceptible to quantified evaluation and decision.

1	single bed	7	office	13	day room (dining)
2	nurses' station	8	toilet	14	staff change
3	clean utility	9	shower	15	disposal
4	bath	10	equipment	16	cleaner
5	dirty utility	11	pantry	17	seminar/doctors
6	six-bed ward	12	day room (TV)		

An adult acute bed unit of 56 beds in a 'Nucleus' cluster, comprising two wards of 28 beds with back to back ancillary rooms in the centre, approached from the hospital street through a shared corridor. Progressive patient care can be practised within each ward, and the nurses' station can have good observation, through glazed partitions, of two six bed bays and two single rooms (half the bed complement), an improvement upon the Harness arrangement. On the other hand there is evidence that storage space and pantry (the latter shared) are inadequate, that day rooms and staff room (12, 13, 14) are too remote and the former difficult to supervise, and that the absence of a treatment room is unsatisfactory. Architects: Department of Health and Social Security

1	single bed	7	sister	14	office
2	nurses' station/	8	toilet	15	relatives
	clean utility	9	bath	16	pantry
3	dirty utility	10	shower	17	visitors
4	four-bed ward	11	day space	18	cleaners/disposal
5	treatment	12	dining	19	supplies
6	six-bed ward	13	seminar		

A typical adult acute unit of 56 beds in the 'Harness' system. It comprises two wards of 28 beds, with their ancillary rooms planned back to back in the centre. The unit is approached from the hospital street through a shared corridor. The nurses' station and clean utility are at the centre of gravity of each ward, and in addition to the day/dining rooms, smaller spaces are distributed as part of the multi-bed bays. Architects: Department of Health and Social Security

Early ambulation and progressive patient care

By no means all patients are confined to their beds all the time. In 1950 the Nuffield survey found that in a general surgical ward, a general medical ward and a gynaecological ward about the half the patients were likely to be bedfast and about a quarter could get up to use a toilet and wash, perhaps with some assistance. The other

1 sister
2 doctor
3 dirty utility
4 kitchen
5 day space
6 sluice
7 bath
8 toilets and showers
9 disposal
10 visitors' verandah

Two of a group of four single storey circular wards for a proposed hospital in Nigeria, approached from a hospital street and surrounded and linked by shaded verandahs. Each ward contains 27 beds, three of them in single rooms with their own toilets. Other toilets, showers and the sluice rooms are in separate units. The nurses' station and clean utility is at the centre of the circle. Architects: Hospital Design Partnership

0   10 m
0   30 ft

1 single bed
2 nurses' station
3 day space
4 four-bed ward
5 five-bed ward
6 bath
7 treatment
8 dirty utility
9 clean utility
10 sluice
11 sister
12 kitchen
13 doctor
14 store
15 cleaner

A 30-bed ward in an 8-storey block at Northwick Park. Although there are two nurses' stations the one nearest the entrance is the one more generally used. All beds have toilets immediately adjacent and, in addition to the small room at the end of the block, day space forms a part of each five bed bay. These paired bays can be worked together or separated from one another if men and women occupy adjacent bays. Architects: Llewelyn-Davies Weeks

patients were fully independent as far as their own toilet was concerned.

It was anticipated that under a more advanced regime of early ambulation only about a quarter of the patients would need to be actually confined to bed, and subsequent experience in Britain has confirmed that this is indeed the case. The implications of this on the provision and location of toilet accommodation and day room space in the ward, and on the journeys nurses need to make with bedpans and other equipment, are far reaching.

The encouragement of early ambulation has led to the dispersal of lavatories throughout the ward so that they are within easy reach of the beds, and in some hospitals to their provision immediately adjoining each multi-bed bay.

The concept of Progressive Patient Care, which in essence means that the patient receives a degree of care that is appropriate to the phase of his illness, can be applied at all levels of the health service as it is inseparable from the concept of primary, secondary and tertiary care. As it affects the accommodation in the general hospital it normally implies only two categories: the general medical, surgical or specialised wards, and the Intensive Therapy Unit or Intensive Care ward, an independent department.

A third category, at the opposite end of the spectrum from intensive care, might be 'self-care' accommodation, of which there are examples in some developing countries although not yet much found elsewhere. It may well be adopted more frequently in the future as the cost of conventional medical care, particularly its staffing, continues to rise so alarmingly.

Ambulant patients who do not need frequent clinical attention but who are nevertheless not ready for discharge might well leave the ward and look after themselves or be cared for by relatives in nearby hostel accommodation. This would leave the beds occupied only by patients whose condition merits supervision by expensive nursing staff.

Within the normal ward Progressive Patient Care has implications on its arrangement. These are partly in the location of the beds for patients who need the closest attention, which are usually placed near the nurses' station for ease of observation, and also in the facilities provided for patients as a consequence of the policy of early ambulation. But the application of the concept of progressive care to actually moving patients around according to the degree of attention they require may decline. Cubicles or single rooms need greater nursing supervision than an open arrangement, and high technology and increasingly sophisticated operations combined with a demand for fast throughput and reasonable economy in nursing staff numbers tend to indicate the need for less subdivision of wards rather than more. They also tend towards a routine requirement for oxygen and other services at most of the beds.

The location of toilet facilities has already been mentioned. There may also be two degrees of day room space, the first adjacent to the actual beds, where one bed is sometimes omitted from a multi-bed bay to give sitting space within immediate reach of the bed area,

A four-bed bay at the West Middlesex Hospital, overlooked from the
nurses' station. The corridor partition is fully glazed with sliding doors.
Architects: Robert Matthew, Johnson-Marshall and Partners

1	single bed	8	dirty utility
2	nurses' station	9	clean utility
3	day space	10	relatives
4	four bed ward	11	sister
5	clinical	12	kitchen work area
6	bath	13	doctor
7	treatment	14	consultants

A typical ward floor at the West Middlesex Hospital. Two 30-bed wards,
each with a sister's room and two nurses' stations. Two thirds of the
four-bed bays and two of the single rooms have lavatories adjoining.
Day space is shared between the two wards. Architects: Robert
Matthew, Johnson-Marshall and Partners

For these reasons, contiguity of planning between one ward unit and another is an advantage, for it offers some measure of nursing flexibility between adjacent units. The breaking down of each unit into smaller bays or rooms can also provide some flexibility in the numbers admitted of each sex. Sometimes a few beds in single

1	nurses' station	9	nursery
2	six-bed room	10	shower
3	single-bed room	11	store
4	day/dining	12	assisted bath
5	pantry	13	dirty utility
6	clean utility	14	visitors' waiting
7	bath	15	charge nurse
8	toilet	16	nursing administration

Maternity Ward at the West Dorset District General Hospital, Dorchester, for the Wessex Regional Health Authority. It provides easy contact between the nurses' station and most of the bed areas, with sanitary and ancillary rooms conveniently close. Other wards in the hospital have a similar plan. By varying the glazed partitions that separate the nurses' station from the two adjacent six-bed rooms these two rooms can be combined into one ten-bed space. Architects: Percy Thomas Partnership, in association with Barry W. Payne, Wessex RHA

and the second by the provision of separate day spaces within the ward. The latter are of particular value for meals and as places where ambulant patients can meet one another and their visitors in a relatively domestic atmosphere. By this method some of the potential disruption that sociability can impose on the routine of the bedfast can be avoided. These day spaces are often provided as two separate rooms, for quiet and noisy activities, and can sometimes be arranged at the interface between two ward units so that they can be shared.

Flexibility

If a hospital is to perform its function efficiently in the delivery of health care it is clear that it must aim to discharge its patients as soon as it is clinically satisfactory to do so. It must also operate with the minimum practicable number of empty beds. Two factors that conspire to hinder this are the relative number of patients needing admission to particular wards at any one time and the relative number of men and women within each category.

Although some hospitals have introduced ward units that accommodate both sexes, and in the case of psychiatric wards this is usually the practice, many wards are for one sex only. Thus in a hospital with wards that are too finite and geographically isolated from one another (for instance if each ward unit is on a separate floor of a multi-storey building) there can be no common ground between one unit and the next into which it is possible for one of them to expand temporarily into its neighbour. If all the units are large Nightingale wards or of similar configuration, allocated to one sex only, beds may be left empty in one when there is unusual pressure on another.

1	single bed	9	kitchen	17	medical typists
2	nurses' station	10	sister	18	nursing supervisor
3	treatment	11	day room	19	laboratory
4	clean utility	12	dining	20	visitors overnight
5	five-bed ward	13	TV	21	seminar
6	dirty utility	14	disposal	22	interview
7	bath	15	doctors on-call		
8	sluice/test	16	consultant		

Half a ward floor at York General Hospital, comprising four 30-bed nursing units, each with one nurses' station. Each unit has five single rooms with five multi-bed bays of five beds; the single rooms in the cross links are 'swing beds' and may be used by either of the two flanking units as required. All multi-bed bays and two of the single rooms have their own lavatories. Day, dining and TV rooms are shared between adjacent units. The ward building is four storeys in height and is naturally ventilated. Architects: Llewelyn-Davies Weeks

1	hospital street
2	courtyard
3	staff toilet
4	wheelchair toilet
5	toilet
6	assisted toilet
7	specimen toilet
8	bath
9	assisted bath
10	office
11	cleaner
12	doctors' office
13	pantry
14	staff lockers
15	sisters' office
16	six-bed ward
17	five-bed ward
18	single-bed ward
19	nurses station
20	clean utility
21	treatment
22	dirty utility
23	day/dining room
24	store
25	seminar

0   10   20 m

Two 30-bed acute wards on the upper floor of Edith Cavell District General Hospital, Peterborough, approached from the main hospital street. Architect: A. A. Crampin, Regional Architect East Anglian Regional Health Authority

rooms occupy the interface between two wards; these are known as 'swing beds' and can be used by either ward according to need.

The peripheral forms of ward planning known as 'banding' may offer some degree of flexibility that might on occasions be useful. Examples of this are at Greenwich and in the most recent building at St. Thomas' hospital, London, or in a linear form at York, or even the Nucleus arrangement where two intercommunicating ward units are placed back to back. All provide some scope for variations in the relative numbers of men and women, not only by virtue of their subdivisions and a proportion of single rooms, but also by their relationship to their next door neighbour.

Subdivision

Although the ward unit is now customarily subdivided into bays and single bedded rooms, opinions differ about the number of beds to a bay and the proportion that should be provided in separate rooms. Bays usually contain between four and six bed spaces and the beds are usually, but not necessarily, arranged parallel to a window wall. Six bedded bays make for compactness

A single room in the ophthalmic department at the Royal Berkshire hospital, Reading. Glare from the sky is reduced by the overhang of the floor above and by the horizontal screen above eye level, which also helps to reduce the scale of the room. Architects: Architects' Co-Partnership

Typical 24-bed ward at Cannock Community Hospital, Staffordshire, for
the West Midlands Regional Health Authority. All wards, whether acute,
geriatric, or for the elderly and severely mentally infirm, have similar
layouts. Architects: Denys Lasdun Peter Softley and Associates

A   hospital street
B   sheltered garden
1   waiting
2   equipment
3   single-bed room
4   four-bed room
5   day/dining
6   quiet room
7   ADL kitchen
8   clean sink room
9   staff
10 doctor
11 sister
12 linen
13 toilet
14 bath
15 store
16 pantry
17 dirty utility
18 clean utility
19 staff base

but have been criticised because the middle bed is an
island and its occupant cannot avoid a neighbour
whichever way he turns – a refinement that may not be of
much significance for the average short-stay patient.

In the UK two and three bedded bays are generally
regarded as unsatisfactory, principally on the grounds
that two patients may prove to be mutually incompatible
and that one of three may be the odd man out. But this
view does not appear to be universally held in Europe,
nor in the USA where two bedded rooms have for long
been common, presumably as the nearest approach to
the seclusion of a single room that patients can afford
under their insurance arrangements.

Some single rooms are normally regarded as essential
for clinical reasons. In the UK the usual number in a
general acute ward of about thirty beds is a minimum of
four, of which two have their own toilets *en suite* to ensure
that the patient can be isolated and the risk of
cross-infection by the transfer of bedpans to the dirty
utility room is eliminated. It has been argued that more
single rooms should be provided and that the greater
their number the greater the flexibility and the fewer the
beds that will be left empty because of sex or medical

incompatibility. It has also been widely held that most
patients dislike the open or semi-open ward and want
privacy, and that the ideal is a hospital consisting entirely
of single rooms.

Although the minority who can pay for the privilege of a
private room seem to prefer to do so, from whatever
motive, for the majority of patients the efficiency of the
nursing is probably of more importance to their recovery
than is privacy. It is clear that a relatively open
arrangement is more conducive to good supervision and
the satisfaction of the patients' needs by a limited staff
than is a cellular pattern. If resources are to be used
economically, single rooms should in the main be
allocated only to those whose medical condition demands isolation, for instance to those who are a source of
infection or are susceptible to it, or who are noisy or
disruptive or otherwise disturb or distress other patients.

Privacy

Where a general hospital offers rooms for a minority of
patients who pay for the privilege of privacy or of other
advantages there may be the possibility of planning them

1 hospital street
2 courtyard
3 pantry
4 staff toilet
5 toilet/bidet
6 toilet
7 bath
8 shower
9 assisted bath
10 store
11 dayroom
12 sister
13 nurses' station
14 single-bed ward
15 five-bed bay
16 six-bed bay
17 clean utility
18 treatment
19 dirty utility
20 doctor
21 flower bay
22 cleaner

Thirty-bed ward for Northampton District General Hospital. It is linked to a similar adjoining ward approached from the same hospital street, the pair enclosing a courtyard. Architects: Yorke Rosenberg and Mardall

1 single bed	6 six-bed ward	11 day room
2 nurses' station	7 treatment	12 seminar
3 preparation	8 pantry	13 medical consultant
4 four-bed ward	9 bath	14 visitors overnight
5 disposal	10 sister	

Wards at Salminiya hospital, Bahrain. Two wards of 60 beds, each arranged in three units with three nurses' stations, pantries, preparation and disposal rooms. Architects: Llewelyn-Davies Weeks

1 private bed	8 treatment
2 nurses' station	9 day space
3 sister	10 private patients' toilet
4 doctor	11 toilet
5 laboratory	12 bath/shower
6 pantry	13 dirty utility/sluice
7 clean utility	14 hospital street

Men's wards, each of 32 beds, at Maiduguri Teaching Hospital, Nigeria. Two private rooms and the clean nursing ancillary rooms are in the link from the hospital street, but toilets and sluice rooms are in a separate block accessible from both wards and are duplicated. A hot dry climate, the wards face north and south and are naturally ventilated, with screens set back from the external face of the building. Architect: John R. Harris

1 single bed
2 nurses' station
3 treatment
4 four-bed ward
5 sluice
6 disposal
7 bath
8 toilet
9 day room
10 sister
11 doctors/students
12 visitors
13 pantry
14 utility

A 28-bed Nuffield type ward at St Thomas' Hospital (1966) with one central nurses' station. Architect: W. F. Howitt

the majority of patients leads them to cherish) but also in the more highly developed world where aspirations and expectations tend to encourage it. Contact and involvement may be more valuable than personal isolation. This hypothesis is unlikely to be proved, but it is at least supported by a survey conducted ten years ago in London. Comparisons were made between the reactions to three occupied wards that had been built over the past hundred years. In the search for quietness and a less regimented atmosphere, ward design has moved away from the communal Nightingale ward and has established a closer relationship between beds and ancillary rooms. The gains resulting from this may appear self-evident, but it is possible that they have been accompanied by losses.

At St. Thomas' hospital in London, some 19th century Nightingale wards, multi-storey Nuffield type wards of 1966, and air-conditioned multi-bay peripheral wards of 1976 with internal ancillary rooms were all in use simultaneously. During 1976/77 over a period of eighteen months these were the subject of a survey of the opinions of patients, doctors, nursing and other staff to assess the

in association with a pair of ward units. They can then share ward staff and some of the centralised ancillary rooms and can also be made available for public rather than private use in an emergency. Today such private accommodation usually has a bath and toilet *en suite* with the room, frequently placed on the corridor side.

In hot dry climates, where protection from the heat and glare is needed and only small windows are indicated, there is much to be said for locating the toilets on part of the room's external wall, and this arrangement may be practicable elsewhere. Whether on the inside or the outside wall it is desirable that the toilets should not screen the head of the patient in bed from observation from the corridor, for his feet do not give much indication of his behaviour. In both private and public accommodation this is particularly important for patients who are occupying single rooms because of their medical condition.

For most people it is improbable that the supposed ideal of personal privacy can be economically attainable within the life span of any hospital built today. It is therefore relevant to suggest that, for universal application, privacy is not only an illusory goal for the near future but may also be a very questionable one. This applies both to countries which are trying for the first time to provide facilities for the mass of the population (for whom privacy may well not be something which the life style of

1 single bed	7 sister	13 clinical investigation
2 nurses' station	8 treatment	14 seminar
3 day room	9 dirty utility	15 student laboratory
4 four-bed ward	10 sluice	16 supply
5 bath	11 clean utility	17 disposal
6 six-bed ward	12 pantry	

A 28-bed ward with one nurses' station at St Thomas' Hospital (1976), comprising one quarter of the floor of a rectangular air-conditioned building. Architects: York Rosenberg Mardall

relative degrees of satisfaction offered by the different types.

The results were not as conclusive as might be expected. Although all three types of ward were found to be operating in ways that the users found largely satisfactory it could almost be inferred that the level of satisfaction was in inverse proportion to the date the accommodation had been built. It was not surprising that doctors and nurses preferred the large and open Nightingale wards for their ease of supervision, observation and control. They used the nurses' time more efficiently and gave greater job satisfaction to the sisters than did the other wards. It was not expected that the patients would have much to say in their favour. The conclusions of the survey team's report included the following words:

'In view of the rejection of the 'Nightingale' type ward in hospital planning since the Nuffield Report of 1955 and the well articulated views that patients hate them it was, however, quite unexpected to find how satisfied patients were with (them). The criticisms that are commonly levelled against such wards were not found to be true here. Patients did not feel a great lack of privacy or lack of dignity, nor were they greatly disturbed by each other. The number who were sometimes disturbed was comparable to those in other wards. Far from finding criticisms, many positive advantages . . . . . emerged. The physical unity and the ease of visual communications meant that everyone, staff and patients, identify very strongly with the ward and with each other. Problems tended to be shared. The sympathy and understanding of the patients for each other and for the nurses was high. Social contacts are easy, both to initiate and to withdraw from. There is plenty going on to watch without the need to actively participate. The resulting high community morale is enjoyable and beneficial for the patients.'

These conclusions do not necessarily suggest a return to the original form of the Nightingale ward. They underline the belief that there are other considerations besides privacy and that to some degree its absence may be helpful to patients. It would be hazardous to assume that patients everywhere in the world or drawn from different social groupings would respond in the same way. However, it is hard to dismiss the possibility that for a high proportion of average short-stay patients there are indications that the supposed ideal of a private room and a private toilet is not only economically unrealistic but is also therapeutically questionable and would do little or nothing to help their rapid recovery. Besides aiming for compactness and convenience, future developments in ward planning may well concentrate on a imparting a sense of community.

6

Principal departments of the hospital

Categories of accommodation

A hospital comprises three categories of accommodation:

medical services which provide diagnosis and treatment for inpatients and outpatients;

medical support services essential for sustaining the medical services and closely related to them functionally;

general support services which are responsible for general administration, the supply of food, linen and stores, the disposal of waste and the maintenance of heating, lighting and energy, piped supplies and mechanical aids.

Each of these three categories is made up of a number of distinct departments. Every hospital will include some departments from each category but few hospitals will include all departments.

In the *medical services* group the principal departments in addition to the various in-patient wards are:

outpatient clinics,
accident and emergency,
short stay wards associated with accident and emergency,
day units for psychiatric or geriatric patients.

The principal specialist diagnostic and treatment services, most of which deal with both inpatients and outpatients, are:

diagnostic radiology,
physical medicine,
dentistry,
radiotherapy,
renal dialysis,
the operating department,
the pathology laboratories.

Medical support services comprise:

the pharmacy,
central sterile supply,
a central milk kitchen associated with maternity wards,
the medical library,
central medical records.

General support services are:

central administration,
general supply and disposal,
linen supply and disposal (which may include a laundry),
the mortuary,
catering,
engineering services including maintenance,
transport,
staff changing rooms and amenities (which may include residential accommodation).

A detailed description of all departments is beyond the scope of this book. There is an extensive literature on the subject. This chapter is confined to an outline of the function of some of the principal departments and of the basic procedures likely to be followed within them. A brief description is included of the type of accommodation which the needs of each department demand and of their relationship to other departments and their desirable location within the hospital. Although the descriptions are based on British practice at the scale of the district general or regional hospital, many of the techniques are recognised internationally. Most functions and procedures are relevant both in the UK and elsewhere.

The plans that illustrate the departments are not meant to be interpreted as models or in any sense as standards. The requirements of different hospitals will vary as to size and the particulars of accommodation and operational policies. The intention is only to show some relatively recent solutions; read in conjunction with the text they may help readers to visualise the procedures and the functional arrangements to which they give rise.

Out-patients

The function of the department is to diagnose and to treat home-based patients and if necessary to accept them as in-patients. A good deal of the diagnostic and treatment accommodation can be of a general nature used at different clinic sessions by different specialists. Too much separate accommodation for specialisms is wasteful, for much of it will be underused most of the time.

Organisation is greatly facilitated and overcrowding reduced if out-patients are filtered by a general practitioner, clinic or health centre and proceed (by appointment) to the department only when it is essential. This method is generally known as a referral system. In some countries, where a referral system has not developed, it may be advisable to have a separate general practitioners clinic adjoining the hospital specifically for this purpose in order to prevent the department (and indeed other parts of the hospital) from becoming grossly overloaded.

For some patients the department will be their first introduction to hospital and many may be nervous and need reassurance. It is important that the atmosphere should be welcoming, comfortable and humane. In a large department, or if there is no adequate referral or appointment system to control the influx of patients, there will be special design problems in retaining a human scale in the arrangements of the large reception and waiting spaces that are likely to be necessary. In some climates shaded open-air areas may be valuable.

The department should be situated so that it is easily reached by both the walking public and vehicles. It should also be close to public transport routes if there are any. A separate entrance is desirable and this should not be located too near the reception point for ambulance and accidents or other departments, such as the mortuary, which are likely to have disturbing associations. Out-patients should not have to pass through any other part of the hospital to reach the department.

It is an advantage if the out-patients department can be entirely at street level, for some patients may find movement difficult. Expansion may need to be anticipated, particularly in developing countries where the facility is being provided for the first time. In countries where local health centres or community hospitals are well established or are increasing steadily in number the future need may be not so much for growth as for change, as the out-patient clinics become more specialised.

Procedure is similar to that in a health centre except that diagnostic techniques and treatment will be more sophisticated. The sequence for patients is reception, registration, waiting, consultation.

The out-patient department at Northwick Park. There are two patterns of consulting rooms; on one side a range of interconnected rooms where doctors may use one, two or three rooms according to their requirements, a very flexible arrangement; on the other side a series of bays serving two smaller consulting rooms each flanked by a pair of examination rooms. Ancillary rooms and a courtyard are in the centre and toilets are distributed. Each waiting space is looked after by a nurse/receptionist. The department is capable of extension on the same pattern. Architects: Llewelyn-Davies Weeks

1 waiting	5 clean utility	9 dietician
2 consulting	6 treatment	10 electrocardiograph (ECG)
3 examination	7 sink room	11 dermatology treatment
4 sister	8 weighing	12 medical social worker

1 male waiting	17 electrocardiograph (ECG)
2 female waiting	18 audiometry
3 patients' toilet	19 audiometrician
4 staff toilet	20 eye treatment
5 staff base	21 perimetry
6 reception/records	22 refraction
7 electroencephalograph (EEG)	23 instruments and equipment
8 clinette	24 orthoptist
9 test	25 electronystagmography
10 consulting/examination	26 consultant
11 preparation	27 orthodontic surgery
12 treatment	28 oral surgery
13 disposal	29 dental laboratory
14 mothercraft	30 dental dark room
15 nurses' duty room	31 store
16 sister	32 cleaner

A large out-patient department for a hospital in Saudi Arabia. Segregation of the sexes is necessary but a degree of flexibility in the allocation of consulting rooms to male or female clinics is desirable. Male and female waiting spaces can be kept entirely separate, and by closing doors at the end of the access corridors the consulting rooms can be used for either sex in any proportion. Architects: Architects' Co-Partnership

In some cases treatment, or referral to another specialist department may be necessary. Prescriptions may be collected at a dispensary on the way out. It is essential to have an enquiry or registration point at the entrance, associated with a general waiting space.

Many of the people waiting may be relatives or friends who may not wish to accompany patients to the actual clinic. Sub-waiting spaces adjoining the clinic to which patients are directed are desirable and the checking of records may be done there. These reduce the scale of the general waiting space and assist the flow of patients through the department. Patients' toilets and telephones should be associated with all waiting areas, with perhaps

1 reception
2 sub-waiting/clinic
    receptionist
3 consulting/examination
4 treatment
5 clean supply
6 dirty utility
7 toilets
8 ECG
9 audiometry
10 pathology outstation
11 sub-waiting, ophthalmology/
    dentistry
12 ante-natal clinic waiting
13 out-patient general surgery
    waiting
14 services' shaft

At Greenwich District Hospital the out-patient department is approached from the hospital's main entrance and waiting area, where there is a shop, a cafeteria, a children's playroom and a dispensary. It shares the pathology outstation with the adjoining ante-natal clinic. The main part of the department consists of ranges of intercommunicating consulting/examination rooms on both sides of a central core of ancillary rooms and sub-waiting areas. Each of the waiting areas is looked after by a clinic receptionist. An arm containing accommodation for ophthalmology and dentistry, with its own sub-waiting area, leads to a further waiting area that serves a group of rooms and a day ward for minor surgery. Architect: W. E. Tatton Brown, Department of Health and Social Security, with the S.E. Metropolitan Regional Health Board

a refreshment counter, a shop and a children's playroom at the general waiting space.

Usually most of the consulting suites are general purpose, consisting either of ranges of combined consulting and examination rooms or of smaller consulting rooms with examination rooms adjoining. Some specialities may need rooms designed for a particular purpose. A clinical room is required for treatments such as dressings, a room for urine tests etc, clean and dirty utility rooms and sister's office. An operating suite for minor surgical conditions may be needed, together with day space and a day ward in which patients can recover before going home. Although proximity is desirable, this operating suite need not be immediately adjoining the department.

Normally there is no need to segregate the sexes in an out-patient department but in some countries segregation may be required. This will inevitably lead to an increase in area and to complications in planning the circulation routes and waiting spaces.

The department needs easy access to the radiodiagnostic facilities, to the dispensary, and if possible to physiotherapy. Out-patients may have to visit any or all of these. Although these departments also serve the rest of the hospital it is an advantage if access to them can be as little associated as possible with other main routes within the hospital. Out-patients can easily get lost and stray into areas from which they should be excluded. Proximity to the pathology laboratories is also desirable for the delivery of specimens.

In some developing countries a major out-patient facility in a new hospital can be much sought after by those who are within reach of it. There may well be a problem in controlling the large crowds who will descend on it and in preventing them from penetrating into other parts of the building. If there is no adjacent GP clinic to act as a filter a more distinct separation of out-patients from the rest of the hospital may be an advantage, in spite of the close relationships which are desirable with other departments. Ample waiting space will be needed outside the department to accommodate the multitude, many of whom may gather there as much for the social occasion as for medical reasons. This space can be in the open, but should be shaded. It is likely that there will be a need for a secure method of containing the waiting crowd and of admitting them to the department in small batches.

Accident and emergency

Injury or sudden illness beyond the capacity of the first-aid box drives most people to a doctor or, if they are near a hospital, to its Accident and Emergency department, where they expect immediate attention and reassurance. Most hospitals must be able to deal with casualties and emergencies without mixing them with other out-patients. For this they need as a minimum a waiting space, a consulting room, examination and treatment cubicles, a small operating theatre and a few beds for recovery.

Many hospitals will, however, be designated as major accident centres and the department will be much more heavily loaded and will require additional and more sophisticated facilities. Some of the accommodation may differ with the locality, for the type of risks to which the population is exposed will not necessarily be the same in all places and the incidence of cases such as burns, fractures and road accidents may vary. Other units in the vicinity may provide particular specialities, notably in a large urban area.

Because the department deals with patients who are the victims of accidents or sudden illness it is subjected to unpredictable peaks of activity at any time of the day or night. Incoming patients may be ambulant or brought by vehicle. Some may be violent, others unconscious. They may come direct or may be referred by a doctor. After examination (which may include X-ray) or resuscitation, patients may be treated within the department and either kept under observation and discharged after a few hours or may be transferred to the wards. Others may go direct to the wards after diagnosis. After discharge some patients may return to the department for follow-up examination or treatment. Certain injuries may have to be referred to specialist hospitals elsewhere.

Because seriously injured patients should be kept separate from others the department requires two

1	walking entrance	22	plaster mould room
2	stretcher entrance	23	plaster/splint store
3	reception/records	24	operating theatre
4	porters	25	anaesthetic
5	trolleys	26	scrub-up
6	interview	27	sink room
7	sister	28	clean utility/lay-up
8	nurses' duty room	29	mobile X-ray
9	resuscitation	30	staff change
10	examination/treatment	31	staff cloaks
11	clean utility	32	doctors' duty room
12	dirty utility/test	33	sister's room
13	kitchen	34	nurses' room
14	waiting	35	store
15	toilets	36	cleaner
16	nurses' station	37	patients' washing/changing
17	tea bar	38	dirty utility
18	orthopaedic/fracture examination	39	four-bed bay
19	consulting	40	single bedroom
20	surgical appliance fitting	41	consultant
21	plaster room	42	secretary

1	reception/porters	7	sluice/disposal/test	13	interview
2	telephone/night reception	8	clinette	14	charge nurse
3	trolleys/wheelchairs	9	cleansing	15	supplies
4	mobile X-ray units	10	examination	16	store
5	resuscitation	11	workspace		
6	treatment	12	waiting		

The Accident and Emergency department for a Mark 2 'Best Buy' hospital. There are separate entrances for stretcher and walking patients controlled by the same reception and porters' room. The ambulance entrance leads to a generous marshalling space and the walking entrance to a waiting area from which small examination cubicles are directly accessible. On the other side of the central workspace and approached from the ambulance entrance there are larger treatment cubicles for patients on trolleys. Architects: McDonald, Hamilton and Montefiore, with the Department of Health and Social Security

A major Accident and Emergency department at King Edward Memorial Hospital, Ealing. The entrance for walking patients leads to a large waiting area with an alcove for children, from which the orthopaedic and fracture section, with its own sub-waiting area, is directly accessible. The reception and records counter communicates with the porters' station for stretcher cases from the ambulance entrance. Opposite the porters there is a trolley park, and straight ahead a large resuscitation room and a sub-waiting space for patients on trolleys. Much of the main examination and treatment workspace is flexibly subdivided. The department includes a pair of operating theatres and a ward of ten beds for preparation, recovery or short stay observation. Architect: John R. Harris independent entrances from outside, one for walking patients and the other for those brought by ambulance. If the unit includes an orthopaedic clinic a third entrance may be desirable, via the out-patients department if the orthopaedic records are kept there.

Walking patients are either attending for the first time or are coming for follow-up procedures. After reception at a counter where particulars are taken or checked, patients in these two categories can, in a large department, be separated into two distinct waiting areas, sharing lavatories, telephones and perhaps a tea bar. A separate waiting room for children may be desirable.

The ambulance entrance, distinct from the walking patients' entrance, should preferably be enclosed and heated and should lead into a stretcher lobby attended by porters. A room for cases needing emergency treatment or resuscitation should open directly from this lobby. Provision should be made for people accompanying a casualty who, although not themselves injured, may be in a distressed condition.

The main examination, diagnosis and treatment area should be directly accessible from the general waiting areas and the stretcher lobby. The area comprises a number of cubicles, partitioned or curtained or a mixture of both, some large enough for patients' trolleys or stretchers, with sluice and utility facilities serving them. The department's own X-ray diagnostic unit with dark room and X-ray viewing area should be adjacent unless the hospital's main X-ray diagnostic department is closely accessible.

If the department has its own operating suite it should be adjacent, probably containing two theatres with scrub-up and gowning rooms, an anaesthetic room and disposal room. A plaster room for the reduction of fractures and the application and removal of plaster casts should be near the operating suite. If all the hospital's operating theatres are centralised there must be quick access to them. In any case it is essential to have quick access to the Intensive Therapy Unit. If the department includes an orthopaedic and fracture clinic, consulting rooms and additional examination and treatment cubicles will be necessary. These should preferably be located near the plaster room, and approached through a waiting space adjoining but distinct from the main follow-up patients' waiting area.

After treatment or operation, and before discharge or admission as an in-patient, some patients will be taken to a small recovery ward in the department. This is a short-stay unit equipped with the usual ward ancillaries on a reduced scale. Patients are unlikely to stay here longer than twenty-four hours.

The department constitutes a highly concentrated unit in which internal relationships are of particular importance in emergencies and lucid planning is vital. This concentration must be combined with generous circulation space to allow easy movement of patients on trolleys or stretchers, as severely injured patients must not be disturbed more than is necessary.

A situation at road level is essential for the reception of emergencies and walking patients, and proximity to the out-patients' department may be an advantage. There must be easy, but not necessarily close, access to the

wards for patients on trolleys but security is likely to be of increasing importance. If the unit is remote from the hospital's X-ray diagnostic department, as it may have to be, it will require its own X-ray facilities. It will also need a small pathology laboratory if it is remote from the Pathology Department.

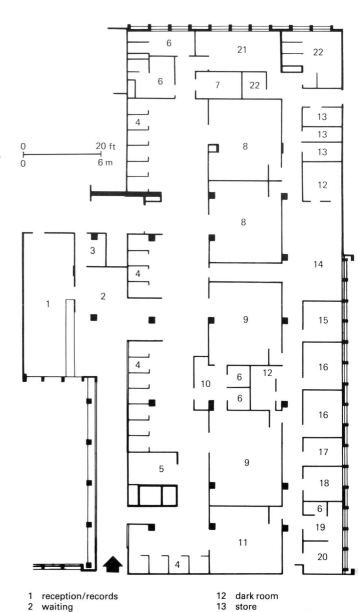

1	reception/records	12	dark room
2	waiting	13	store
3	porters	14	film sorting/viewing
4	dressing cubicles/sub-waiting	15	radiographer
5	recovery	16	reporting
6	toilets	17	typist
7	linen	18	clean utility
8	general radiodiagnostic	19	lavage
9	fluoroscopy	20	dirty utility
10	barium kitchen	21	staff common room
11	100 mm camera	22	staff cloaks

The Radiodiagnostic department at the King Edward Memorial Hospital, Ealing, located adjacent to Accident and Emergency and close to Out-patients. The X-ray rooms form the core, flanked on one side by a reception and records office which commands the entrance to the patients' sub-waiting areas and dressing cubicles, and on the other by processing, viewing and staff rooms. Architect: John R. Harris

Radiodiagnostic

The department receives in-patients, out-patients and casualties. Its function is to photograph, process the film and provide facilities for its interpretation and storage. Patients may arrive on foot, in wheelchairs or on trolleys, and may be wearing dressing gowns, theatre gowns or their normal clothes. After registration they may need to wait, to change their clothes or to undergo preparatory procedures before their X-ray, and following the X-ray they may need a short period for recovery.

X-ray rooms are equipped with photographic machinery of considerable sophistication (some of which is large and heavy and incorporates moving parts needing floor tracks and ceiling support). The recent introduction of computer linked scanners, which replace the use of X-rays, has introduced a new element into the design of these departments, although in general it has made little change in the total area needed for them. The X-ray rooms need dark rooms nearby for the processing of the films (which may be taken there either manually or by conveyor) and a room for viewing and film sorting.

Ancillary accommodation includes rooms for meetings and conferences, reception and records with arrangements for the storage of current exposed films, offices for radiologists, radiographers and secretaries, general storage and utility rooms, staff cloakrooms, and ample changing cubicles near the X-ray rooms for patients who arrive fully dressed. Some radiodiagnostic procedures are carried out under a general anaesthetic and appropriate facilities and accommodation need to be provided. Barium examinations require separate preparation rooms for rectal washouts, with toilets immediately adjoining, and small recovery rooms in which out-patients can rest before leaving the hospital.

Adequate waiting space of a cheerful and unclinical character adjoining the reception office is needed for ambulant and wheelchair patients. There must also be space for in-patients on trolleys. Toilets should adjoin the waiting space. A nurse will normally escort patients to the appropriate X-ray or preparation room. Some serial examinations may be spread over several hours with intervals of waiting between them, and for these separate sitting rooms for each sex are desirable. The traffic of patients' trolleys, equipment and people within the department is likely to be considerable.

Special precautions are necessary with X-ray machines to minimise the risks of irradiation to which staff are exposed. The controls to the X-ray tube are operated from behind a protective screen. The tube is normally capable of pointing vertically downwards or horizontally. The layout of the room depends partly on the equipment, but the basic principle is that the tube should never be able to be pointed towards the control unit or a door, or towards the dark room if it is adjacent.

The location of the department should be convenient for trolley access from the wards and close to the out-patients' department. Unless the Accident and Emergency department has its own X-ray facilities, it is essential that there should be easy access to the X-ray department. It is of advantage to other patients if the reception of accidents can be kept separate from the general waiting spaces. The department is not associated with radiotherapy, which is an entirely different technique. Expansion and change should be anticipated.

Physical medicine

The function of the department is the rehabilitation of patients. It comprises two related sections;
physiotherapy
occupational therapy.

Physiotherapy is principally treatment by massage, exercise, heat or electricity for the restoration, for instance, of the function of limbs, sometimes after injury or surgery, or for the education towards independence of patients with severe physical disabilities.

Occupational therapy is the treatment of physical and mental disorders by means of craft or manufacturing activities, frequently related to the patients' lifestyle outside hospital.

0 —— 50 ft
0 —— 15 m

1 reception/records	12 special radiodiagnostic room
2 waiting	13 anaesthetic
3 porters	14 preparation
4 radiologist	15 disposal
5 patients' toilets	16 recovery
6 mobile X-ray	17 conference
7 staff toilets	18 staff rest room
8 store	19 staff duty room
9 dressing cubicles/sub-waiting	20 radiographer
10 radiodiagnostic room	21 dark room, manual
11 lavage	22 dark room, automatic
	23 film sorting/viewing

The Radiodiagnostic department for a hospital in Saudi Arabia, located between Accident and Emergency and the operating department and close to the specialist clinics. There are separate sub-waiting and changing areas for each radiodiagnostic room. Architects: Architects Co-Partnership

The functions of the two sections overlap: both deal with in-patients and out-patients but the latter predominate.

Physical medicine should be close to the out-patients' department, from which it should, if possible, be directly accessible. In-patients also need to be able to reach it easily without passing through the out-patients' waiting areas. As many patients will arrive by vehicle road access is necessary. Throughout the department the planning must take particular account of the requirements of wheelchair users and of others with disabilities that make movement difficult.

The physiotherapy accommodation consists of two distinct areas; one for passive treatment such as massage or radiant heat, and the other for treatment requiring the patient's active participation, such as exercise in a gymnasium or movement in a hydrotherapy pool. From the reception and waiting space patients pass either to male or female changing rooms and thence to the passive treatment section or to the gymnasium. Alternatively, they may go direct to the pool, which will have its own changing rooms.

The passive treatment section consists of a number of separate rooms or cubicles or, alternatively and more flexibly, one area subdivided by adjustable curtains. Its ancillary spaces are a small bay for the preparation of dressings, etc and a room for paraffin wax treatment and plaster splint making.

In the active treatment section the gymnasium is conventional, preferably high enough for ball games and if possible with access to a terrace for exercise in the open air. The hydrotherapy pool is raised like a bath above the pool surround so that staff can handle patients; it is entered by a flight of steps. In addition to changing cubicles, lockers, toilets and showers it needs staff changing space, a utility room for rinsing, drying

1	reception/records	10	staff duty room
2	male waiting	11	appliances store
3	female waiting	12	staff change
4	trolleys	13	standard treatment cubicle
5	superintendent	14	large treatment cubicle
	physiotherapist	15	patient change
6	consultant/examination	16	hydrotherapy
7	paraffin wax	17	exercise room
8	preparation	18	gymnasium
9	disposal	19	cleaner

The Physical Medicine department for a hospital in Saudi Arabia. The treatment area is subdivided into bays to provide the opportunity to deal with male and female patients with some degree of privacy. In addition to the gymnasium there is a separate exercise room, primarily for children who have suffered cerebral palsy. The department is close to the specialist clinics and is entered only from within the hospital. Occupational therapy is located elsewhere with a psychiatric day unit. Architects: Architects Co-Partnership

and dry storage, and a rest room where patients can lie down after treatment.

Three distinct areas are customary for occupational therapy.

a heavy workshop for woodwork and light metalwork supervised by a technician, which is likely to be relatively noisy;

a light workshop for handicrafts and clerical rehabilitation including typewriting;

a domestic section for re-education, particularly of the disabled, in the every day activities of getting in and out of bed, bathing and using a toilet and working in the kitchen.

In all these areas some patients are likely to be working in wheelchairs. The workshops need storage space for raw materials and equipment, and for finished products. In some hospitals there may also be a need for gardening facilities immediately adjoining the department.

Maternity

Faced with sudden injury, incapacity or pain, most people in most countries will turn to a hospital for help if they can. But faced with childbirth the reaction may be different, for custom, religion, superstition and family pressures intervene. The need for and the attitude towards institutionalised help varies widely from one country to another, but where maternity facilities are provided (and they must be provided for some pregnancies) certain basic requirements are universal.

Unlike most other departments of the hospital the maternity department is normally concerned with a natural rather than a pathological event. It is also dealing

1	waiting	8	gymnasium
2	consulting	9	teaching bed-bay
3	examination	10	teaching kitchen
4	office	11	light workshop
5	treatment	12	heavy workshop
6	wax	13	hydrotherapy
7	ultraviolet light treatment	14	research

The Physical Medicine department at Northwick Park Hospital and Clinical Research Centre. There is an independent main entrance for out-patients but it is also entered direct from the hospital. The central core of the department contains heavy and light workshops, teaching kitchen, bed bay and bathroom, gymnasium, and a large treatment area off which open smaller rooms for wax and ultraviolet light treatment. The department includes a range of research laboratories. Architects: Llewelyn-Davies Weeks

1	clinic entrance and pram park	35	sluice
2	admissions entrance	36	GP admissions
3	visitors' entrance	37	first stage/delivery
4	service entrance	38	soundproof lobby
5	records	39	sink room test
6	mothercraft	40	dayroom
7	waiting and tea bar	41	equipment
8	children's waiting	42	pantry
9	toilet	43	toilet and shower
10	history taking	44	duty room
11	blood taking	45	delivery
12	medical social worker	46	sterile room
13	health visitor	47	scrub-up
14	district midwife	48	sink room
15	medical staff	49	theatre
16	sub-waiting	50	anaesthetic
17	examination	51	female changing
18	consulting	52	male changing
19	sister	53	doctors' duty room
20	cleaner	54	milk pantry
21	linen and equipment	55	demonstration
22	consultant paediatrician	56	six cots
23	clinette	57	single cot
24	clean utility	58	doctor/sister
25	treatment	59	gowning/scrub-up
26	dirty utility	60	dirty utility
27	porter	61	mother's bedroom
28	flying squad	62	visitors' waiting
29	nurses' station	63	nurses' cloak
30	visitors	64	midwifery superintendent
31	bath	65	consultant
32	utility	66	clerical office
33	linen	67	administration/staff room
34	GPs' coats		

Ground floor of the Maternity department at Chase Farm Hospital, Enfield. The ante-natal clinic is a single storey building and is linked to a three storey in-patient block. There are separate entrances for clinic, admissions and for visitors, each leading to clearly defined territories.

In the clinic the history and blood taking rooms open off the main waiting area. The examination rooms are ranged along a separate corridor and are entered by patients through undressing cubicles and by doctors through intercommunicating doors. The records office serves both the clinic waiting area and the in-patient admissions entrance.

The inpatient floor comprises four territories: a group of twelve first stage and delivery rooms grouped around a nurses' station, three larger rooms and a theatre for major deliveries, a special care baby unit, and an administrative unit through which visitors enter to reach the lying-in wards on the two upper floors. Architects: Stillman and Eastwick-Field

with a continuous process, from pregnancy through delivery to after-care of both mother and child. It is not principally concerned with curing a condition but with fulfilling it. Thus not only are its accommodation requirements different from those of other wards but it is important that it should not be associated psychologically with illness.

For this reason, and to avoid risks of infection to newly born babies, it is greatly to be preferred if the maternity department can to some degree be separate from the rest of the hospital, perhaps not geographically but certainly with its own entrance. It should retain close communication links with the hospital for meals and supplies and reasonable links with other departments to

which mothers may sometimes need access.

Whatever its size the department has two main parts; the *out-patient clinic* and the accommodation for *in-patient delivery and aftercare*. The clinic, which may be associated with the out-patients' department or may be separate, is primarily ante-natal. Depending on the arrangements of the particular hospital and the attitude of the gynaecologists and obstetricians concerned, the same rooms may serve for post-natal examinations, family planning consultations and gynaecological out-patients.

Ante-natal patients are usually seen at the time of booking, at about the thirty sixth week of pregnancy, and then weekly until admission for delivery. This clinic will preferably be approached separately from the department's ambulance entrance, and the accommodation will comprise a waiting space, rooms for history taking and examination with three or four undressing cubicles to each room, a urine testing room and lavatory, and space for offices and records. Easy access to the X-ray department and to pathology is an advantage.

The ante-natal clinic should have a non-clinical atmosphere, for in many areas it provides a valuable social meeting place for expectant mothers. This function can be of particular importance in new communities.

The in-patient accommodation falls into two closely related divisions, one concerned with labour and birth and the other with the lying-in wards. The labour suite, which should be accessible without passing through the wards, consists of first-stage rooms, each with one bed, and delivery rooms, both on a scale of one room to about ten post-natal beds. Pairs of delivery rooms can share wash-up and scrub-up. If there is no separate operating theatre for the department, or the hospital's main operating suite is not nearby, one delivery room needs to be suitable for caesarean operations, with scrub-up and anaesthetising room adjoining. The delivery rooms should be well insulated acoustically from the first-stage rooms and from the ward. A comfortable day room for visitors is needed near the entrance to the labour suite.

The ward has day room and ancillaries similar to a normal ward except that a treatment room is unlikely to be needed. It will probably be divided into four or six bedded rooms with perhaps about a quarter to a third of the mothers in single rooms. Cots beside the mother's beds, or 'rooming-in', is usually preferred to a central nursery because it presents less risk of cross infection. Some countries adopt an arrangement in which a small nursery is situated between each pair of two or three bedded rooms, with communicating doors.

In addition a Special Care Baby Unit, capable of temperature and in some countries humidity control, should be provided. This consists of separate rooms, each containing about six cots, and incubators, an isolation facility, and a gowning room for staff entering the unit.

A central milk kitchen is required, divided into a clean room for the preparation of milk feeds and the sterilisation of equipment, and a dirty room for wash-up. In a very large department it may be convenient to provide more than one kitchen, for instance on each ward floor. Cleanliness is of critical importance here, for newly born babies have little immunity from infection.

Operating theatres

The function of the department is to receive patients after diagnosis, to anaesthetise them either before or after transfer to the operating table, to operate, and to supervise their post-operative condition before returning them to the wards.

The department consists of one or more operating suites which share ancillary accommodation such as staff changing and rest rooms, arrangements for the reception of patients, and facilities for the disposal of soiled material. The suites may also share a unit for the supply of sterile material and instruments. Each operating suite normally consists of a theatre, an anaesthetic room, a preparation room and a scrub-up. In some countries it is the practice to anaesthetise in the theatre itself.

For reasons of staffing, engineering services, flexibility of programming and the sharing of ancillaries operating suites are usually located together in one department if possible. Operations for accidents and emergencies, and sometimes for maternity, may need to be located

1	link and waiting	14	kitchen
2	on call	15	staff office
3	disposal	16	nursing officer
4	staff cloaks	17	wheelchairs
5	toilet	18	staff base
6	assisted toilet	19	dining
7	bath	20	day space
8	shower	21	six-bed ward
9	assisted bath	22	isolation suite
10	equipment	23	isolation room
11	cleaner	24	delivery
12	dirty utility	25	sluice
13	clean utility	26	nursery

Maternity Unit at Barking District General Hospital. An independent 26-bed isolation unit with its own delivery suite, built to replace an existing ward in poor condition and linked to the main hospital department. Corridors are virtually eliminated and the six-bed post-natal wards open off the day room and dining space. Architects: Harris Stow Partnership

1 anaesthetic
2 theatre
3 scrub-up
4 clean utility
5 dirty utility
6 recovery
7 equipment store
8 staff changing

0   6 m
0   20 ft

A single theatre addition at the London Hospital, Mile End. A clean access corridor provides the approach to the suite for patients, staff and stores, and for the patient's transfer to the Recovery Room after the operation. Soiled material from the theatre is passed through a hatch to the dirty utility room for disposal by lift or, after washing, for autoclaving and retrieval in the clean utility room on the other side. The door between dirty and clean utility rooms is for emergency use. Architects: T. P. Bennett and Son

elsewhere, and there may be an independent suite for minor operations, principally associated with the out-patients' department. Accident and emergency cases needing major surgery will nevertheless probably be dealt with in the main operating department.

Before the introduction of shadowless artificial lighting, surgery used to need adequate natural light and for this reason many operating departments were usually located on a top floor. Today better light and good ventilation can be provided artificially and this location is no longer necessary. Indeed the vibration that can arise from the proximity of air-conditioning machinery on an upper floor may make it undesirable. In countries where there are dust storms a top floor location will not necessarily avoid their effect, as dust can be blown up to heights of 50 m or more.

Although the requirements of theatres can be met by an entirely internal situation, from the point of view of staff who spend long periods in the department, some natural light can be a valuable asset. This should be provided for some of the ancillary staffrooms and should have some prospect of the outside. Whatever the location of the operating theatre, it is important that the communication routes from all the wards (not only the surgical ones, for the balance may change) should be direct, easy and if possible short. The department should be on a *cul-de-sac* so that access to it can be strictly controlled. Access from the accident and emergency department should be particularly easy.

If there is an Intensive Therapy Unit it should be nearby, and preferably adjacent. Proximity to the X-ray diagnostic department is not usually of great importance, for if X-rays are needed during operations the work will normally be done with mobile machines.

The original operating theatre, built about 1900, at University College Hospital, London. With entrance through an anaesthetic room and exit through a recovery room, from which it can be separated by sliding doors, it is conveniently but somewhat dangerously located off the main circulation core of the building. Steeply tiered seating allows spectators close observation of the procedure and there are basins for the surgeons to wash themselves. Architect: Alfred Waterhouse

0   10 ft
0   3 m

1 surgeons' changing and rest room
2 nurses' changing
3 scrub-up
4 sterile supply
5 sink room
6 theatre
7 anaesthetic
8 recovery
9 sluice
10 sister

A single theatre suite in the Ophthalmic unit at the Royal Berkshire Hospital, Reading, served by a central sterilising department elsewhere in the building. Staff enter the theatre from their changing rooms via the scrub-up. Supplies reach the sterile supply room by lift from the CSSD and thus direct into the theatre. Soiled material from the theatre is passed into the sink room and is disposed of or taken by separate lift for central sterilisation. Patients leave the theatre directly into the recovery ward, which communicates with the clean lobby by which they entered. Architects: Architects' Co-Partnership

It used to be normal practice in Britain to sterilise instruments within the suite, a pair of theatres sharing between them a sink and disposal room which was separated from a sterilising room by autoclaves. Both sink and sterilising rooms communicated directly with theatres. More recently this arrangement has tended to be avoided if possible, not least because of the difficulties it can present for temperature and humidity control in the theatres. Instead cleansing and the supply of sterile goods is done in a separate Theatre Sterile Supply Unit (TSSU) which can serve a larger number of theatres via a small preparation room attached to each of them. Alternatively, if there is a Central Sterile Supply Department (CSSD) for the whole hospital the work can be done there. The method of sterilisation and supply affects fundamentally the planning of the department.

Of prime importance in the design of the department is the need to reduce to a minimum the risk of infection at the operating table. This is vital for any operation but has become increasingly important as a result of advances involving deep surgery and lengthy exposure. Ensuring the sterility of instruments and other apparatus is relatively simple, but no less important is the reduction of risks of airbone infection. This depends upon management procedures and the physical arrangement of the department and of its ventilation system. The physical arrangement should ensure that not only are these procedures facilitated but that as far as possible they are inescapable.

The suite can be regarded as a sandwich in which the centre consists of the theatre, the anaesthetic room, the scrub-up in which those working in the theatre can wash and gown, and the supply, preparation or lay-up room through which instruments and materials are passed into the theatre. This centre is flanked on one side by a clean area from which patients, staff and sterile supplies reach

1	transfer zone	16	equipment transfer
2	porters	17	store
3	trolleys	18	recovery
4	anaesthetic	19	nurses' station
5	theatre	20	intensive care
6	exit bay	21	sluice
7	lay-up	22	sister
8	scrub-up	23	doctor
9	disposal	24	kitchen
10	laboratory	25	relatives
11	endoscopy	26	instrument processing (TSSU)
12	dark room	27	autoclaves (TSSU)
13	X-ray	28	sterile pack store (TSSU)
14	rest room	29	blood bank (TSSU)
15	orderlies	30	plaster room

A large operating department at Northwick Park Hospital and Clinical Research Centre, with its own Theatre Sterile Supply Unit and a recovery ward associated with the Intensive Care Unit. There are eight theatres and an endoscopy suite. Patients enter and leave the inner clean zone through a transfer lobby. Entirely separate dirty corridors connect each theatre's disposal room to the TSSU, where instruments are processed, autoclaved and passed into a sterile pack store, from which they are taken via the clean zone to the theatre lay-up rooms. Because of the research function laboratories adjoin the Recovery and Intensive Care Unit and each of the theatres. Architects: Llewelyn-Davies Weeks

CSSD

1	scrub-up	8	plaster room	15	staff lockers
2	anaesthetic	9	recovery	16	supervisor
3	theatre	10	sisters	17	sterilising room
4	supply room	11	changing room	18	sterile store
5	lay-up	12	clean-up room	19	emergency cupboard
6	sink room	13	workroom		
7	X-ray	14	store		

Two pairs of operating theatres with recovery ward at Wexham Park Hospital. Lay-up rooms and sink rooms are separated by autoclaves. The suites adjoin the central sterile supply department, which comprises a clean-up room from which goods are passed into a workroom and thence via the sterilising room to a sterile store: from this they are distributed either to the hospital or direct to the theatre corridor and the supply rooms that serve each pair of theatres. Architects: Powell and Moya. Consultants: Llewelyn-Davies Weeks the centre, and on the other side by a dirty area or disposal route through which soiled or infected material leaves it. Theatre staff enter the clean area through changing rooms.

To minimise the risk of infection the method of artificial ventilation should ensure that within each suite there is a supply of pure air sufficient to reduce the bacterial count below a critical level. There should be a positive pressure in the theatre and preparation room to provide a flow of air from the clean to the less clean areas. Where there is more than one operating suite in the department, as will usually be the case, each should have its own self-contained ventilation system in order to reduce the risk of cross infection. There should be no movement of air from one suite to another.

Patients are wheeled to the department either in their own beds or on trolleys. They are likely to have received a 'pre-medical' injection in the ward and to be unaware of what is happening. Whether in bed or on a trolley they are usually transferred to a theatre trolley in a transfer zone or lobby at the department entrance and ample space may be needed outside this zone for a bed or trolley park.

In the UK and some other countries the patient is trolleyed from the transfer zone to the anaesthetic room adjoining the theatre, and after anaesthesia is trolleyed into the theatre and transferred to the operating table. Sometimes the table itself is mobile and the transfer takes place in the anaesthetic room. On the other hand, in the USA and many countries, a separate anaesthetic room is unusual and anaesthesia is induced in the theatre itself. But whether or not there is an anaesthetic room the anaesthetist needs a wide variety of equipment, instruments and drugs which calls for considerable storage space.

After the operation the patient is transferred from the table to a trolley and is wheeled through an exit bay into the clean area and thence to a recovery area. After recovery from the anaesthetic the patient is returned by the route through which he entered, either to his own ward or to the Intensive Therapy Unit if his condition is critical.

The recovery area serves all the theatres in the department (assuming that they are all on the same floor). The usual British practice is to provide about three bed spaces for a pair of theatres. Because post-operative conditions may demand constant attention by nurse or anaesthetist, and sometimes visits by the surgeon, the recovery area needs to be easily super-vised and readily accessible from the theatres.

The procedures carried out in the operating depart-ment are probably the most precise and critical of all the functions performed in a hospital. The suite itself makes the most exacting demands upon detailed design and is frequently the most remote from the average designer's direct experience. Ventilation and lighting are probably open to more refined improvement than in any other part of a hospital building. For these reasons there may be much to be said for a design approach that anticipates future flexibility and change instead of attempting precise original design with materials and equipment that may be difficult to alter later.

1	porters
2	senior nursing officer
3	sister
4	transfer
5	clean corridor
6	anaesthetic
7	scrub
8	preparation
9	ENT theatre
10	day theatre
11	general theatre
12	plaster theatre
13	plaster and exit bay
14	exit bay
15	disposal
16	dirty corridor
17	recovery
18	store
19	mobile X-ray
20	male staff change
21	boots
22	female staff change
23	staff rest
24	beverage preparation
25	medical staff rest
26	courtyard
27	plant

A suite of four theatres at the Edith Cavell District General Hospital, Peterborough, with separate clean and dirty corridors. Architect: A. A. Crampin, Regional Architect, East Anglian Regional Health Authority

There are already available commercially prefabricated operating suite units, analogous to other items of hospital equipment. These integrate the enclosure and its components with the lighting, engineering services and ventilation and can stand like huts or tents within the building structure. It may be that units of this nature are valuable not only for introduction into old buildings where the operating suites no longer provide the facilities necessary for modern surgery, but also for new buildings. In the latter case the prefabricated units can be installed from the outset within an adequately spacious permanent shell in the knowledge that they will function efficiently and in anticipation that even more sophisticated units are likely to supersede them in the future.

Within the theatre itself a further development in the effort to reduce the risk of airborne infection is a glazed sterile enclosure around the operating table. Inside this the operating team can work. The enclosure can be combined with a body exhaust system in which the team wear hoods and gowns connected to an extract system so that they do not contaminate the air within the enclosure.

There are occasions when an operating theatre has to be added to a hospital, perhaps temporarily whilst an existing suite is being renovated or undergoing major alteration. There may also be emergencies when a suite is needed urgently, as occurred recently in the Falklands when the theatre at Port Stanley was destroyed by fire. One solution to situations such as these has been developed that uses three standard ISO containers, delivered fully fitted on low-loaders. Placed together side by side with a passage link to the existing building, they are capable of being installed in a few days.

Intensive therapy

The purpose of the unit, variously known as the Intensive Therapy Unit or Intensive Care Ward, is to give the most highly skilled care to the most acutely ill and to be able to do so continuously and in a concentrated manner throughout the twenty four hours. Its patients are relatively short stay. They may be in the unit for perhaps four to eight days before transfer to an ordinary ward if their treatment has been successful. It is entirely different from other wards, for all the patients are bedfast and are likely to be connected to monitoring or life support systems. Their condition demands that they must all be visible all the time and under the constant control of the nursing team.

All necessary services must be readily available at the bedside. Although there is a tendency for some of the

1	clean corridor	4	scrub	7	disposal
2	pass-through cupboards	5	anaesthetic	8	gas store
3	preparation	6	operating theatre	9	electrics

Relocatable theatre suite by Trojan Structures Limited. Three standard 12 × 2.4 m ISO containers arranged side by side. The unit includes a flexible corridor link for connection to existing buildings and a roof mounted air conditioning package. Electrical switchgear and medical gases are accessible from outside the unit. Architects: Architects Co-Partnership

1 intensive therapy beds
2 coronary care beds
3 staff base
4 clean utility and supplies
5 fire escape
6 beverage kitchen
7 disposal/sluice
8 equipment
9 equipment laboratory
10 staff change
11 doctors' and overnight room
12 charge nurse
13 staff lounge
14 relatives' lounge

The Intensive Therapy Unit in a Mark 2 'Best Buy' hospital. The staff base in the centre of the ward overlooks five intensive therapy beds, of which two are in single rooms with lobby entrances and glazed partitions, and also a separate enclosure for three coronary care beds. Only the clean utility bay communicates directly with the ward; all other ancillary rooms are off the entrance corridor. Architects: McDonald, Hamilton and Montefiore, with the Department of Health and Social Security equipment to become more compact than it used to be, which makes wall or even ceiling mounting possible and avoids obstructing the bedside, it is still necessary to have generous space around the bed for some bulky specialist machines. Some of the machines are heavy, and wall, floor and ceiling loadings may be critical.

The unit invariably has fewer beds than the normal ward (between 1% and 2% of the total number of acute beds) and will usually not contain more than eighteen beds, broken down into sub-divisions of about six with a small proportion of single rooms for isolation. In addition to clean and dirty utility rooms its ancillary accommodation is likely to include waiting space for relatives, bedroom accommodation for overnight visitors or relatives, additional rooms for staff and generous storage space for portable equipment.

Access to the unit must be strictly controlled. It is usually situated close to the operating theatres and if possible to the Accident and Emergency Department. It has a higher claim to full air-conditioning than do the other wards.

Pathology

The essential function of the department is to carry out diagnostic tests on specimens from in-patients and out-patients. It may also be concerned with work for clinics, health centres, local practitioners and the public health services. Apart from other considerations an efficient laboratory that produces accurate results rapidly can be an important factor in reducing the patients' length of stay and thus contribute substantially to the economy of a hospital.

Within the department the main divisions are those for histology and morbid anatomy, which involve the microscopic examination of tissues and cells; haematology, the study of the blood; biochemistry, the study of living tissues and fluids; and microbiology, the study of

One of the two floors of a large Pathology department at Northwick Park Hospital and Clinical Research Centre. Services run in vertical shafts at a regular module on both sides of the central corridor and feed into the laboratories horizontally on the bench lines, above floor level. Benches and partitions may be rearranged and the functions of individual rooms changed. Internal rooms are cold rooms, centrifuges, dark rooms etc. The external escape stair can be taken down and re-erected if the building is extended. Architects: Llewelyn-Davies Weeks

1 male waiting	20 disposal
2 female waiting	21 haematologist
3 records/reception	22 haematology labs and blood bank
4 examination	23 microbiology labs
5 clinette	24 media preparation
6 office	25 sterilising
7 blood donors	26 outfit preparation
8 post donation rest room	27 inflammable spirits
9 staff change	28 chief technician
10 library	29 staff duty room
11 specimen receipt	30 temperature controlled stores
12 pathologist	31 hot room
13 chemical pathology labs	32 animal colony
14 morbid anatomy labs	33 animal reception
15 cytodiagnosis	34 staff room
16 studio	35 animal observation
17 dark room	36 animal investigation
18 workshop	37 disposal
19 wash-up	38 general store

A pathology department for a single storey hospital in Saudi Arabia. Services are in vertical ducts and run out horizontally along the bench lines as at Northwick Park. Washup and sterilising are centralised. There is a separate animal house. Outside the laboratory area there is provision for blood donors and the collection of specimens from patients. Architects: Architects Co-Partnership

1 specimen reception	7 histology
2 blood donor	8 sterilise/wash-up
3 cross matching	9 store
4 pathologist	10 refrigerator
5 haematology	11 blood bank
6 chemist	12 fume cupboard/safety cabinet

A small pathology laboratory in a private ophthalmic hospital in Saudi Arabia. Architects: Architects Co-Partnership

micro-organisms. Each of these divisions may require sub-departments, their extent depending on the context and policy of the laboratory.

Although each division carries out a different type of work and needs particular ancillary accommodation the boundaries between them tend to become blurred, some techniques may be shared, and the basic laboratory bench requirement does not differ essentially from one to another. A standardised modular plan and a system of service spurs feeding relatively deep bays at right angles to a corridor or open aisle can accept a wide variety of bench arrangements and ancillary spaces and offices. It can also provide reasonable flexibility for the future changes which will undoubtedly be demanded.

In addition to those originating from outside the hospital specimens will be delivered from the wards, the operating theatres, the mortuary, the out-patients' department, or from the accident and emergency department if it is nearby. Some specimens, particularly blood and urine, will be obtained from out-patients on the spot, and for this a patients' waiting space, lavatories, and several consulting/examination rooms are necessary. Nearly all specimens will pass through a central reception and sorting office before distribution to the appropriate laboratory divisions.

If diagnostic reports are to reach the originator of the request quickly in an emergency, it is clear that the pathology laboratory should ideally be close to the theatres and to accidents even if advances in Information Technology allow the transmission of results by electronic means. But an overriding consideration may be its relationship to out-patients, not for reasons of speed but for their convenience. However, small ancillary units are often sited in the Intensive Care Ward (for speedy blood gas analysis), in an accident unit, or in out-patient units if they are not close to the main laboratory facilities.

In addition to the likelihood of the department's internal requirements changing it may well need space for expansion. This would be particularly necessary if an increasing role in servicing demands from outside the hospital is to be anticipated.

Pharmaceutical

The pharmacy serves the whole hospital. It stores pharmaceutical products manufactured elsewhere and may also store dressings. It usually manufactures some sterile and non-sterile products in bulk and dispenses prescriptions, sometimes direct to out-patients. It supplies all wards and other departments, often on the basis of daily deliveries. For small hospitals, manufacture and dispensing may be done at a larger centre elsewhere and the function of the department may be restricted to storage and distribution.

Because supervision of drugs is essential and security is of first importance, manufactured goods are sometimes received direct by the pharmacy rather than via the hospital's main stores. The basic work flow in the department is reception of goods, unpacking and checking, then storage in either a dressings store or a drugs store, and finally dispensing and distribution. The reception point needs ample provision for disposable

	7 autoclaves
	8 clean-up
	9 bulk preparation
	10 bottle wash
	11 drug store
	12 dispensary
1 bond store, inspection and	13 quality control
labelling	14 information
2 air lock	15 pharmacist
3 aseptic room	16 despatch store
4 sterile products	17 out-patient waiting
5 filling	18 clerks' office
6 preparation	19 staff cloaks

The Pharmacy at King Edward Memorial Hospital, Ealing. Goods are delivered by road elsewhere in the hospital and reach the pharmacy from within the building. The department is situated next door to out-patients and has its own sub-waiting space for the collection of prescriptions. Architect: John R. Harris

packaging and returnable empties. Some of the products (poisons and dangerous drugs) require special security measures. Others need refrigeration, and some flammable liquids may demand particular precautions against fire or explosion involving storage outside the building.

From the drugs store, goods pass to the dispensing section either direct or via a bulk preparation room. In the dispensary they are broken down into correct quantities, and from there distributed to the hospital or collected direct at a counter on prescription by out-patients. A separate waiting space is necessary for the latter unless it is combined with the out-patients' main waiting area. Ancillary accommodation includes staff offices and lavatories, a laboratory, and a suite for the manufacture of sterile products, comprising preparation room, wash-up, autoclaves, and a room for inspection, labelling and storage.

If the pharmacy is to serve out-patients direct rather than through a separate dispensary proximity to the out-patients department is the main consideration in its location. For this reason it is usually situated at road level. Its relation to the rest of the hospital is relatively unimportant provided it has easy access to the communication routes. Road access for deliveries is highly desirable.

Central sterile supply

A hospital consumes a large quantity of new material that needs sterilisation before use. It also processes other material that has to be cleaned and sterilised before it can be used again. This sterilisation used to be carried out where and when the material was wanted, for instance in the wards or the operating suite. Nowadays items can be supplied by manufacturers in sterilised packs appropriate for particular purposes and an increasing number of them are disposable (which affects both the storage and the disposal areas needed). However, the hospital still needs to sterilise most items and also to control the supply of properly sterilised material to wherever it is needed.

The purpose of a central sterilising department is to concentrate the skill and the responsibility for the supply of this material and to reduce the risk of error. The department also enables the nursing staff to do their work with patients more effectively. Where there are several hospitals in fairly close proximity one department may provide this service for them all.

The department receives clean material from a laundry and new material from manufacturers and suppliers. These deliveries normally arrive by road. It also receives, for re-use, dirty articles from within the hospital. These are normally brought by trolley but may also arrive by road if the department is servicing more than one hospital.

Clean and dirty materials require separate delivery points, the clean one serving a bulk store for new materials such as towels and masks, and the dirty one serving a clean-up room where all re-usable goods including instruments and syringes are washed, cleaned and dried. Rubber gloves may either be dealt with here or passed through the clean-up room to a separate glove room for treatment.

From the clean-up room syringes and instruments are passed to another room for inspection, maintenance and dry heat sterilisation before being placed in a sterile store. Other goods pass from the clean-up room, the glove room or the bulk store into a workroom. Here packs

are made up and stored temporarily before being autoclaved and taken into a sterile store.

From the sterile store goods are issued to a trolley loading bay for distribution. This will need easy access to a vehicle loading bay if the department is supplying more than one hospital. Except for the delivery and dispatch points the department is planned on a closed circuit production flow. The ancillary rooms for staff communicate with the main workroom.

The department should be in the hospital's service zone to simplify the reception of goods (and of deliveries to other hospitals if it is intended to serve them as well). Proximity to the boiler house is an advantage if steam is raised there. Good communication routes to most of the other departments of the hospital are essential.

The advantages of complete centralisation of sterile supplies do not necessarily extend to the operating department. Here the large number of instruments that are used have customarily been sterilised locally (indeed some of them may be regarded by some surgeons as their personal tools). Nevertheless, it is becoming increasingly recognised that there are advantages in concentrating sterilisation for all the operating suites either in the Central Sterilising Department or in a Theatre Sterile Supply Unit (TSSU) instead of providing separate sterilising facilities for each theatre suite. One of the advantages of this concentration is that the absence of local autoclaves avoids the problem of heat and humidity in the operating suite and simplifies the supply of correctly conditioned air.

Catering

Suitable food well cooked and presented is an important part of the patient's treatment. In the developed world the trend has been towards an increasing degree of individual choice of menu together with dietary supervision. There is an increasing sophistication in the methods of cooking and distribution with the object that meals should reach the patient in as attractive a form as practicable yet demand the minimum amount of labour.

Food has to be supplied to both patients and staff, and in a modern hospital the total number of staff may be roughly equal to the number of beds. One central kitchen usually supplies all the food and because it simplifies service the staff dining rooms are generally sited adjacent to the kitchen.

Several methods are in use for delivery of meals from kitchen to wards. They differ in the method of processing, the palatability, the means of transport and the amount of labour that is necessary. Food may be transported to each ward in a bulk container by heated trolley and served on to plates by the ward staff. This method has for a long time been the normal method and is simple and effective; it allows for immediate adjustments in the quantity given to individual patients but is relatively labour intensive in the wards.

More recent methods are for individual meals to be portioned and plated up in the kitchen or served there on to insulated and compartmented trays, and delivered complete by trolley or conveyor. Alternatively and more rarely food may be cooked centrally, then frozen, and

0   10 ft
0   3 m

1 lobby and trolley park
2 autoclaves
3 clean-up
4 bulk store
5 workroom tables (hardware)
6 workroom tables (soft goods)
7 sterile store
8 office

The Central Sterile Supply Department for the Royal Berkshire Hospital, Reading. Soiled material from within the hospital arrives on trolleys; from the lobby it is passed across a counter into the clean-up area. Clean material is taken through a doorway direct into the bulk store. Packs are assembled at the tables in the workroom, which is not separated from the storage area; they pass through the autoclave room before reaching the sterile store. The two small lifts adjoining the sterile store serve an ophthalmic operating theatre, one into its preparation room and the other from its disposal room. Architects: Architects Co-Partnership finally reheated in the ward kitchen, or even prepared centrally and cooked in the ward kitchen.

There is an increasing use of bulk frozen foods, with consequent implications on the storage requirements, and also of the bulk purchase of ready-made frozen meals from commercial sources. The catering may be run by the hospital or contracted out to external organisations. The different methods are reflected in the size, equipment and planning of both central and ward kitchens. Only conveyor delivery is likely to affect fundamentally the strategic planning of the building, tending to put a premium on concentration and vertical stacking. This system is fairly widely adopted in the USA but it demands a high degree of technical efficiency and is unlikely to be relevant to any but the most sophisticated and mechanically dependent hospitals.

The washing up of crockery and utensils has in the past been done in the ward kitchens. This is now usually centralised in the main kitchen, with the advantages of more efficient steam sterilisation, less work for the ward staff and less noise in the ward itself.

In some countries it is usual, for economic, cultural or religious reasons, for friends or relatives to supply patients' meals, bringing in food from their homes if they live nearby. It is sometimes customary for members of the family to accompany a patient to hospital and to stay in the vicinity or even in the ward until he is discharged, purchasing, cooking and serving his food. Sometimes simple communal visitors' cookhouses are provided for this purpose outside the hospital.

This practice seems likely to continue, particularly in rural hospitals. Provided there is control over what the patient is permitted to eat there seems little reason to change it, for family support can be of importance to a patient's recovery besides easing the burden on the hospital. Where these practices are general some much reduced provision for food to be cooked by the hospital will nevertheless be necessary.

7

Teaching hospitals

Arrangements for the training of medical and other hospital staff and the administrative relationships between hospital and educational authorities, such as universities, may differ from one country to another. Most hospitals, however, have some teaching function and many general hospitals have training schools for nurses. Specialist staff, such as radiographers, may be trained in a variety of establishments. In Britain the term 'teaching hospital' has the specific meaning that whatever other training it may do, it is a place where medical students are taught to become physicians or surgeons. It is this category of hospital, with its highly integrated training, that is considered in this chapter.

Interdependent functions

Teaching hospitals combine three interdependent functions:

the treatment of the sick;
undergraduate and postgraduate education including nursing;
research;

Compared with many general hospitals teaching hospitals are larger in size, partly because of the number of beds and the range of specialities that are desirable to give students a wide experience, but principally on account of the additional accommodation needed for education and research. Their diagnostic and treatment departments also tend to be particularly specialised and to employ the most highly sophisticated equipment.

The teaching hospital is rightly regarded as a centre of excellence and an important centre of research. Because of these attributes there is a tendency for it to admit a relatively high proportion of patients who are suffering from 'interesting' or specially critical ailments, or who are of particular value from the point of view of research. This is inevitable in any primary, secondary and tertiary referral system.

The clinical experience offered by a teaching hospital may therefore not be entirely typical of the more common illnesses that the average young doctor is likely to encounter in general practice. For this reason, and although teaching hospitals may do their best to make their services available to the community in which they are situated, a period of the doctor's training is often in a general hospital. Where this is the policy it will have implications on the accommodation that is desirable in those establishments. The same consideration applies to the training of other medical, nursing and auxiliary staff.

The education of doctors is normally in two parts, undergraduate and postgraduate. The undergraduate stage usually lasts three years; the early part is mostly academic, or 'pre-clinical', dealing with the basic sciences and conducted in a medical school; the latter part is increasingly clinical, in which the student assists in the wards and some of the specialist departments, perhaps opting towards the end of the period for a particular specialism. In most countries the student then has a period of postgraduate training in hospitals, with some degree of responsibility, before he can practice as a doctor. Those intending to become hospital consultants may spend ten years in various hospital posts,

beginning as house officers and ending as senior registrars, and usually spend two or more years in university or research work combining research with teaching.

In the past the pre-clinical period has been separate, but where the standard of education of students entering medicine has been high the trend has been for this period to become less strictly academic and for students to be brought into contact with patients at a relatively early stage of their training.

The training of nurses is more closely integrated with the day-to-day work in the wards and other departments and is similar to a sandwich course. Practical work with patients, supervised by the sister and other senior nurses, alternates with periods of academic work in a school of nursing. The responsibility given to the student nurse in the hospital increases during the period of basic training, which normally lasts three years.

Background

The role and administrative position of teaching hospitals in the UK has changed in post-war years, since the introduction of the National Health Service. Originally their traditions, buttressed in many cases by substantial endowments and guarded by the powerful Boards of Governors who were responsible for their financing, gave

1	student laboratory	5	doctors
2	seminar	6	visitors
3	clinical investigation	7	registrar
4	students		

0   15 m
0   50 ft

A ward floor at St Thomas' Hospital, London. There are four wards, each occupying one quarter of the perimeter. Clinical teaching accommodation in the form of student laboratories, seminar rooms and clinical investigation room is embedded in the middle of the building, with access both from within the wards and from the central lift lobby and corridor through which the wards are approached. Architects: Yorke Rosenberg Mardall them independence from the regional organisation of the service. However, in 1974 the Boards were abolished and after 1982 the teaching hospitals became fully integrated with the national organisational structure, with commitments to districts and regions.

This historical independence, combined with their special requirements and the fact that, compared with district general hospitals, relatively few new ones were needed, meant that to a large extent they were free from the constraints of the national programme. Because each responded to a particular problem, often in an innovative manner, they display a range of individual solutions.

Twenty of the forty-eight universities in the UK have medical schools. The University of London alone includes nineteen schools of medicine and specialist post-graduate institutes.

The hospital and the medical school

The accommodation provided in a teaching hospital differs from other hospitals in two principal ways. Space is needed for research, and also for a medical school for academic instruction. Both of these are to some degree separate from the hospital's ongoing function of caring for the sick. Space is also needed in the wards for clinical teaching, and in the past this has sometimes been interpreted as more room around the beds for large groups of students under instruction (the traditional teaching round).

Although such visitations still prevail, the student groups nowadays tend to be smaller and training is mainly done by discussion, demonstration and practical work in separate rooms which are now generally provided as an integral part of the ward. Thus the ancillary rooms necessary in the ward may be increased by seminar space for group discussions with the clinical

staff and by clinical demonstration space to which a patient may be brought from the ward. Laboratories are also required for simple work by students on specimens from patients, and also rooms where students can read and write up their notes.

The teaching and demonstration function used to require the special design of some of the hospitals' operating theatres, with galleries or other devices from which students could watch procedure. This requirement has today been largely superseded by colour film and closed circuit television, which have also immensely extended the range of demonstration in other medical fields.

Teaching accommodation not directly associated with clinical observation is provided in the medical school. In addition to the social and ancillary spaces generated by

1 wet (or high) bench
2 dry (or low) bench
3 & 5 storage units
4 fume cupboard
6 projection screen
7 free-standing equipment
8 preparation bench
9 ancillary accommodation

1 reception
2 consultant
3 head
4 laboratory
5 tutorial
6 demonstration
7 interview
8 senior registrar
9 house officer
10 examination
11 kitchen
12 sister
13 showers and toilets
14 bath
15 disposal
16 nurses' station
17 treatment
18 clean utility

0   50 ft
0   15 m

The ward plan at Ninewells Hospital. Two units of 24-beds are approached through a cross link which contains offices, laboratory, tutorial room and clinical demonstration room. Three day rooms and a balcony are shared between the units. Architects: Robert Matthew, Johnson-Marshall and Partners

1 wet bench
2 dry bench
3 reagent shelves
4 fume cupboard
5 glass storage
6 projection screen
7 free-standing equipment
8 preparation bench
9 ancillary accommodation

0   30 ft
0   10 m

Two basic layouts for multi-discipline laboratories in which the student has his own home base for wet and dry laboratory studies and for reading and written work. Each laboratory is for 16 students and a pair share an interlab with preparation bench, freestanding equipment and fume cupboards if required. Architect: Audrey Williamson the needs of a large number of students it will include lecture theatres, seminar rooms, staff rooms, and the specialised plant of pre-clinical laboratories and dissecting rooms.

Pre-clinical teaching laboratories have traditionally been largely devoted to special subjects and have been specially designed for each purpose, such as biochemistry, physiology, histology, pharmacology, and anatomy. Each speciality has tended to retain its own territory and the students have moved in classes from one to another.

A more recent development that allows more intensive use of the accommodation and can be less divisive, less wasteful of space, and encourages a teaching unit more suitable for seminars, audio-visual aids and project work, is the smaller multi-discipline laboratory. Here most of the student's work can be done in one place (with the exception, probably, of anatomy, for which the centralised storage of cadavers is likely to be more practicable). In the multi-discipline laboratory the student has a place of his own, a home base, where he can do both his laboratory work and also his reading and writing.

Research

Laboratories for research present an entirely different picture from the large and relatively static teaching laboratories for instruction in particular specialities or the multi-discipline laboratories which provide bases in which students can study. Research projects may both come and go, ebb and flow, and throw up differing needs and differing sizes of teams. They need accommodation that will permit the flexibility that these changes demand.

Specialised spaces such as offices, preparation rooms, balance rooms, constant temperature rooms, autoclaves and workshops are likely to be necessary. It

1 wet bench
2 dry bench
3 fume cupboard
4 blackboard and projection screen
5 ancillary accommodation

0   30 ft
0   10 m

Multi-discipline laboratoriesa at Nottingham University Hospital and Medical School. Two laboratories share a preparation room and store. Wet benches with underbench lockers are served with gases and electricity and with water over drip cups; they alternate with lower tables for written work, serviced with electrical outlets for microscopes. Each laboratory has a sink and fume cupboard, and a chalkboard and projection screen on the back wall. Architects: Building Design Partnership

is desirable that most of the other working space should be standardised as far as possible in its planning module and in the servicing arrangements for electricity, water, piped gases, drainage and ventilation. Most laboratory work can function satisfactorily with movable benches and storage units located along or around predetermined service lines or pedestals, arranged in undifferentiated bays.

The requirements of different research projects change and the boundaries between different specialities also tend to become less distinct. The planning of research laboratories should discourage the establishment of separate research empires with territorial rights and inviolable tailor-made rooms. The sharing of specialised facilities and the opportunity for expansion and contraction as research programmes demand should be encouraged.

Initial design decisions can assist but not resolve the solution of this problem. However flexible the accommodation may be it is unlikely that it will be adequate for future requirements. Therefore, not only should the inevitability of change be recognised but the probability of growth should be anticipated and should be reflected in the siting of the accommodation.

Relationships

In some of the great teaching hospitals of the past the physical relationship between hospital, medical school and research accommodation has tended for various reasons to be less close than is now thought desirable, indeed they have even been organisationally and physically separate institutions. In part this has reflected the attitudes towards medical education at the time, and buildings have been developed on a succession of constricted sites which have offered little alternative. Apart from any psychological disadvantages, this separation can waste the time of staff in moving from one place to another and can sometimes tend to inhibit such movement if it can be avoided.

Although all the research accommodation usually needs to be planned as one unit sharing centralised facilities, it should when possible also be arranged so that it is near its associated hospital department. Although many of the research workers will be scientific rather than medical personnel, many of the medical specialists who lead the research projects will combine clinical work with research. If the medical school can also be closely associated with the hospital so much the better for many of the hospital staff will also be involved with teaching. The more that the rigid division between the student's pre-clinical and clinical experience disappears and medical education is integrated with the work of the hospital the more valuable will these close physical relationships become.

Comparative examples

An example of a newly designed teaching hospital which made a determined attempt at close integration of the clinical, teaching and research functions was the new Charing Cross Hospital in London. Planned on a

A multi-discipline laboratory at Nottingham. Tables for dry work alternate with higher benches for wet work. Architects: Building Design Partnership

1 multi-discipline laboratories
2 ancillary rooms
3 MDL lecture theatre
4 classrooms
5 discussion and tutors' rooms

A floor of multi-discipline laboratories and associated rooms, including a large lecture theatre, in the medical school block at Nottingham. The block has five main levels, with an animal house on the roof. The lowest level contains library, lecture theatres and workshops; the second seminar rooms, offices, common rooms, professors' and readers' laboratories; the third multi-discipline laboratories and ancillary rooms; the fourth professors', lecturers' and teaching laboratories and film and medical artists; and the fifth dissecting laboratories, specialist professors', readers' and lecturers' laboratories, and laboratories for 3rd and Final Year honours. The link block is on four levels and houses the nurses' training school. Architects: Building Design Partnership relatively restricted site in an urban area the ward block took the shape of a multi-storey cruciform in which one wing of the cross contained research, teaching laboratories and clinical teaching space, and the other three wings were occupied by beds.

A later London example, also on a restricted site but part of the phased redevelopment of an existing hospital, is to be seen at St. Thomas' Hospital. Here clinical investigation rooms, seminar rooms and clinical laboratories for student work are embedded with the other ward ancillaries in the core of a rectangular multi-storey block, and the beds and day spaces occupy the whole of the perimeter. Laboratories occupy some of the lower floors of this ward block and a research institute shares with diagnostic and treatment, operating and outpatients departments an adjacent building linked closely to it below the level of the wards.

An entirely different type of solution, impossible on the urban sites of the two previous examples, is the Ninewells Hospital at Dundee in Scotland. With more space to spread, low-rise buildings of not more than three storeys were practicable. The three elements – the wards, the paraclinical laboratories and lecture theatres, and the pre-clinical laboratories and library – are disposed in parallel lines with cross-links between them. There is also a fourth element, medical physics, on a line which is most remote from the wards. This building, opened in 1974, is the earliest UK example in which clinical and paraclinical departments are fully integrated with the hospital itself.

Compared with the restraints imposed by a condensed multi-storey arrangement this pattern clearly has the advantage of providing some opportunity for future growth by the lateral extension of any of the elements. Here again the T-shaped wards show the close juxtaposition of clinical teaching accommodation and

1 dental hospital and school
2 lecture theatres
3 medical school
4 hospital departments
5 wards
6 day hospital
7 post-graduate medical centre and physical medicine
8 administration

A staff, patients, visitors
B maternity
C dental patients
D staff and students
E animals and cadavers
F supplies
G accidents

Development plan for the Royal Victoria Infirmary and Medical School, Newcastle upon Tyne. There are three parallel lines of accommodation with cross-links. On the north are the medical school, lecture theatres and dental school; hospital departments are in the centre and wards on the south face. The day hospital, physical medicine and post-graduate medical centre extend to the south, linked to an existing administrative building. Architects: Robert Matthew, Johnson-Marshall and Partners

1 wards
2 laboratories
3 pre clinical labs
4 lecture theatres
5 library
6 operating
7 administration
8 polyclinic
9 maternity
10 medical physics
11 laundry and plant
12 residences
13 nurses' school

Ninewells Hospital and Medical School, Dundee; an 865 bed hospital and medical school for 400 students. There are in principle three parallel lines of accommodation, with cross links. The wards, which include clinical teaching rooms, are situated on the south face; there is then a line of paraclinical laboratories, theatres and diagnostic departments. On the north are the preclinical laboratories, lecture theatres and medical library. Operating theatres and administration are at the fulcrum. Medical physics, the department least associated with the wards, is in a separate building on the extreme north. To the east the laundry, plant, nurses' training school and residences leave space for expansion of the main building. Architects: Robert Matthew, Johnson-Marshall and Partners

A main entrance
B service entrance
C nurses' training school
D bridge to University

1 medical school and medical sciences
2 diagnosis and treatment
3 works department

Nottingham University Hospital and Medical School provides 1400 beds in three large quadrangular blocks; accommodation for the medical school and medical sciences is in the fourth. The blocks are linked by a ring system of corridors; one of these links contains the nurses' training school. Diagnostic and treatment departments are in the central area. A bridge over a main road connects the medical school with the university campus. Architects: Building Design Partnership patients, with tutorial and demonstration rooms in the area through which the beds are approached.

A similar gradation from pre-clinical to clinical and community departments, with cross links, is seen in the plan for the Royal Victoria Infirmary at Newcastle. Here the parallel lines of accommodation contain firstly the medical school and dental hospital and school; secondly the main hospital departments, and thirdly the wards, with physical medicine and the day hospital in a further unit beyond the wards.

The University Hospital and Medical School at Nottingham demonstrates another type of solution to the close integration of pre-clinical and clinical work. Four blocks, each forming a hollow rectangle, are linked by a larger square containing a corridor ring, of which one side is largely occupied by the Nurses' Training School. Within the ring is a central area of diagnostic, treatment and service departments. Three of the hollow blocks contain wards and the fourth is the Medical School, one of whose six floors is entirely occupied by multi-discipline laboratories and their ancillary accommodation.

Interstitial space

It is for buildings of this complexity, presenting considerable areas of highly serviced accommodation and the probability of future changes in their disposition, particularly in the research accommodation, that the advantages of interstitial space are most likely to be relevant. We have referred to this type of space arrangement in Chapter 4, particularly in connection with the Health Service Centre at McMaster University in Canada, but although they are not on so grand a scale there are examples of it in Britain, for example the Greenwich District General Hospital and the teaching hospitals at Leeds and Nottingham. However, if the interstitial approach is adopted it is vital that it is adequately thought through in all its detailed aspects. There is a risk that having decided on a type of design that appears to be relatively expensive in first cost there will be a temptation to economies in dimension and material that may lead to the advantages of the concept being seriously reduced if not nullified.

Interstitial space has been defined as a fully accessible walk-through space under the main floor structure and above the ceiling of the floor below, devoted entirely to the distribution of mechanical and electrical services. Its principal advantage in the long term is to reduce the need for access into the occupied spaces below in order to carry out maintenance, repairs and alteration. In the shorter term, during construction, it provides a discrete zone in which mechanical and electrical contractors can proceed with the installation independently of the building contractor, thus potentially reducing the overall contract period by parallel working.

Services installations normally account for between 35% and 40% of the cost of a hospital building, sometimes more. But the life of many elements of mechanical and to some extent of electrical services is shorter than that of the building fabric. With some elements it may be no more than about 30 years, even less. There are already cases where areas of relatively recently built hospitals have had to be taken out of use in order to replace the services concealed above their suspended ceilings. In low-rise buildings such horizontal service runs may be largely accommodated in a roof space, as in 'Nucleus' hospitals, but in the multi-storey structures so often unavoidable in urban situations, not least in large complexes such as teaching hospitals, the advantage of an independently accessible interstitial service zone is obvious, particularly if the building is air conditioned.

The technical design of such spaces is critical, but certain principles may perhaps be suggested here. Firstly, the clear height of the service space needs to be at least two metres and it is questionable whether a lattice structure as at McMaster is desirable if it can be avoided; the diagonal members impede the layout of service runs. Secondly, the deck of the interstitial floor unit must not only be capable of taking traffic but should be reasonably quiet to walk on. In order to pass services through to the floor below it must also be easily perforated, and easily made good. And thirdly, a suspended ceiling is necessary below the deck to provide some tolerance for emerging service runs before they drop to their precise positions.

Independent hospitals

The introduction of the National Health Service in Britain provided comprehensive care for all people free of charge at the time they needed it, funded by taxation. When the Service came into being, voluntary hospitals were vested in the Minister of Health. But the Act allowed the Minister to exclude those that were not required within the public sector and in the event these were principally most of the hospitals connected with a religious body or supported by Freemasons or Trades Unions and those providing for employment-linked contribution schemes. The Act did not affect the ownership of private establishments such as the majority of nursing homes, nor convalescent homes unless they belonged to hospitals that became part of the National Health Service.

The Act provided the opportunity for part-time contracts with National Health Service consultants, who could thus supplement their 'salary' by private practice. The intention of this incentive to combine public and private work was to avoid senior specialists quitting the public sector. The Act also established private pay-beds in National Health Service hospitals but in 1966 the number of these was reduced. A policy of abolishing them altogether was introduced in 1976, resulting in a drop in their number from 4444 at that time to 2533 by 1980, when a different government reversed the policy and the number of pay-beds began to increase.

Provident associations

The intended abolition of pay-beds and the strains that National Health Service hospitals were experiencing, particularly the long waiting time for non-emergency surgery, stimulated the growth of various sorts of independent hospitals. But long before this happened there had been major developments in the independent sector in the field of provident schemes. Provident associations are the main providers of private health insurance in the UK. All surplus revenue is ploughed back into the associations' reserves. Subscribers are either individuals, paying their own premiums, or are enrolled through arrangements with, for example, their professional body or company, to which they pay their subscriptions, or are part of a group whose premium is paid partly or wholly by their employer. Today nearly five and a half million, 9% of the population of the UK, are covered by such schemes.

Perhaps the most significant of these developments was in 1947 when 17 provident associations combined to form the British United Provident Association (BUPA). In 1957 it established the Nursing Homes Charitable Trust Ltd, which later became the Nuffield Nursing Homes Trust, now Nuffield Hospitals. There are currently thirty two Nuffield hospitals with a total of over 1300 beds. In 1980 the earlier, tenuous connection between Nuffield hospitals and BUPA ceased; the latter has 17 hospitals and also twenty three medical centres with screening and diagnostic facilities.

In the last decade the number of acute-care beds belonging to the religious and charitable bodies has remained much the same but the number in the independent sector has rapidly increased very consider-

ably, particularly amongst British and American groups. Since 1984 the total number of private beds of one sort and another has increased from about 8640 to 10500. In addition to hospitals the independent, charitable and voluntary sector is almost entirely responsible for nursing and convalescent homes and hospices.

Other developments

A development that began to accelerate in the 1970s was the establishment of hospitals that, unlike the original BUPA and Nuffield hospitals, were run commercially for profit by investor-owned companies. At first these were mainly in London and the south-east of England. They were costly and luxurious, within reach of London West End consultants. They attracted many patients from overseas, notably from the Middle East. In the early 1970s the prestigious Harley Street Clinic was taken over by American Medical International (AMI) and the foreign and American involvement in this for-profit sector is now substantial. For example, AMI own twelve hospitals in England, with a total of 965 beds. Some of them are newly built. Humana, another US chain, owns the Wellington Hospital in London, and Hospital Affiliates International has built the Cromwell Hospital in West London.

1	main lifts	8	suite with bathroom
2	bed lifts	9	toilet
3	nurses' station	10	pantry
4	sister	11	dirty utility
5	single ward with bathroom	12	cleaner
6	twin-bed ward with bathroom	13	store
7	three-bed ward with bathroom		

London Bridge Hospital. Typical ward plan of this 119 bed hospital with cardiac and renal facilities. It occupies the carcass of a 19th century warehouse from which the interior structure has been removed and the four ward floors rebuilt around an inner court with a glazed roof. Beneath these floors the whole area within the original enclosing walls is occupied by two floors of central facilities – operating, radiology and treatment, stores, CSSD and administration. There is a link to another building containing consulting rooms and dental suite. Architects: Llewelyn-Davies Weeks

*The internal courtyard of the ward floors at London Bridge Hospital.
(Photo: Jo Reid and John Peck)*

The attraction of independent hospitals (and today there are 205) is not merely the privacy, comfort and cooking, or the freedom they provide to be treated by the consultant of the patient's choice but, to a much greater extent than has proved practicable with National Health Service hospitals, the opportunity to make arrangements for treatment in advance, at a time when it is convenient for the patient.

Characteristics

All independent hospitals need to make a profit, which has encouraged short-stay patients and non-acute surgery. They have therefore concentrated on elective surgery rather than accident and emergency cases. For example, in England they carry out 17% of all such elective surgery, including 28% of all hip replacements and 19% of all coronary artery by-pass grafts. Unlike the hospitals of the National Health Service they have not been available to everyone without charge and only now are beginning to provide comprehensive care. Nor does this part of the independent sector cater for the mentally ill, the chronic elderly, the handicapped or the terminally ill. In the main private hospitals have been accessible only to the minority who can pay for their services, either personally or through insurance – and insurance schemes have not provided for long-term care of those over 65.

These characteristics have been reflected in the scope of their accommodation and their specialist departments.

Their emphasis has been on the routine range of surgical and acute medical activity, without provision for accidents and emergencies, but with special facilities for out-patient consultation and treatment. This is not to say that the services they provide are not good ones, or that they are not equipped with advanced diagnostic facilities for their purposes or with excellent operating arrangements. By complementing the National Health Service, the private hospitals have progressively relieved the nation of the total burden of health care, even if only marginally.

It is interesting to compare the difference between typical recent National Health Service hospitals – for instance the district general hospitals described in Chapter 4 which aim to serve the whole community and are based on a catchment area – with one or two of the most prestigious and sophisticated examples of recent private hospitals in London, namely the Wellington and the Cromwell, all from the past two decades. Although by no means typical of private hospitals they demonstrate the relative scale of the accommodation needed and the relative luxury in both space and facilities of their 'wards', and also emphasise that unique solutions and ingenuity may be demanded by the nature of small sites in restricted and sensitive central urban areas where land values are high and where proximity to a pool of private consultants is of vital importance to their activities. It is also likely that, because the available sites will be used to maximum capacity, growth and change will be made more difficult. Indeed, the later Wellington Humana hospital, although within easy reach of the original Wellington, is necessarily an entirely separate building.

Compared with the typical new district general hospital these examples are small in size. The largest, the Cromwell, provides only 164 beds. But there is nothing small about their operating suites or their diagnostic departments, which provide for a relatively rapid throughput of short-stay patients. Nor is there anything small about the plans of their ward floors. At first glance these might be thought to be luxury hotels, each bedroom discreetly screened from the public corridor by its own private bathroom lobby. Indeed, this is the atmosphere it is intended to create and for many clients is an important attraction. The close and involuntary contact between patient and nurse, the objective of so many British ward plans to which some designers have paid so much attention, is subordinated to the imperative of patient privacy. For much of the time contact depends upon telecommunication in one form or another.

Nuffield and BUPA hospitals

Although they perform a similar function the typical BUPA and Nuffield hospitals are not only more numerous but are by contrast more modest than these prestigious examples. Except in major urban centres, such as Newcastle upon Tyne (Nuffield's 78 beds) and Manchester (BUPA's 93 beds), most of them are also smaller, providing between 30 and 50 beds, and some are on relatively green sites. They do not resemble five-star hotels in character, but in plan form and facilities they are in some ways more akin to the homely 'cottage hospital'.

Ground floor
1 lifts
2 reception
3 shop
4 porter
5 administration
6 loading bay
7 courtyard
8 waiting
9 consulting suite
10 day surgery theatre
11 recovery
12 pathology
13 pharmacy
14 consultant
15 ultrasound
16 radioisotope
17 lavage
18 diagnostic radiology
19 viewing/sorting

Lower ground floor
1 lifts
2 courtyard
3 anaesthetic
4 scrub
5 preparation
6 theatre
7 recovery
8 intensive care
9 physiotherapy
10 pathology
11 kitchen
12 restaurant
13 TSSU
14 stores
15 mortuary
16 staff changing
17 staff rest room

First floor
1 lifts
2 coffee lounge
3 single bed and
   bathroom
4 dirty utility
5 nurses' station
6 clean utility
7 equipment
8 floor sister
9 waiting
10 pantry
11 treatment
12 disposal
13 conference
14 director
15 office
16 matron
17 bedsitting room
18 common room
19 kitchen
20 laundry
21 bath

Cromwell Hospital, South Kensington, London was opened in the early 1980s. The first phase, shown here, provided 120 beds in single rooms, supported by clinical and diagnostic departments. An extension on all floors in a second phase brought the number of beds up to 164. The Lower Ground floor, at basement level, now occupies the whole of the urban site. Densely planned, it contains a suite of four operating theatres and recovery ward, TSSU, intensive care, physiotherapy and staff changing – also oncology and radiotherapy which were completed in the second phase. Two sunken courtyards provide visual relief to the centre of the plan. Below this floor a further basement houses plant. On the ground floor the main block occupies nearly all the Cromwell Road frontage and contains a suite of consulting rooms, a day surgery for out-patients, and diagnostic radiology. Above it are four floors of wards. In a two storey block behind it, enclosing a garden, is a generous main entrance hall, administration, loading bay, stores etc., and, in the second phase, parking for 15 cars. On the first floor the racetrack plan provides 41 single rooms in the two phases, each with its own bathroom, a pattern repeated on the three floors above it. Some pairs of adjacent bedrooms can be used as VIP suites. A coffee lounge extends into the upper floor of the two storey block at the rear, where in addition to administrative offices the two phases of this block provide 24 bedsitting rooms for on-call staff. Architects: Building Design Partnership

Not all are newly built; some are in old buildings converted and extended. For example, the Nuffield Hospital in a residential area in Hull, with 36 beds, began as a house containing administration and consulting rooms to which was added in the 1960s an extension including wards, and in the 1980s a new operating theatre block and an upgrading of the wards. Newly built hospitals are usually of at most two storeys, with on each floor one mother and child room and one four-bed bay overlooked by the nurses station. All other beds are in single rooms with their own bathrooms. However, in contrast with the passage lobby of the more prestigious establishments that ensures almost total privacy, an oblique wall to the bathroom ensures that observation of the patient is possible from the corridor.

The accommodation in some fairly recent independent hospitals reflects a degree of luxury not found in the National Health Service. Standards of spaciousness for the patients, particularly in the circulation and communal areas, are more generous. Privacy is a prerequisite, not a clinical imperative for the few. The atmosphere created by their furnishings and decorations is also more relaxed and their small size makes them less intimidating.

Second floor
1 bedroom and bathroom
2 staff base
3 rest room
4 interview
5 cleaner
6 kitchen
7 dirty utility
8 treatment
9 examination
10 utility
11 flowers

0   30M
├──┼──┼──┼──┼──┼──┼──┼──┤
0   100Ft

Ground floor

1	main entrance	6	ECG	11	rest
2	shop	7	eyes	12	lavage
3	office	8	lung function and audiometry	13	staff dining and coffee
4	consulting and examination	9	radiography	14	senior staff dining
5	pathology laboratory	10	viewing	15	apartment

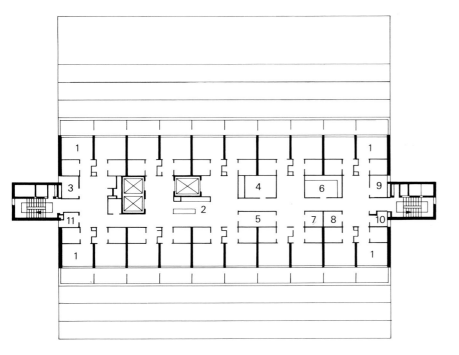

Fourth floor
1   bedroom and bathroom
2   staff base
3   interview
4   dirty utility
5   clean utility
6   kitchen
7   linen
8   store
9   doctor
10 cleaner
11 flowers

The Wellington Hospital, St John's Wood, London was opened in the 1970s. It provides 90 beds in single rooms, and clinical and diagnostic departments. A railway line into Marylebone Station passes through the length of the site under the building. The ground floor is at road level; it contains the main entrance hall, consulting rooms, diagnostic rooms and pathology laboratory, together with offices, staff dining and two residential apartments. From the entrance forecourt a vehicle ramp leads down to the lower ground floor and a service yard and goods entrance below the forecourt. Half of this floor is occupied by a suite of three operating theatres and recovery bays, and half by the TSSU, stores and kitchen. From the service yard a car lift descends to a deep basement through a mezzanine that accommodates parking for 15 cars and maintenance and staff changing rooms. A further 15 cars are parked in the basement below, at the level of the railway tracks, where the remaining part of the site not occupied by the railway tunnel is devoted to plant rooms. Above the ground floor there are five floors of wards, with 24 single bedrooms and bathrooms on each of the first two floors and 20 on the two floors above. The top floor contains eight single bedrooms, two double size suites of bed and sitting rooms, and a patients' lounge. The building profile steps back on each floor, with terraces outside the bedrooms; the deeper two floors are on a racetrack plan surrounding treatment and ancillary rooms; on the three upper floors the bedrooms are approached from a generous central access core. Architects: Yorke Rosenberg Mardall

Ground floor

1	main entrance	13	pantry	26	specimen toilet	39 medical secretaries
2	office	14	linen	27	specimen reception	40 nursing office
3	wheelchair toilet	15	dayroom	28	laboratory	41 physiotherapy office
4	assisted bath	16	pharmacy	29	X-ray	42 treatment/clean utility
5	cleaner	17	restaurant	30	process and view	43 dirty utility
6	toilet	18	conservatory	31	ultrasound	44 hydrotherapy pool
7	equipment	19	kitchen	32	sub-waiting	45 shower
8	one-bed room and bath	20	staff change	33	reception	46 changing
9	mother and child bedroom	21	matron	34	mammography	47 exercise room
	and bath	22	pharmacy store	35	bulk store	48 treatment cubicle
10	nurses' station	23	consulting room	36	reception and change	49 stair
11	clean utility	24	test	37	waiting	
12	dirty utility	25	screening office	38	reception	

Upper floor
1   void over entrance hall
2   store
3   assisted bath
4   office
5   cleaner
6   toilet
7   equipment
8   one-bed room and bath
9   mother and child bedroom
     and bath
10 nurses' station
11 clean utility
12 dirty utility
13 pantry
14 linen
15 day room
16 plant
17 meeting/interview
18 day patients wait and change
19 sister's office
20 two-bed room
21 store
22 ward tea bar
23 clean utility
24 nurses' station
25 linen
26 dirty utility/cleaner
27 toilet
28 bath
29 female staff change

30 male staff change
31 staff rest room
32 doctors' rest room
33 tea bar
34 cleaner
35 trolley bay
36 transfer zone
37 linen
38 sister
39 equipment
40 anaesthetic
41 sterile room
42 theatre
43 scrub-up
44 exit bay
45 dirty corridor and disposal
46 recovery
47 incoming supplies
48 packing and holding
49 autoclaves
50 theatre sterile store
51 ward sterile store
52 telephone equipment
53 stair
54 temporary fire escape stair

The first phase of the BUPA Hospital at Harpenden, Hertfordshire, planned around a central courtyard that provides an amenity space for patients and staff, was completed in 1982. A later phase added the wing that contains on the ground floor a day surgery, hydrotherapy pool and exercise room and on the floor above an 11-bed ward. Except for three two-bed rooms in this ward all the beds are in single rooms (or in the four mother and child rooms) with their own bathrooms and toilets. The total number of beds excluding the four children's beds is now 63. Diagnostic rooms adjoin the main entrance. Above these are operating theatres and the autoclaves and sterile stores. Architects: Percy Thomas Partnership

Sixth floor
1 nurses' station
2 clean utility
3 conference
4 treatment
5 bedroom with bathroom
6 soiled utility
7 catering
8 assisted toilet and shower
9 clean linen

0   20M

Third floor
1 nurses' station
2 clean utility
3 conference
4 treatment
5 bedroom with bathroom
6 clean linen
7 soiled utility
8 catering
9 assisted toilet and shower
10 lounge
11 bar/servery
12 store

First floor
1 lift lobby
2 reception, preparation and supervisors office
3 blood bank and test laboratory
4 trolleys
5 steriliser
6 anaesthetic
7 theatre
8 scrub
9 instrument store
10 preparation
11 disposal
12 recovery
13 staff base
14 soiled utility
15 doctors' change
16 doctors' lounge
17 nurses' change
18 nurses' lounge
19 laboratory
20 radiologist
21 cardiologist
22 preparation
23 disposal
24 control room
25 catheterisation procedures
26 dark room
27 changing
28 sorting
29 lavage
30 fluoroscope procedures
31 tornographic procedures
32 echo ultrasound
33 staff base
34 venepuncture
35 staff resting
36 clean utility
37 soiled utility
38 porters

The Humana Hospital Wellington, on a separate corner site near the Wellington Hospital, was opened a few years after the original one. The same railway passes under the site. The building provides 86 single bedrooms with bathrooms, an operating suite, maternity accommodation, and diagnostic and treatment rooms. It shares some of the earlier hospital's supporting departments, such as the TSSU. The basement, intersected by the railway tunnel, is not so deep as that of the original Wellington; it contains principally plant rooms but also staff changing, the kitchen and the pharmacy. Entrance and reception is on

the ground floor, approached from a forecourt beneath the building, and the remainder of this floor comprises storage and service access, staff dining and offices. Half the first floor is occupied by a suite of four operating theatres and the remainder by rooms for diagnostic procedures. Ward accommodation begins on the second floor, where 14 bedrooms with bathrooms adjoin a delivery room and its associated ancillaries. On the four floors above this the bedrooms surround a central core which diminishes in size as one face of the building steps back in terraces on each floor. Architects: Yorke Rosenberg Mardall

Upgrading patients' bedrooms in a two storey wing at the Nuffield Hospital, Hull. Fully fitted prefabricated units containing toilets and showers were erected by crane, connected to external services previously prepared, and subsequently faced with a brick skin matching the existing brickwork. Architects: Architects Co-Partnership

Problems of success

In many of the earlier post-war independent hospitals, even of twenty years ago, this luxury was not so marked. Although private bedrooms were usual it was not always thought essential that every bedroom should have its own bathroom. Competition and the higher expectations of the insured have made this provision more important and have led to problems of up-dating solidly constructed buildings without dislocating the running of the establishment or closing it down during alteration work.

In at least one example this difficulty has been met by the addition of compact prefabricated and fully fitted sanitary modules erected against the external face of the building, each module containing two compartments that can be separately approached from an adjacent pair of single bedrooms. An arrangement such as this can leave at least half the frontage of a typical single room available for glazing, which in any circumstances is entirely adequate, and all supply and drainage services can be prepared in advance outside the building with a minimum of dislocation to the interior.

The Government White Paper

It is too early to predict the effect of the 1989 White Paper on the development of the independent sector, except that it seems bound to give it encouragement. The proposal for tax relief on private medical insurance premiums for retired people, whether paid by themselves or their families, is not the only indication of this encouragement. Some contractual arrangements already exist between the National Health Service and the private sector, albeit of a relatively minor nature. The White Paper claims that its reforms will 'open up further opportunities for the two sectors to work together for their mutual benefit'.

Clearly the intention is not only to foster co-operation but to increase competition between the two sectors, not least in the light of the proposal that general practitioners should be able to use National Health Service funds in their budgets to pay for their patients' treatment in private establishments 'if this offers better quality or better value

One of the prefabricated units being placed in position at the Nuffield Hospital, Hull. In the background, brick cladding on completed units. (Photo: Kenn Dalley)

for money than buying NHS services'. The initial reaction of the medical profession has been strongly hostile; the outcome remains to be seen.

The White Paper also encourages joint building ventures between the National Health Service, the private health sector, and developers. Between the latter two there are examples of this already, notably in housing for the elderly by developers, associated with private sector health-care accommodation in the 'village'. But taking the thrust of the White Paper as a whole – its full implications are unlikely to be felt before 1991 – it would be rash at this stage to anticipate what building opportunities for private hospitals might emerge as a consequence.

An increase in the number of beds seems likely, but it is reasonable to wonder whether these will be entirely in single rooms, for the economics in nursing staff might suggest otherwise. In some locations an increase in diagnostic, out-patient and day-patient facilities might also result. But whatever pattern emerges it seems possible that hospital buildings in the private sector may experience more acutely than in the past the problems of growth and change already familiar in the National Health Service.

9

Psychiatric services

Mental illness can afflict people of any nationality, culture or background, and of any age or intellectual capacity. It can incapacitate them as seriously as many other identifiable diseases. It is not, as is sometimes popularly supposed, essentially a product of the stressful developed world. A World Health Organisation expert committee on mental health estimated in 1974 that in the developing countries over 40 million men, women and children were suffering from serious untreated mental disorder.

However it is only relatively recently that a substantial body of opinion has attempted to explain this form of illness. Although its mechanisms are still imperfectly understood and it is not always possible to effect a cure or to remove the factors that cause it, psychiatry, a newcomer to medical science, has reached a stage at which the majority of cases will respond to treatment.

Psychiatry has seen a period of change as rapid as conventional medicine, not only in its methods of treatment but more fundamentally in its social objectives. In the relatively recent past people whose behaviour was bizarre, unacceptable or dangerous were offered asylum or had asylum forced upon them in order to withdraw them from a society inconvenienced by their activities.

The aim today can perhaps best be characterised by the objective of modifying their patterns of living and their ability to adjust to other people so that they can learn to return, perhaps by degrees, to 'normal' life. Instead of being regarded as unreliably peculiar the treatment of mental illness is becoming increasingly integrated with general medicine in the 'normal' hospital and with the associated health and social services.

Psychiatric treatment is increasingly available on a voluntary basis rather than as a sequel to compulsory detention. Its range of care has also extended widely. Severe mental disorder was formerly its principal preoccupation but today, besides its concern with the ability of people to cope with the strains and stresses of everyday living, it embraces personality disorders, alcoholism and drug addiction, delinquency and emotionally disturbed children and adolescents.

Old methods of treatment

The 19th century conception of care for the 'mad' is epitomised by the huge and forbidding mental hospital or asylum. In these buildings patients were confined in the atmosphere of a prison, preferably far away from any large centre of population, so that normal society could go its own way protected from their vagaries and violence. Little if any distinction was made between the mentally ill and the mentally handicapped. In these institutions the inmates could be regarded as an isolated and self-contained community safely removed from the world to which it was unlikely that they would return.

In a WHO paper of 1959, '*Psychiatric Services and Architecture*', there is a description of the impact that the vast old mental hospital would have on the patient. It bears repeating not only because it emphasises what should be avoided but also because by implication the antithesis is so clear.

'It is common for the hospital to be approached by a stately drive which culminates in a direct approach to the centre of an enormous block of buildings . . . . . Such buildings make the visitor feel small, powerless, and insignificant. The effect on the patient is to increase any tendency he may have to run away, to destroy this frightening object or such parts of it as he can, or to retreat into inert submission.

Once inside the door . . . . . the patient is usually taken from an entrance hall to a records department where his documents will be examined by a member of the lay staff. After this he will be escorted down long corridors where he will see numbers of patients sitting or walking aimlessly, perhaps exhibiting gross evidence of desocialization and eccentricity. He may then arrive at an admission unit, where he will be examined by a doctor before being taken to yet another unit which will be his ward for initial observation and treatment. He will then be put to bed and left to observe his surroundings. He will see the many beds, all alike, and the absence of other furnishings, the walls of dull, uniform institution buff or brown, and the windows small, high, barred and often dirty. There will be evidence of locks and he will hear the keys of his attendants. The ward will have a stale smell and often provide evidence of the inadequacy of the sanitary arrangements. He will also find within the ward no privacy, or opportunity to create it. He will be forced to perform even the most private activities where he can be seen both by other patients and the staff. Within a crowd of such patients there will be no opportunity to form friendships with a small group, or to feel any drive to identify himself with those around him. Within this environment our patient feels no encouragement to develop human relationships, and he will see that his life is without purpose. Any tendency to aggressive behaviour caused by his illness will be reinforced by the architecture and by the regime which the design of the building tends to perpetuate.'

Institutions like the above still exist and, in some parts of the world, mental patients are still kept chained in conditions of mediaeval squalor, shunned by their relatives and friends. But with the spread of communications and education, the growth of industry and urbanisation and the changes in traditional communities and beliefs it seems inevitable that mental illness, like other forms of sickness, will come to be regarded everywhere as something that demands and will respond to a different form of treatment. However constituted the health service will have to provide for its alleviation.

Treatment today

There are still occasions when physical confinement of the mentally ill is necessary but this is not the general rule. New approaches to treatment have made it possible to guide most of the mentally ill back to normal life. Since the 1950s the development of drugs has not only removed some of the need for physical restraint but has enabled doctors and nurses to maintain human contact with a patient who would otherwise have repudiated any effort of assistance.

In some countries the growth of social services in the community has helped in the work of readjustment, rehabilitation and support that the patient needs after responding to treatment and re-entering society. The social services also have begun to provide the type of care that can ameliorate and sometimes avoid the factors that seem to contribute to this form of illness.

Treatment is based increasingly on out-patient clinics, day hospitals and various types of community care and less on the admission of patients to residential care in a hospital. It takes many different forms, or combinations of forms, including physical treatments such as drugs or electro-convulsive therapy (ECT), and various techniques of socially interactive therapy. The latter are possibly the most important in their bearing on the design of the accommodation. From 'talking' treatment on a one-to-one basis in a comfortable consulting room they may range through small discussion groups to larger ones of a dozen or more. It may offer encouragement for participation in a variety of everyday activities that can contribute to the patient's self-reliance and readjustment to society.

Psychiatrists differ in their approaches however; some use drugs and electro-convulsive therapy as their main avenue, others use 'talking' therapies. Still others may use 'role playing' methods in which rehabilitation is based on training in social skills and work skills.

The old type of mental institution, relying upon confinement behind locked doors and formidable boundary walls, did not need many people to run it. Staff did not require a particularly high degree of training, for they were custodians rather than nurses. In most establishments caring for mental illness today a higher ratio of staff to patients is usual; a variety of skills is available and an entirely different emphasis needs to be placed on the nature and character of the buildings. Whereas the old institution deliberately imparted a sense of withdrawal and physical restraint imposed by authority the new will try to avoid too overt a feeling of segregation from society. It will aim to foster an atmosphere of security of a very different sort – as normal and as domestic as is practicable within an establishment that in scale is usually larger than domestic – and in which supervision, although necessary, will be incidental to the other activities in which the staff are engaged with the patients.

Varieties of care

Buildings for the mentally ill are for most patients 'staging posts' where they can be encouraged to find their way back to normal patterns of everyday life and to their families, friends and occupations. Unlike short stay patients in a surgical ward, for example, who may often be discharged soon after treatment, their process of readjustment is likely to be much slower.

Thus to a greater extent than other buildings for health care, this type of building must provide opportunities and encouragement for social and occupational activities that can assist the patient's progress towards the goal of 'normal' life. The main object is to give physical and psychological shelter; the strictly clinical facilities are relatively few. Most patients are fully ambulant and the bed is much less the focus of attention than in medicine or surgery, for only a small minority of patients need that type of care and then only for short periods.

But even with the most advanced psychiatric care there will remain a small proportion of patients who need more or less permanent support in a hospital environ-

ment. For example, there are some patients with degenerative and irreversible mental symptoms associated with old age, and some who are continuously behaviourally disturbed or persistently violent. These patients must be treated in conditions of physical security. There are some with dangerous or criminal propensities for whom a particularly high degree of security is necessary.

Patients without families or friends to whom they can go after discharge or who, although they have homes to return to, may not be able to sustain the strain of normal society or employment without further support, may need continued partial psychiatric care. These patients may be well enough to find a place in society during the working day but may need to return to the protection of a hospital for the night. Alternatively, they may need to spend part of the day at an institution and return to their homes in the evenings to sleep. Whatever the pattern it is generally recognised that the aim must be to avoid arrangements whereby they are encouraged to depend on constant in-patient care and become institutionalised and chronically sick. It should also be recognised that it is no use discharging them into the community if appropriate community care is not available.

It will be seen from the preceding paragraphs that mental illness demands several varieties of care and that there are many gradations between one degree of care and another. Compared with acute medical and surgical cases the course of sickness and cure is less mechanical and proceeds in less of a straight line. It may also be much slower. Thus the types of accommodation that are needed are more varied and less specific, and because of the state of knowledge can be regarded as considerably more experimental.

Because mental illness seems to be caused by personal stresses arising from the patient's relation to the family or to society the manner of treatment and the appropriate institution (if indeed an institution is appropriate at all) may vary greatly from one culture to another to a much greater extent than does the short stay hospital.

Social customs and religious beliefs influence, and may determine, not only the way in which mental illness can best be tackled but also the readiness of sufferers to seek help. Thus generalisations, which are dangerous enough in any discussion of health facilities that embraces both the developing and developed world, are doubly so in the field of psychiatric services. The range of facilities will clearly differ from one country to another. However, in much of the developed world, where the birth rate is more or less static and the population is ageing and health services are fairly readily available, there will be an increasing need for facilities which care for the elderly and the geriatric.

In the developing world where the population is continuing to expand and there is a higher proportion of young people, the emphasis is more likely to be on children and adolescents. The range will also depend on the extent to which other supportive facilities have been established in the community. This will have a considerable influence on the need for in-patient care as distinct from out-patient or day-patient partial care supplemented by various forms of community care.

It is now usually accepted that community care is the more desirable approach, both for its preventive advantages and for the avoidance of chronic institutionalisation. Although there must still be a place for the specialist mental hospital, the majority of cases are better treated in other forms of institution in which the patient is withdrawn as little as possible, or for only brief periods, from the society to which his cure is attempting to re-adapt him.

The general hospital

Over the past few decades there has been an increasing tendency in western countries for the psychiatric treatment of adults (as distinct from children and the geriatric) to be integrated with the general hospital where this is possible. Apart from other advantages this can help to reduce the unfortunate social stigma that is still often associated with mental illness.

Thus many general hospitals include emergency clinics for walk-in patients, in-patient psychiatric wards, out-patient psychiatric clinics, and day hospital facilities for rehabilitation and occupational therapy. In large district general hospitals in the UK these facilities may constitute a separate large department with upwards of sixty in-patient beds. However, experience has shown that such units cannot satisfactorily deal with all patients in need of psychiatric services, such as those whose behaviour is very bizarre or violent, or those whose illness is chronic.

Emergency clinics for walk-in patients in the general hospital are only likely to be necessary in some urban areas. Ideally they should perhaps be separate from the accident and emergency department, whose work in dealing with casualties may otherwise be disrupted. But, in general, the accident and emergency staff are likely to have to cover this service with the help of a psychiatrist.

If separate, the emergency clinic should not be in an isolated location but close to a department which is well staffed at all times so that if necessary it can be called upon to help deal with sudden aggressive emergencies. The accommodation needed is of the simplest: a manned reception point, some waiting space, and some interview rooms.

Some walk-in cases may be violent or suicidal, and at least one of the interview rooms should be arranged with this in mind. It should be furnished so that the fittings cannot readily be damaged and, in addition, do not offer the patient the opportunity of damaging himself. The same considerations apply to some degree to all this accommodation.

Out-patient clinics may well form part of the hospital's general out-patient department, or be associated with it. Psychiatric out-patients can share the waiting areas, will use the hospital pharmacy, and may need access to other facilities which are used by the department. Normal consulting rooms for doctors, psychologists and other professionals will be needed, but larger and more specialised rooms may be required for group therapy. These should be capable of seating about twelve patients and staff informally and equipped with a one-way screen between the group room and an adjacent room from which behaviour can be observed, with facilities for microphones and recorders.

Wards for in-patients usually contain between twenty and thirty beds. In the UK thirty is favoured as the optimum and two wards of this size as probably the minimum viable for a district general hospital. Psychiatric wards usually accommodate both men and women, with separate sleeping arrangements for the sexes. As in all other accommodation for psychiatric patients, the planning should aim to help observation through interaction between staff and patients rather than rely on strict custodial care.

Three degrees of care can be identified, according to the degree of the patient's dependence on nursing, and the sub-division and arrangement of the ward can reflect this. These degrees may be termed High Dependency, Intermediate, and Minimum (or Low) Dependency.

They may be reflected both in the planning of the ward and in the use which the patients can make of other parts of the ward, such as day spaces, and of the facilities which the hospital provides outside the ward.

Some High Dependency patients may be on their beds for much of the time. They may be seriously disturbed or heavily sedated, and a few may need nursing in bed. They should be accommodated in single rooms close to the staff base; their doors should be capable of being opened outwards, for they may be barricaded by the patient from within. Observation panels, windows, mirrors, etc should be of toughened or splinterproof material. A washbasin will probably be provided, but it should be indestructible. These precautions may be functionally necessary but they need not result in the atmosphere of a prison.

An assisted bath, a shower and a toilet should be closely accessible from this group of rooms, for it is tedious for staff and upsetting for other patients if the highly disturbed have to be escorted along corridors to reach them. Five single rooms of this nature may be a reasonable complement for a thirty bed ward, two of them capable of taking a baby's cot at the side of the mother's bed.

The Intermediate category of patient may be ambulant some of the time and perhaps dressed. They may be wandering around the ward but cannot safely be allowed to so so unless they can be kept under observation. Some of them may be encouraged to use the day areas within the ward or to sit in the corridors (particularly if these have been designed with this in mind).

These patients are progressing and although some of them may spend part of the day on their beds they do not need single rooms and should not be encouraged to want them. Perhaps two rooms of about five beds, each including a little day space (about the equivalent of a six-bed room) can help to encourage group relationships at this stage of illness. They should be near the staff base and should preferably have toilets adjacent.

Minimum or Low Dependency patients are those who have progressed to the stage at which most of them can participate in group therapy activities or make use of the occupational therapy and other facilities that the hospital provides. They will be fully ambulant and dressed, and for much of the day many of them may not be in the ward but in the day hospital, mixing and taking part in activities with the day patients.

On the ward they can profit from more individualised bed spaces than can the Intermediate category. They may well be in five-bed rooms which can be flexibly sub-divided into personal corners and cubicles by screens and storage furniture. In a thirty-bed ward about half the beds might be provided in this manner.

The ward should provide bed areas, the sanitary and utility accommodation and staff base (which should include a treatment room with particularly secure storage for drugs). In addition there should be a ward office and one or more rooms in which doctors and others can interview patients and their relatives, a beverage pantry to which patients have access, and some variety of patients' day spaces.

As a minimum, these day spaces should include an active area and a quieter one capable of being separated from it, and should provide some opportunity for occupational therapy. They may be used as a dining area by patients who cannot leave the ward; alternatively there may be advantages if a larger dining area can be shared by more than one ward. At times the day areas may be used for group meetings of patients and staff and a degree of flexibility can be useful for purposes such as this. In addition there should be somewhere for patients to wash and dry their own clothes and a room for hairwashing and hairdressing.

This type of psychiatric ward may not, however, be able to deal with all patients admitted to the hospital. There are likely to be some who are so disturbed and disruptive that they cannot be treated alongside other patients while they are in this condition. For these patients an annexe of about ten beds may be valuable, separate from the wards but with easy access for staff from one of them.

It will be necessary to be able to lock up the annexe, for security will be of particular importance, but the atmosphere should remain as domestic as possible in the circumstances. At a reduced scale it will need much the same ancillary and day accommodation as the normal ward, including a small staff base. British practice for a unit of ten beds in this category tends to be to provide six in single rooms and the remainder in one multi-bed room.

The day hospital

The purpose of the day hospital is to provide some clinical facilities, but principally occupational, recreational and social accommodation for day patients who are living in the community and for those in-patients who are well enough to visit it from the psychiatric wards. It is entered by patients separately from other parts of the hospital and may usefully be in an independent building. It should be linked to the main hospital and if possible to the out-patients' department, for some psychiatric day patients may make use of the hospital's occupational therapy and gymnasium facilities.

The bulk of the accommodation will provide spaces for everyday activities such as housekeeping, the preparation and cooking of food, dressmaking, laundering,

ironing and child care. There should also be accommodation for occupational activities such as woodwork, metalwork, pottery, weaving, painting, music, typing, according to the cultures of the country or district in which it is situated.

There will be a central dining area for some of the day patients and for those in-patients who can leave the wards, and space for concerts, films, dancing and parties or assemblies, perhaps by multiple use of the dining area. The rest of the accommodation will be made up of offices and cloakrooms for nursing, social work, domestic and administrative staff, consulting and interview rooms, and group therapy rooms, some of which

1　reception
2　interview
3　waiting
4　coats/toilets
5　meetings
6　kitchen
7　utility
8　general purpose
9　rehabilitation
10　administration
11　rehab. office/store
12　sister
13　consulting
14　social worker

15　cleaner
16　void
17　staff toilets
18　changing
19　ECT treatment
20　recovery/nurse
21　seated recovery
22　clean utility
23　dirty utility
24　shower
25　store
26　bath

0　　　　　　10 m

A psychiatric day hospital at Evesham. It is the first phase of a new Avonside general hospital and will remain a separate unit at the extremity of later hospital development along a linear hospital street. Rehabilitation and social areas are off the main entrance downstairs; upstairs there are consulting rooms and a suite for electro-convulsive therapy and recovery. Waiting spaces are slightly withdrawn into partially screened alcoves. A void over part of the social area helps to give a sense of unity to the two levels. Architects: Derek Stow and Partners

1	waiting
2	reception
3	administration
4	nurse in charge
5	consultant
6	clinical
7	toilet
8	general purpose
9	rehabilitation
10	patients' preparation
11	ECT treatment
12	recovery
13	nurse
14	bath
15	consulting
16	group therapy/staff common room

0   15 m
0   50 ft

The conversion of an old building into a psychiatric day centre at Malvern, Worcs. The main entrance is from the road at the north end; there are gardens on the east side and car parking on the west. Nearly all the existing walls of the building have been used and only a few new openings have been made or partitions demolished. On the ground floor the general purpose room (the main social area) leads through to a light rehabilitation workshop. Upstairs are consulting rooms and electro-convulsive therapy and recovery, and a group therapy room which is also used as a staff common room. A lower ground floor, approached from the main entrance hall, accommodates dining room and kitchen. There is a separate caretaker's flat below the rehabilitation workshop. Architects: Derek Stow and Partners

may need one way screens for observation from an adjoining room.

Facilities for electro-convulsive therapy (ECT) may be required in the psychiatric unit and may possibly be sited in the day hospital. Some psychiatrists use this form of treatment more than others. When it is required, the ECT suite is likely to comprise a small waiting space for perhaps half a dozen patients, a sound-proofed treatment room in which the patient is anaesthetised and the treatment administered, with services for resuscitation in case of emergency, and a recovery room, with oxygen and suction, divided into two areas for anaesthetised patients on trolleys or couches and for those sufficiently recovered to be able to sit in chairs and rest. The recovery room needs a pantry nearby for the preparation of tea or coffee.

Detailed design

In accommodation for the mentally ill it is easier than in most parts of the hospital for designers to achieve a comfortable and reassuring domestic atmosphere. Many of the constraints imposed by equipment and sterility are absent and most of the floorings and furnishings can be soft. But there are likely to be problems arising from the

sheer size of the building or department which militate against domesticity.

Although it is important for confused and disorientated patients that planning should be lucid and routes easy to follow, long corridors can be intimidating, however decorated or adorned, particularly if they are internal and offer no prospect of the world outside. They can, however, be planned so that they provide opportunities for social meeting or withdrawal, with alcoves or bays where it is inviting to sit down. In some cases they can be combined with day areas.

0   6 m
0   20 ft

1	visitors	9	activity	17	clean linen
2	interview	10	TV	18	baths/showers
3	male staff	11	duty room	19	toilets/wash
4	female staff	12	treatment	20	disturbed patient
5	staff rest room	13	sister	21	single bed room
6	quiet room	14	sluice/dirty linen	22	4 bed room
7	dining	15	store	23	5 bed room
8	kitchen	16	cleaner	24	6 bed room

A ward for 28 men for a mental hospital at Jumiera, United Arab Emirates, with an additional room for a disturbed patient. A mix of one, two, four, five and six bed arrangements are centred on the duty room, and there is a variety of social rooms for dining, quiet and noisier activities and television. A visitors' space and interview room are arranged off a separate entrance lobby. Architect: John R. Harris

1	visitors	6	interview	11	sluice/dirty linen
2	kitchen	7	consultant	12	store
3	dining/day	8	staff change	13	toilets/wash
4	nurse	9	staff rest room	14	bath/shower
5	quiet	10	cleaner	15	single bed room

The ten-bed protected ward at Jumiera for disturbed patients who need to be segregated. All bedrooms are single and have their own toilets. All the beds are approached from a corridor which can be separated from the rest of the accommodation, but the nurses' room communicates with bedrooms and day space

There are also likely to be problems arising from the demands of security and safety; it should not be easy for patients to escape without being noticed or for those with suicidal tendencies to find opportunities of indulging them. There must be adeqate provision for escape in case of fire (and some patients may be prone to setting things alight) but the escape routes may need to be monitored, perhaps electrically. All windows accessible to patients, particularly on upper floors, should be restricted in the amount they can be opened.

Great ingenuity may be exercised in overcoming these constraints and the use of toughened glass or plastic may be advisable in some areas. Furniture and fittings can also be vulnerable and may provide a patient with something with which to damage himself or other people. Some furniture, such as seating in alcoves, may of course be fixed.

Design should offer patients the opportunity of going outdoors. This presents few problems in the case of the day hospital, where space should be provided for sitting out, for strolling and for games; in some localities there may with advantage be facilities for gardening and horticulture. Such outdoor areas are usually best reached from the dining and social areas, from occupational therapy and from the nursery, if there is one.

Where security is of importance care needs to be taken that outdoor areas help the staff to contain patients without creating the impression that they are locked in. High wire fences are not the only answer; properly planted walled gardens or courtyards are better, particularly in single-storey buildings. Dense hedges may be equally effective provided these are properly situated in relation to the building so that staff can exercise unobtrusive supervision.

Mental hospitals

Psychiatric in-patient facilities in the general hospital are primarily suitable for short-stay patients. In time it may be possible to house long-stay patients in hospital hostels or in hostel wards, but even so there will almost certainly remain a need for the specialist mental hospital, or something analogous, particularly for patients whose condition demands some degree of security while they are being helped to re-enter the community.

Mental hospitals are frequently situated away from town or city centres and are not physically associated with the general hospital. If possible, they should be developed at relatively low density in buildings of domestic scale in adequate grounds.

Whereas in the general hospital the relationships between different departments induce close communications and compactness of planning, there is no reason why a mental hospital should be arranged as a single building. Indeed if the site is adequate there are many advantages in planning it as a collection of separate and dissimilar buildings more analogous to a loosely spaced village. These could be connected in some places by covered ways if the climate justifies it. This arrangement can help to avoid some of the dangers of institutionalisation and with some activities can foster the feeling that it

is natural to go out for work or entertainment or to meet with other people.

The elements of accommodation will be similar in function to those in the general hospital, but not identical. Admission wards will provide the same facilities but may have to cope with more patients in an acute stage of illness and are likely to justify a higher degree of security. The long-stay living accommodation may well take a form more akin to separate houses or hostels where a patient can have his own territory. This may be no more than the equivalent of a cubicle for keeping personal belongings in safety and perhaps creating a congenial atmosphere even if it is only his own muddle.

The size of each house or hostel should be the smallest that is compatible with the needs of the patient for privacy and society, and the availability of staff. Cooking may well have to be centralised but the more that dining can be broken down into smaller units the better. Comfortable sitting room or lounge spaces for

A mental hospital at Jumiera, United Arab Emirates; a single storey building with beds for 111 in-patients. The entrance gatehouse is at the bottom of the picture; administration, kitchen and laundry occupy the south side of the rectangle; separate wards for ten children and thirty-five women are on the east side, and two twenty-eight bed wards for men on the north. Next to the gatehouse, on the west side, is the social centre, which leads through to the treatment and therapy complex that occupies a quarter of the centre of the rectangle and is accessible to out-patients. The other unit within the rectangle is a protected ward for ten patients who need segregation; this has a small secure internal courtyard. Covered walkways subdivide the centre of the hospital into garden courts. Housing for staff and servants lies outside the hospital to the north and west. The buildings for plant on the east leave space for the addition of further men's and women's wards. Architect: John R. Harris. (Photo: Henk Snoek/Crispin Boyle)

The entrance gatehouse at Jumiera is in the foreground on the right, with the social centre on the left. (Photo: Henk Snoek/Crispin Boyle)

reading or watching TV will be needed in each living unit. Other social activities may well take place in a separate community centre having facilities for indoor games and sports, entertainments, cafe refreshments and so on.

Working activities may extend from normal occupational therapy to rehabilitation workshops, where suitable

The community centre at Bethlem Royal Hospital, Beckenham, Kent. Two parallel blocks two storeys high are linked together in the middle. One contains light occupational therapy, education, and rooms for social purposes and light refreshments; the other has a small swimming pool and a general purpose hall for theatre, cinema and dances. Architects: Architects' Co-Partnership

contract work for local business can be undertaken in sheltered conditions under expert guidance. This may even provide some income for the patients.

Other facilities for the mentally ill

The day hospital, the general hospital and the mental hospital are likely to be able to cater for only a proportion of patients. For many people these establishments will not be near enough at hand and may not in any case provide the right environment. Something more local and smaller in scale may be desirable, even when the support of local medical practitioners, health centres and the social services are available.

There have been some programmes, notably in the USA but also elsewhere, that aim to fill this gap by providing community based mental health centres with facilities for diagnosis, therapy, rehabilitation and social activity. Residential accommodation is sometimes provided, linked to the hospital service but not psychologically associated with it. Generally these units are in urban areas and are in physically independent buildings whose character is as far as possible the reverse of clinical.

Some centres have been housed in converted domestic buildings; others have been newly constructed for their purpose. They may provide beds or may be run in conjunction with separate sheltered residential accommodation in ordinary houses in the neighbourhood, or they may be based on a combination of both.

Plan for a medium-secure residential unit for 40 patients at Frierne mental hospital, Middlesex. It is arranged in four residential 'houses' of ten patients. Each house has its own day and dining spaces, and its internal circulation is separate from the main access corridor. The four houses permit the unit to operate on the basis of progressive patient care, the high dependency patients being in house A. Bedrooms for houses C and D are on an upper floor. All houses open on to garden areas with a secure perimeter. The only access to the unit is past the control room in the link with the main hospital. Architects: Hutchison Locke and Monk

1	single bed	16	rumpus yard
2	wash/toilet	17	courtyard
3	staff base	18	staff change
4	staff toilet	19	staff rest room
5	living/dining	20	staff garden
6	kitchen	21	control
7	lounge	22	waiting
8	store	23	nursing office
9	medical store	24	consultant
10	interview	25	social worker
11	office	26	dirty utility
12	four-bed room	27	general purpose/treatment
13	utility	28	secure perimeter
14	conservatory	29	garden
15	rumpus room		

1	lobby
2	records
3	nurses' station
4	dining
5	living
6	servery
7	patients self-catering
8	activities and workshop

9	viewing room
10	remedial teaching
11	launderette
12	treatment
13	seclusion room
14	single bedroom
15	double bedroom
16	shower
17	assisted bath
18	toilet
19	bath
20	female changing
21	male changing
22	office
23	refuse
24	dirty linen
25	clean linen
26	boiler house

Medium Secure Unit for the South East Thames Regional Health Authority, one of four 15-bed in-patient clinics built in hospital grounds to serve specific catchment areas and related to a central 30-bed clinic at Bethlem Royal Hospital. They provide intermediate care for mentally disordered patients who are not so ill that they need to be in a maximum security hospital but are too disruptive for the ordinary psychiatric wards. Patient accommodation is in the two larger wings adjoining the dining and living space and nurses' station, which opens on to a grassed area enclosed by a security fence. Staff rooms are in the smaller wing. Architects: Hutchison Locke and Monk

1 main entrance
2 secondary entrance
3 waiting
4 garden
5 dining and coffee lounge

6 servery
7 toilet
8 bath
9 shower
10 assisted bath
11 bedroom
12 seclusion room
13 nurses' station
14 interview
15 trunks
16 TV/remedial teaching
17 treatment/medicine
18 linen

19 rumpus room
20 hair/beauty
21 launderette
22 patients' kitchen
23 multi-use room
24 pottery/art
25 store
26 OT office
27 workshop
28 sister/charge nurse
29 family visiting
30 office
31 group-use room
32 staff tea point
33 staff coffee
34 case conference room
35 secretarial

0   20 m
0   60 ft

*Medium secure 30-bed in-patient clinic with assessment and
supervision services at Bethlem Royal Hospital, Kent, which works in
conjunction with the South East Thames Regional Health Authority
15-bed clinics. Two separate grassed areas, each enclosed by a
security fence, are accessible from the bedroom wings, one of which
opens onto a smaller enclosed garden. Administrative, staff changing
and teaching rooms are in the other wing, which is partly of two storeys.
The plan is intended to permit closing off a variety of sections of the
building for day, evening and night time use or for specialised activities.
Architects: Hutchison Locke and Monk*

The function and facilities of such centres will vary
according to the needs of the district in which they are
located. Primarily they are likely to aim at providing
comprehensive after-care and rehabilitation for men and
women who have been discharged from psychiatric
hospitals, to help them to readjust to normal community
living. This may be combined with care for referred
patients for whom the only alternative, and a less suitable
one, would be admission to hospital.

Unavoidably they may have on occasions to deal with
walk-in cases, even if only temporarily. Some of them
may be called Day Centres, others might more appropri-
ately be called Day and Night Centres. They are truly
half-way houses. They are essentially community buildings and are most likely to be acceptable in the

community if they are part of it and if externally they look
as if they belong to it. Internally their design needs to
foster a feeling of friendliness, of a club in which patients
and staff are living together; it needs also to encourage
social encounters as much as possible and an awareness of all the activities that are going on in the place.

The design will tend towards compactness, but there
may be conflicts between this and the needs of security
and even of segregation. This is particularly the case if
the centre provides not only residential accommodation
but also some normal in-patient beds and thus may at
times have to deal with badly disturbed people.

Accommodation is likely to include an entrance hall,
welcoming and habitable in character but supervised;
perhaps the entrance lounge of a small hotel is the best

A entrance from public road
B entrance up from hospital
   grounds
C service entrance
1 team area
2 nursery
3 OT suite
4 heavy workshop
5 plant
6 offices
7 waiting and coffee stall
8 reception
9 research
10 group room, classroom,
   library
11 OT kitchen
12 main kitchen/dining
13 laundry, hairdresing, TV
14 intensive supervision beds
15 high supervision beds
16 low dependency beds
17 OT/day space

Exploded view showing the four storey arrangement of a psychiatric centre at the Maudsley Hospital to serve the Camberwell district. On a tight urban site, it combines day care for 111 patients with residential care for 34. Although intended principally for day patients it is possible for some patients to occupy a bed for a period without interrupting the continuity of care by admission to a mental hospital or a psychiatric ward elsewhere. Beds are on the top floor and social facilities on the floor below; on the two lower floors there are three distinct team areas, each for about 36 patients in groups of 13. Suites for light and heavy occupational therapy are at ground level. Parts of the building provide offices for a Medical Research Council Unit. There is a difference in level of one storey between the hospital grounds and the public road. Architects: Architects Co-Partnership

Mental handicap

A distinction must be made between the nature of the services and accommodation appropriate for the mentally ill and those needed for the mentally handicapped. The mentally ill are generally curable to some degree and the cure may involve different forms of continued support for differing periods of time; they present a range of problems and there is a range of ways for dealing with them.

Those patients who are variously defined as mentally subnormal, handicapped or retarded constitute a different category, in which the development of the mind is incomplete or arrested and the capacity for learning severely limited. Mental handicap is also sometimes associated with physical disability and sometimes with behaviour disturbance.

Legislation in Britain has used the term 'subnormal' for the mentally handicapped who need special care and training and 'severely sub-normal' for those needing protection. The World Health Organisation and the USA use the term 'mental retardation' and classify it as 'mild', 'moderate', 'severe' or 'profound'.

In terms of appropriate buildings, however, the mentally handicapped can be considered in three main

analogy. There will be rooms for the various daily activities, craft rooms or manual and clerical workshops, rooms for laundry, ironing and hairdressing, for withdrawal or quiet reading, one or more classrooms, a dining room and kitchen, perhaps with facilities for a few patients to do their own preparation, cooking and washing-up. There should be a few discussion rooms for groups of about a dozen, and rooms where doctors and other staff can work and talk with three or four other people. A large space is likely to be needed for meetings, parties or entertainments attended by everybody using the building. There may be a need for a creche or nursery.

If the centre includes beds, some of these are likely to be arranged similarly to those in a psychiatric ward. For patients of minimum dependency accommodation may well be in single rooms of a hostel type more akin to student study-bedrooms, a few rooms being large enough to take a mother and child.

Some of the patients may be in the building both day and night, others may come only for the day or part of the day, and others may come only in the evenings and to sleep. If the centre caters for this sort of mixed occupancy it may be necessary to plan so that some of the daytime areas can be shut off easily and naturally in the evening; this will avoid residents straying into unsupervised parts of the building.

A low dependency area
B high supervision area
C intensive supervision area
1 single bedroom
2 nurse base
3 amenity space
4 patients kitchen
5 store
6 bath/shower/toilet
7 toilets
8 lockers
9 cleaner
10 quiet room
11 day area/OT
12 servery
13 medicines
14 sluice/dirty linen
15 sister
16 interview
17 clinical
18 four-bed room
19 two-bed room
20 day room

The top floor at the Maudsley District Services centre. It provides for three levels of care: low dependency in single bedrooms of domestic character; high supervision in four-bed rooms with day space, a room for occupational therapy and a kitchen for serving meals to patients who cannot go to the main dining room on the floor below; and intensive supervision in two-bed rooms whose occupants share a small dayroom which gives access to an inner suite of single rooms for patients who need to be segregated. By opening or closing interconnecting doors the degree of movement between these zones can be controlled according to the types and severity of illness being treated. Architects: Architects Co-Partnership

1	training unit	21	living
2	domestic instruction unit	22	bath
3	special care unit	23	bedroom
4	entrance and waiting	24	coats and wheelchairs
5	office	25	office
6	manager	26	group room
7	deputy manager	27	dining/training
8	female cloaks and changing	28	covered court
9	male cloaks and changing	29	recreational area
10	admission and assessment	30	female toilets
11	retiring room	31	bath
12	staff room	32	male toilets
13	male staff	33	resource room
14	female staff	34	laundry
15	dining	35	store
16	dining	36	training area
17	kitchen	37	covered training area
18	group room	38	hard courtyard
19	kitchen	39	soft courtyard
20	dining	40	boiler house

Chilwell Social Education Centre, an Adult Training Centre for daytime use by mentally handicapped people aged between 16 and 65. It is combined with a Special Care Unit for those who are both mentally and physically handicapped and need greater care and supervision. The Centre aims to be a focal point for the teaching of mentally handicapped people and their families and to help individuals to achieve their maximum level of independence as members of the community. The building encloses two courtyards: a hard one for ball games and a soft one with artificial turf and special planting for use by the Special Care Unit. The covered court (28) has a fully glazed roof. Elsewhere many rooms have large lights in the pitched roofs. Architect: H. T. Swain, County Architect, Nottinghamshire County Council

groups: first, the severely handicapped who depend on almost continuous attention; second, those who although less severely handicapped need fairly constant help; and third, those whose handicap is less severe and who in many cases are capable of being found a place in society but may need sheltered occupation and housing.

The purpose of care is not so much to enable patients to return to normal society as to attempt to help them to develop to the greatest extent possible such rudimentary skills as they possess. This includes providing assistance in the tasks of everyday living such as washing, dressing and eating, speech and movement, and teaching simple crafts and skills that can do something to enrich the quality of the life they can lead. This can help to relieve the burden on their families or on the health and social services that have to look after them.

In Britain there have for many years been non-residential establishments known as Adult Training Centres, provided and run by the local authorities, with workshops where mentally handicapped 'trainees' are organised to undertake simple contract work, often of a highly repetitive nature such as assembling components or packing, sometimes for almost the rest of their lives.

1	staff rooms
2	laboratories
3	staff cloaks
4	boilers
5	kitchen
6	day rooms
7	observation
8	playroom
9	training
10	teacher
11	three-bed room
12	four-bed room
13	single bed room
14	mother and child
15	laundry
16	toilets/bathrooms
17	paved play area
18	grassed play area

Hilda Lewis House, a residential unit for mentally handicapped children at the Bethlem Royal Hospital, Beckenham, Kent. Designed to accommodate 24 children, some of them long stay, the main purpose of the unit was to carry out research into their treatment and care. The residential part of the building consists of a central toilet area (for reasons of incontinence) with bedrooms and dayrooms grouped around it. The dayrooms are separated by sliding screens to allow flexibility of groupings. Architects: Grahame Herbert Associates

More recently there have been pressures to change these Centres into something more positive and constructive so that they offer the opportunity of education in social skills and independent living together with greater freedom of choice of occupational programmes and a closer integration with the local community.

Relatively few of the mentally handicapped are incapable of learning anything. Most can be taught to look after themselves to some degree and many can achieve simple occupations which are useful. In all societies some mentally handicapped people, whether children or adults, live with their families, but there will always be some whose families cannot sustain the burden continuously or who have no family to support them. For these some form of residential care is necessary.

Residential homes for the mentally handicapped

Today's approach is the antithesis of the huge and intimidating asylum, with its atmosphere of a gaol. The aim is for small institutions, broken down into units of domestic character. In these surroundings most of the patients can usually be trained to identify themselves with such places and to perform simple basic domestic activities. The staff can work in congenial surroundings, which relieves some of the considerable strain to which they are exposed. Unlike the remote asylum, on which society has turned its back, these small units will be sited

The playroom at Hilda Lewis House, which opens on to a paved play area behind the wall in the foreground

0 ————————— 20 ft
0 ————————— 6 m

1 general activities/dining	4 store	7 staff toilet
2 staff	5 boilers	8 six-bed room
3 dirty utility	6 patients' toilet	9 bath

A unit designed to be linked to existing facilities at Northfields Hospital. It is for severely mentally handicapped people, all of whom have great difficulties of mobility and most of whom are in wheelchairs. Three six-bed spaces cluster round a central dining and general activity area off which are the staff and ancillary rooms. Meals are trolleyed from the main building and there is no separate servery. Each bed has its own corner, the island ones formed by low screens, and all patients' spaces have direct access to the open air. Architects: Derek Stow and Partners

whenever possible in places where they are in touch with the community.

Opinions differ, but it is probably true to say that much current thinking today would restrict the size of new residential accommodation for the mentally handicapped to between 100 and 200 beds at the very most. However, it is recognised in the UK and elsewhere that conditions cannot be changed rapidly without a massive financial injection. This means the inherited building stock of the large old institutions, and their occupants, will remain with us for some time to come, however much we would like to be able to do without them. Even with present restrictions on capital expenditure much can be done with existing buildings.

The aim is to reduce their overcrowding, to break them down into smaller nursing units, and to increase their amenities without adding unduly to their physical size. In parallel with this, new provisions tend to be in the form of residential homes that are domestic in conception, some of them small and local enough for the handicapped to be cared for reasonably near their families. It is in this direction that the most interesting developments have taken place in recent years.

For those who have to leave their family but do not need the special medical or nursing care that a hospital provides the British government paper of 1971, '*Better Services for the Mentally Handicapped*', envisaged small residential homes, usually for residents of both sexes. These would house twenty-five adults or twenty children (but many of them less than this) where staff and residents could become a substitute family group. It was considered that most of the adults should have single bedrooms and that no rooms should contain more than four beds.

Northfields mentally handicapped unit. The link to the main hospital is on the left: this elevation is at the right-hand side of the plan above.

Architects: Derek Stow and Partners

1	day space	8	sister	15	cleaner
2	quiet	9	toilets	16	store
3	dining	10	bath	17	staff toilet
4	kitchen	11	shower		
5	four-bed room	12	staff room		
6	single-bed room	13	dirty utility		
7	linen	14	calorifier		

An adult residential unit for the mentally handicapped at Chase Farm Hospital, Enfield, housing two groups of 14 residents, each with day spaces and dining areas. There are five residential units for adults, two for children, and a day centre

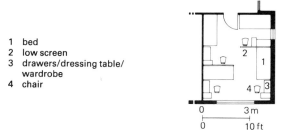

1 bed
2 low screen
3 drawers/dressing table/
  wardrobe
4 chair

Typical bedroom arrangement at Chase Farm Hospital. Each adult bed is in a corner, with its own storage for clothes and personal belongings. Architects: Stillman and Eastwick-Field

1 single bed
2 wash/toilet
3 disposal
4 four-bed room
5 store
6 living area
7 dining
8 kitchen
9 rest room
10 waiting
11 cleaner
12 office

One of four residential buildings for mentally handicapped adults at Lightwood House, Norton, Sheffield. Each building is divided into two 'houses' for twelve people, sharing a kitchen. Covered ways link the residential buildings to a 15-place Day Centre: this is arranged around a large social area with facilities for training in physical mobility, and contains suites of inter-communicating teaching spaces, a central kitchen, consultants' rooms and administration. Architects: Hutchison, Locke and Monk

The central social area at Lightwood House, lofty enough to permit climbing equipment, showing the link to the teaching spaces and residential buildings. (Photo: Richard Bryant)

A day care centre
B patients' residence
C staff residences and garages

Residential unit for forty-eight mentally handicapped adults at Boston, Lincolnshire, comprising two residential buildings for patients, a day care centre planned to accommodate in addition sixteen patients from the neighbourhood, and ten separate staff houses. Garden walls separate the patients' territory from the staff and public areas. Architects: Architects' Co-Partnership

1	living room	10	four-bed room
2	dining/activity	11	single bed room
3	kitchen	12	cloaks
4	wheelchairs	13	staff room
5	toilet	14	office
6	bath, shower and toilet	15	cleaner
7	disposal	16	courtyard
8	linen	17	patients' residence
9	two-bed room	18	day care centre

One of the two residential buildings for twenty-four patients at Boston. It is divided into two social groups of twelve, each with its own living and eating area but sharing a kitchen/servery. Bedroom areas are further subdivided into units of six, with their own sanitary accommodation and linen storage. All bedroom units and living areas have access to sheltered courtyards, and the building is linked to the day centre by an enclosed walkway

Health and local authorities have responded to the concept of residential homes in different ways. Although most people are agreed that large institutions are undesirable, the problem is how to organise care for large numbers of people when only relatively small resources are available.

To some extent size may depend upon the degree of handicap. At one end of the scale accommodation has been provided in only slightly modified houses of truly domestic size, either specially built or converted for the purpose, closely integrated with an existing community. At the other end of the scale larger and more self-sufficient establishments have been constructed, centred around more specialised facilities. Although composed of 'houses' of relatively domestic size these units nevertheless have some of the characteristics of the large establishment, albeit in a more humane form. The fact that their architectural character strives to avoid the

traditional atmosphere of an 'institution', sometimes successfully, does not necessarily neutralise the organisational regimes that their administrative conception implies.

The larger residential homes for adults provide about 100 beds, with a central place for day care that may serve, in addition, a few handicapped people from the district, and with nearby residential accommodation for staff. Whilst many people would prefer to restrict living units to between six and eight handicapped people there

1	reception	20	locomotion/adventure
2	wheelchairs	21	cleaner
3	shop	22	joinery and store
4	telephone	23	dirty linen
5	administration	24	industrial therapy
6	visitors' toilet	25	disposal
7	housekeeper	26	patients' toilet/bath or shower
8	psychologist/testing	27	dressmaking
9	patients' toilet	28	basketwork
10	training organiser	29	pottery
11	treatment	30	boilers
12	consultant	31	education
13	interview	32	individual tuition/therapy
14	seminar	33	staff change
15	nursing administration	34	staff room
16	domestic training	35	staff coffee/sandwiches
17	kitchen	36	staff dining
18	day patients' dining	37	housekeeping store
19	social area	38	kitchen

The day care centre at Boston. Four wings relate to the central entrance hall and activity space: one for visitors, administration, consultation and treatment, a second for kitchen and staff amenities, a third for relatively heavy or noisy industrial and woodworking therapy, and a fourth, which leads to the patients' residential accommodation, for education and light occupational therapy. Residents have meals in their own buildings, trolleyed from the kitchen. Day patients eat in the dining room off the central activity space. Architects: Architects Co-Partnership

0   10 m
0   32 ft

A teaching space at Lightwood House. (Photo: Richard Bryant)

1 patients' cloaks
2 male staff
3 female staff
4 office/overnight stay
5 waiting
6 toilet
7 shower
8 bath
9 wheelchairs
10 day area
11 quiet room
12 sister/charge nurse
13 OT store
14 servery/washup
15 dining/occupational therapy
16 plant
17 six-bed room
18 single bedroom
19 nurses' station
20 preparation
21 disposal
22 sluice
23 clothes
24 utility
25 equipment
26 domestic service room

One of eight 30-bed 'cottages' for the mentally handicapped at Kirklands Hospital, Lanarkshire. All the six-bed rooms and single rooms have toilets en suite and are grouped around a nurses' station.
Architects: Scottish Health Services, Common Services Agency Building Division

1   bedroom
2   shower
3   toilet
4   bath
5   sitting area
6   dining
7   kitchen
8   bar
9   laundry
10 staff bedroom
11 staff bath
12 staff lockers
13 staff

Bingham residential centre for 24 mentally handicapped adults with a moderate degree of handicap, some of whom will be in wheelchairs. It is part of a residential estate where there are community facilities. Each of the two smaller units in the group of three 'bungalows' has a kitchen and dining/sitting area. The long stay and short stay wings in the larger unit are grouped with a central kitchen and dining room, and a bar which is open to visitors. All bedrooms are single. Architect: H. T. Swain, County Architect, Nottinghamshire County Council

Bungalows at Bingham residential centre. The larger communal unit containing dining room and bar is in the background. (Photo: Terry Cotterill)

1	bedroom	6	store
2	bath	7	utility
3	toilet	8	office
4	living/dining	9	staff cloaks
5	kitchen	10	staff room

0 ———————————— 15 m
0 ———————————— 50 ft

seems little doubt that the basic residential groups should not exceed about twelve; in some cases two 'houses' for groups of this size are joined to share a kitchen.

Because physical disability is a major constraint, the house for each group is generally on one floor only, with access to garden space outside. The building is arranged as normally as circumstances permit around a comfortable living room and dining area, with bedrooms containing from one to four beds. They aim to be domestic in character, with storage for personal belongings, and to be generously planned with easily accessible bathrooms and toilets. Units of this nature are linked to a centre for day care, and it is accepted that it is desirable that the handicapped should move to such a centre daily rather than have everything artificially at hand within a single building, as happens in so many institutions. Detailed planning must recognise the requirements imposed by the wheelchair and that some of the residents, although not chairbound, will at times need the assistance of another person to perform quite simple activities. Designers must also take account of the considerable difficulties presented by incontinence, which demand adequate and strategically placed toilets and showers, and pose special problems in the selection of finishes and methods of cleaning.

The function of a day centre in such a community is both social and educational, and is likely to be combined with administration and a central kitchen. It will include craft rooms and a laundry available to residents and day patients from the district. Its principal space, around which the life of the centre may well revolve, will probably be a major area equipped with gymnastic apparatus for physical activities and physiotherapy. This area can also be used for social functions, entertainments, parties and dances.

Residential households

In the UK there have been developments that provide care in even smaller residential units and rely to a lesser extent on centralised activities and institutionalised arrangements. There are examples of units for small households, arranged around a living room and dining room, with a kitchen and utility room planned on the assumption that the residents will prepare some of their own meals and do their own housework, and that to as

Chilwell Residential Centre houses 16 mentally handicapped adults of moderate degree handicap who use the nearby Chilwell Education Centre. It is in a residential area. Each of its four linked houses has four single bedrooms and its own entrance porch, living/dining room and kitchen. Whilst each house has its own sense of identity staff can pass from one to another, but unlike the earlier housing at Bingham, meals and social facilities are not centralised. Within an institution that aims not to feel like one the mentally handicapped are encouraged to be self-sufficient. Architect: H. T. Swain, County Architect, Nottinghamshire County Council

1	living room	13	toilet
2	dining	14	bath
3	kitchen	15	store
4	utility	16	single bedroom
5	goods/dirty entrance	17	double bedroom
6	staff toilet	18	courtyard
7	dirty linen		
8	refuse		
9	linen		
10	plant		
11	shower		
12	garden store		

0 ———————————— 9 m
0 ———————————— 30 ft

A house plan for the mentally handicapped in South West Wales. Each house is for eight residents. A variety of single and double bedded rooms or three bedded spaces divided by screens is possible, centred on their own day time accommodation and with access to a courtyard. All meals are served in the house. Breakfast and evening meals are made in the kitchen and staff and patients eat and wash up together whenever possible. Patients are encouraged to do their own laundry in the utility room. Architect: W. H. Simpson, Welsh Health Technical Services Organisation, Welsh Hospital Board

A group of three of the houses shown on p. 139. These single storey
domestic buildings are situated as part of the community, on hospital
sites in towns. Standard house plans can be combined in various ways
to produce layouts enclosing sheltered courtyards. Each site houses
about thirty-two patients and incorporates a therapy room which also
serves as a community hall

Courtyard of one of the residential buildings for mentally handicapped
adults at Boston, Lincolnshire. Architects: Architects Co-Partnership.
(Photo: Peter Nixon)

great an extent as possible residents and staff will function as a family that lives, works and eats together. Units on this scale, which can be aggregated if local needs demand it, are more likely to be able to provide care that is geographically close to the family of the mentally handicapped and to offer opportunities for a more normal relationship with the local community.

The severely handicapped can behave in ways that can be extremely disturbing, making great demands on the people who look after them. Although staff numbers may be high the staff are often faced with situations which are very difficult to contain. The planning of residential units must take this into account, particularly if the category of residents is likely to give rise frequently to disruptive behaviour that will communicate itself to others and get out of hand. Open plans of both work and living areas need rigorous scrutiny from this point of view. In the case of the most severely handicapped, a disturbance can spread like wildfire. It may thus be desirable to be able to contain small numbers of residents in separate spaces where one or more members of staff can shut the door and deal with a situation before it infects a larger group.

Whether care is in the hands of nurses or, as some people now suggest, of residential care staff, looking after the mentally handicapped is probably the most demanding of all forms of 'nursing'. It is also inevitable that it requires a very high ratio of staff to handicapped residents. For this reason it is arguable that very small and self-contained domestic units, for all their virtue, may present problems when staff is difficult to recruit, train and retain (as it is in all branches of medicine, whether in the developed or the developing world).

Although a one-to-one ratio of staff may be desirable for the most severely subnormal patients it is not usually possible to provide this degree of attention. Both for this category and for the less severely handicapped it is generally necessary to stretch resources further. Because the small and virtually independent 'family' house may present problems in this respect there are likely to be practical advantages if such small domestic units are related in a way that allows staff to be shared between them to some degree without the units losing their own identities.

If staff have the opportunity of sharing the territories of adjacent units and of acquiring some personal knowledge of adjoining residents it should make staff movement between one unit and another easier and more effective in an emergency, or when there is some temporary hiatus in staff numbers.

10

Care of the elderly

Improvements in living conditions and sanitation, the supply of uncontaminated water, the virtual elimination of killing epidemics and the extension of primary health care not only save people from an early death but also help them to live on into old age. And advances in medical science, particularly in the industrialised countries of the western world, have enabled an increasing number of the elderly to reach old age in tolerable comfort. The heart, for example, may still be doing its job thanks to a by-pass operation or a hip still be permitting mobility thanks to mechanical engineering. In 1900 only 4% of the population in Britain was over 65. This has now increased to over 15% and by the year 2000 will probably have reached 20%. In 1976 only one in 104 patients in National Health Service hospitals were over 85 years of age; by the end of the century it is predicted that this proportion will have increased to one in 64. In Britain over the next 40 years the number of people over 85 is expected to double.

Not all the handicaps of ageing are curable, but some of them can be ameliorated so that the elderly can continue to live with dignity, a sense of identity, and often with a degree of independence. Continuous family support is frequently not available, or not practicable. The extended family, perhaps even the family itself, is on the wane. Working mothers are not at home to keep an eye on grandmothers suffering from difficulties of

movement, incontinence or dementia. In Britain these factors have led to a variety of provision for the care of the elderly, a hierarchy of residential care where they may live with domestic and perhaps nursing support, and also day centres which they can visit regularly.

Geriatric day hospitals

Many elderly, including the disabled and those recovering from illness, are able to live in their own homes as members of the community, or in homes for the elderly, and are sufficiently mobile to visit a day unit and benefit from organised therapy which can help them to cope with their disabilities and to manage their everyday tasks. A few elderly people may be able to reach such a unit independently but most are collected at their homes and

1	reception	15	staff rest room
2	waiting	16	female staff toilets
3	dining/waiting	17	coats
4	dining	18	interview
5	occupational therapy/dining	19	speech/dental/ophthalmic
6	rest	20	hair/chiropody
7	kitchen and utility	21	store
8	servery	22	physiotherapy office
9	bedroom	23	OT office
10	consulting/examination	24	physiotherapy cubicles
11	baths and toilet	25	physiotherapy exercise
12	treatment	26	terrace
13	dirty utility	27	lawn
14	office	28	boilers and tanks

A geriatric Day Hospital for fifty patients in the grounds of Ellesmere Hospital, Walton-on-Thames. Four zones for different activities are arranged around a small central courtyard, with access to sheltered lawns and terraces outside the building. Except for the areas for individual therapy, physiotherapy exercise and clinical work the circulation space, although defined, is not separated from the relatively intimate bays which adjoin it. Architects: Derek Stow and Partners

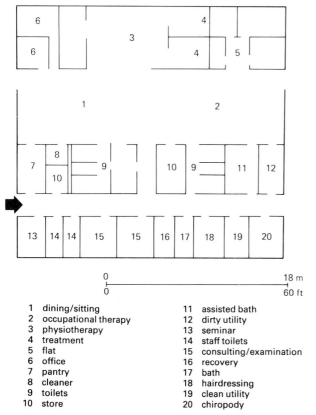

1	dining/sitting	11	assisted bath
2	occupational therapy	12	dirty utility
3	physiotherapy	13	seminar
4	treatment	14	staff toilets
5	flat	15	consulting/examination
6	office	16	recovery
7	pantry	17	bath
8	cleaner	18	hairdressing
9	toilets	19	clean utility
10	store	20	chiropody

The ground floor of a standard geriatric unit providing day accommodation for 50 patients (with in-patient accommodation on the upper floor). Vertical circulation is separate, outside the entrance, designed to suit the requirements of the particular site, and can if necessary form the link to a second unit. Architect: R. G. Brown, North Western Regional Health Authority returned to them at the end of the day in small 'buses provided by the ambulance service or by volunteers using their own transport.

Day facilities for this purpose in Britain are normally attached to general hospitals; but they are usually built as separate units with their own identity, not merely because they may be new extensions to an existing establishment but principally because in function and atmosphere they profit from a sense of independence.

They are likely to provide places for about fifty elderly people and to work a five-day week. In addition to medical attention they offer physiotherapy and occupational therapy, the opportunity for chiropody and hairdressing, sociability and mutual assistance and a communal meal. On a small and relatively domestic scale, with particular attention to the needs of the elderly, the accommodation they provide is not unlike that of the department of physical medicine in a general hospital.

Ellesmere Day Hospital. The occupational therapy area, with the central courtyard on the right. (Photo: Richard Einzig)

Ellesmere Day Hospital. The main entrance, with a large canopy to shelter patients arriving and departing by ambulance. (Photo: Richard Einzig)

1 reception
2 shop
3 office
4 hairdresser
5 chiropodist
6 community development worker
7 social worker
8 toilet
9 district nurse/health visitor
10 occupational therapy
11 ADL kitchen
12 ADL bath
13 ADL bedroom
14 laundry
15 workshop
16 physiotherapy
17 clinic
18 assisted bath
19 speech therapy
20 sitting/dining
21 kitchen
22 nurses' office
23 dirty utility
24 clean utility
25 dentist
26 seminar room
27 staff room

The Whittington Centre, Streatham, London. A small day centre on a suburban site, given coherence by its fully glazed circular corridor enclosing a secluded central garden. Architect: Edward Cullinan

1	reception	11	office
2	female patients' cloaks	12	ADL kitchen
3	male patients' cloaks	13	ADL bathroom
4	male staff toilet	14	ADL bedroom
5	female staff toilet	15	quiet room
6	toilet	16	OT store
7	sister	17	physiotherapy
8	day/dining room	18	office
9	pantry	19	store
10	occupational therapy	20	speech therapy

21	office
22	examination room
23	consulting room
24	linen
25	bath
26	clean utility
27	treatment
28	dirty utility
29	dressing room
30	cleaner
31	courtyard

Geriatric day hospital at North Cambridgeshire Hospital, Wisbech, part of an extension that includes geriatric wards linked to the main hospital building. It provides 40 day places, some of which are for in-patients prior to discharge. The day/dining room and occupational therapy spaces are divided by movable screens. The latter space adjoins an Aids to Daily Living flat. Physiotherapy opens on to an exercise courtyard. Architect: A. A. Crampin, Regional Architect, East Anglian Regional Health Authority

The form that the accommodation takes may vary, from a simple central area for the communal activities of dining and occupational therapy around which are grouped the individual rooms for specialised functions, to more complex configurations in which the communal spaces are broken down into a variety of areas for relatively small groups of people.

Whatever the arrangements the space for physiotherapy is likely to be separated to some extent and to comprise both an open floor for exercises and some bays for individual treatment. There is usually a flat with bedroom, kitchen and bathroom where everyday domestic jobs can be relearnt, known as 'Aids to Daily Living' (ADL). Toilets need to be well distributed and easy to reach, large enough for wheelchair use and for staff to help a patient, with outward opening doors. An assisted bath is essential.

Residential care

Residential care has been developed principally, but by no means entirely, by voluntary bodies, sometimes with government support. Since 1980 in Britain the growth in the number of private residential and nursing homes has been stimulated by government policy, which has increased supplementary benefit payments to much higher levels than previously. Private provision for the elderly and physically disabled has trebled. The total provision of institutional care for the elderly is now almost equally balanced between the public and independent sectors, and if present trends continue the latter will become the principal provider. Not surprisingly the geographical incidence is uneven, with the heaviest concentration along the southern coast of England.

Under the Registered Homes Act of 1984 all private homes for the elderly are obliged to register and are subject to inspection. A home providing purely residential care for four or more people must be registered by the Local Authority. Such a home will offer accommodation, meals, communal facilities and personal care such as assistance with bodily functions if needed. But if one or more people living there is ill and needs nursing care the home must be registered by the District Health Authority. As the distinction between residential care and nursing care may be unclear it may be helpful to describe the latter.

Proposal for an Extra Frail and Geriatric Day Unit in an urban area, for the West Lambeth Health Authority. It provides bedsitting rooms and medical care for 24 extra frail elderly residents and a separate day unit. Each bedsitting room has direct access to outdoors. The day unit is on two floors, served by a lift. The upper floor includes a gym, hairdressing, chiropody, a room for meetings and speech therapy, and a room for the social workers. The dining room is shared by residents and day patients. Architects: Hutchison, Locke and Monk

1 extra frail entrance
2 geriatric day unit entrance
3 dayroom
4 dentistry
5 consulting room
6 dirty utility
7 toilet
8 secretary
9 laundry
10 manager
11 kitchen
12 dining
13 bedsitting room
14 tea area
15 dirty utility
16 clean utility
17 bath
18 seminar
19 cleaner
20 linen

Nursing care

The National Association of Health Authorities has defined the need for nursing care as when a resident's general health deteriorates to a level that needs constant nursing care and when one or more of the following procedures is required periodically over 24 hours: the administration of medicines by injection; dressings to an open or closed wound; artificial feeding requiring nursing skills; basic nursing care of the type given to the bedfast or predominantly bedfast; frequent attention as a result of double or single incontinence; intensive rehabilitative measures following surgery or debilitating disease which is likely to continue for more than a short period; management of complex prosthesia or appliances.

However, there can be dual registration under both residential and nursing categories. The elderly do not necessarily fall neatly into one or the other; some need nursing care at some times and many will eventually need it continuously. If they move into a homely institution for their declining years it seems preferable that if possible they should remain there and not be uprooted. Thus the range of accommodation for the elderly is various, with many gradations from sheltered housing at one end of the spectrum to the hospice at the other. In this chapter we are principally concerned with buildings in which there is a degree of nursing support.

Standards for nursing homes

Because the registration and inspection of an independent nursing home is the responsibility of the local health

1 hospital street
2 bathroom
3 linen
4 cleaner
5 single-bed ward
6 two-bed ward
7 four-bed ward
8 assisted toilet
9 nurses' base
10 pantry
11 sister
12 day room and dining
13 quiet room
14 staff toilet
15 disposal
16 dirty utility
17 clean utility
18 courtyard
19 entrance to communal area

Two of the ten-bed units at the Tonna Hospital for the psycho-geriatric in West Glamorgan. Four such units on each side of a central street provide 80 beds. There is also a large communal area off which open a café servery, clothing shop, hairdresser and dispensary. The single storey building has hipped and gabled roofs. At the offsets in the street and at the centre of the units by the nurses' base and the sister's room rectangular pyramids with clerestorey windows rise above the main roof. All units surround courtyards to which they have access, and all dayrooms open on to enclosed patio areas around the serrated perimeter of the building. Architect: William H. Simpson, Chief Architect, Welsh Health Common Services Authority

0 ____ 30 ft
0 ____ 10 m

authority, the National Association of Health Authorities in England and Wales publishes a handbook of guidance on the standards expected. This handbook, incidentally, also covers a wider variety of establishments in the independent sector, all classified under the Act as 'nursing homes', and ranging from those for the elderly to large acute general hospitals.

The Association's recommendations are useful guide-lines, and are not mandatory directions. They apply, of course, not only to new buildings but to old ones put to nursing use. They suggest that the location should as far as practicable be free from noise, environmental pollution and heavy traffic, with easy access for ambulances and other vehicles. It may be added that it can be a disadvantage if the location is too isolated; the ambulant elderly can benefit from being near shops and other manifestations of a social life.

As to standards of space, a minimum of 8 m^2 per patient is suggested for multi-bed rooms and 10 m^2 for single-bed rooms, with 2.3 m^2 per patient for sitting rooms used by the ambulant. The latter is an absolute minimum of communal space, for there should be adequate day space for private and individual occupa-tions and an area suitable for physiotherapy and other remedial activities. Guidance is also given on minimum sanitary provision, namely a washbasin in each patient's

room or one basin to 8 patients, one bath to 8, and one WC to 8 if separate from the bathroom or one to 6 if combined with it. There should also be a basin with elbow action taps in each ward for the use of medical and nursing staff, and sluicing facilities for cleansing and if necessary sterilising soiled articles including bedpans and commodes. Staff must have separate toilet facilities and their own dining and rest room, and there need to be changing rooms for non-resident staff.

1 wheelchairs and trolleys
2 office
3 sister
4 assisted baths
5 waiting
6 assisted toilet
7 staff cloaks
8 cleaner
9 ward pantry
10 hairdresser
11 store
12 disposal
13 single bedroom
14 eight-bed ward
15 day/dining room
16 conservatory quiet room
17 nurses' base
18 linen
19 dirty utility
20 clean utility
21 treatment room
22 assisted shower
23 nursing officer
24 plant
25 link

One of two 20-bed wards in a single storey unit for the care of the elderly, situated in the grounds of Aberdare General Hospital in Mid Glamorgan, with a link to the main buildings and to a potential geriatric day hospital. The plan of the wards is derived from those at the earlier Mold Community Hospital illustrated in Chapter 2, but with some changes following an operational appraisal by the Medical Architecture Research Unit of the Polytechnic of North London. Architect: William H. Simpson, Chief Architect, Welsh Health Common Services Authority

1 single room
2 two-bed room
3 bath
4 disabled toilet
5 window seat
6 basins
7 hanging cupboard and storage

Proposal for upgrading bedrooms at the Goldsmiths nursing home, Highgate London, which was originally built in the early 1960s on the assumption that most residents would be able to walk and would not need toilet assistance. All now need assistance, most are in wheelchairs, and individual or double rooms are preferred to wards. The small rooms on one side of the corridor were single bedrooms. Bay windows with seats, built-in storage, hanging cupboards and basins have been added. The larger rooms were four-bed wards and are converted to double rooms with similar bay windows and storage peninsula. A bathroom and disabled toilet are incorporated, accessible from the corridor. Architects: Douglas Stephen and Partners

The degree of dependency of the elderly will vary considerably: some will be ambulant and able to look after themselves to some extent, others will need wheelchairs or walking frames, others may be primarily bedfast. Some are likely to be mentally confused, others visually handicapped. The degree of dependency will clearly determine the design, but in general all patient areas should be accessible for wheelchairs and stretchers. Ramps and other strategic locations should have handrails, floor finishes should be easy to clean (notably if these are carpets) and strong floor patterns which the visually handicapped can mistake for obstructions should be avoided. Bathrooms should have non-slip floors. Baths are likely to need space on both sides for nurse assisted bathing, and the need for mechanical aids for lifting must be foreseen. Because of the likelihood of incontinence the routes from bedrooms and sitting areas to WC's should be short and direct.

In spite of these precautions it is likely that ambulant patients will be encouraged to go out freely, and shopping expeditions may be organised for the more dependent. Their leisure occupations and hobbies are likely to be encouraged, and there should be appropriate facilities for them. Above all, their surroundings should be domestic in character; many will have treasured personal possessions and others will bring in items of their own furniture. The opportunity for them to retain their individuality is of great importance.

A hospital street
B entrance to dispensary
C entrance to elderly and severely mentally infirm day hospital
D entrance to geriatric day hospital
E link to rehabilitation department
F sheltered garden

0   5m

1 wheelchairs and linen
2 reception
3 waiting
4 dining/sitting
5 occupational therapy
6 physiotherapy exercise
7 toilet
8 cleaner
9 staff cloaks
10 clean utility
11 shower/toilet
12 bath/toilet
13 enema/toilet
14 dirty utility
15 seminar
16 store
17 nurses
18 examination
19 interview
20 consulting
21 quiet room
22 pantry
23 office

Geriatric Day Hospital at Cannock Community Hospital, Staffordshire, for the West Midlands Regional Health Authority. The main entrance to the hospital is on the right and the Rehabilitation Department on the left. The plan of the EMSI Day Hospital on the opposite side of the hospital street is similar. Architects: Denys Lasdun Peter Softley and Associates

Terminal care

Whatever the degree or nature of health care available to keep people alive and to look after them in old age, or to help them to look after themselves, eventually everyone has to die. Heart disease, stroke and cancer (which alone accounts for one fifth of all deaths in Britain) are now common causes of death. Nearly a third of the deaths occur in people's homes, but the majority die in hospitals or similar institutions where, however sympathetic the medical and nursing team, the accent is necessarily on cure and preserving life rather than on making the process of dying tolerable, and where the pressure of medical routine is unlikely to leave time for adequate psychological support for the patient, the family and the bereaved.

Terminal care has in the past been a characteristic of religious foundations, not surprisingly in view of their theological beliefs and a long tradition of compassion. But with increased longevity there can be little doubt that government will play a greater part, not least by providing financial support.

Hospices

The 'hospice movement', as it is called, is of relatively recent origin. It puts the emphasis on care rather than cure. Mother Frances Dominica of the Helen House Hospice for Children, which was opened in 1982, has said that a hospice is a philosophy rather than a facility. Although a dictionary may still define 'hospice' as a home of rest and entertainment for pilgrims, travellers or strangers or as a home for the destitute, in the context of health care today the word has a different meaning.

The hospice movement as it is now understood in Britain and elsewhere was pioneered by the work of Dame Cicely Saunders, who was instrumental in the foundation of the St. Christopher's Hospice in South London. It was opened in 1967 and was the first hospice in the world to be concerned not only with care for the dying but with teaching and research into the control of pain in terminal illness. Two years after its opening it began a service for caring for terminally ill patients in their own homes, and two years later introduced the first bereavement service to care for patients' families.

At such a hospice the concentration is on care, on concern for the quality of life of the dying patient, or 'guest', and on giving strong emotional support both to the dying and to their family. A characteristic of its medical care is the administration of pain relieving drugs at regular intervals before the unmistakeable need for them arises, thus not only relieving pain but also reducing the anxiety that can make pain worse for both patient and relatives.

Hospices are generally initiated and run by voluntary bodies, some of them religious ones, and are funded from charitable sources. They are complementary to the National Health Service, with which they work in co-operation. Some of them are supported by a Health Authority, perhaps by the gift of surplus land or buildings or by financial grants or a contractual arrangement for beds. There are now some 120 hospices in Britain offering in-patient care, providing a total of about 2300 beds. There are about the same number providing home care only. The running costs are considerable: a 12-bed hospice with day centre and home care can cost about half a million pounds a year. Some face formidable financial difficulties.

Home support, day care and in-patient care

Hospice care can comprise three elements: home support, day care, and in-patient care. Many hospices, but not all, combine all three. The home support element, usually of nurses and medical and other professionals expert in the relief of pain and other symptoms, can advise and support the health service staff in the community and provide counselling and bereavement care. The team may be attached to an in-patient hospice or to the community nursing service, but does not usually provide actual bedside care. It can assess the needs of the patients, liaise with the family practitioner and the community services, and help the patient to remain at home.

Day care provides for those who are being looked after at home but are able to attend the centre – people who need not be in hospital or hospice but can benefit from more help than a family practitioner or hospital out-patient department can provide. The staff will include medical and nursing skills, and perhaps those of an occupational therapist, a physiotherapist and a social worker.

The in-patient element, staffed by a specially trained multidisciplinary team, will necessarily have a high ratio of staff to patients, perhaps as high as 1.5:1. Not all the patients admitted will die in the hospice; some will return home if their symptoms have been adequately controlled, others if they have been admitted temporarily to give a brief respite to those who are looking after them.

St Christopher's Hospice, the first to be purpose-built in Britain, provides 62 in-patient beds and an out-patient clinic and home care service. Relatively few of the subsequent hospices have been newly built. Some are conversions of older buildings, perhaps with extensions. St Christopher's is large in comparison to other hospices; the preferred optimum appears to be between 15 and 25 beds, but many hospices are smaller than this. The greater the number of beds the more difficult it is to create an atmosphere of secure domesticity and avoid the character of an institution.

Accommodation

With buildings for the National Health Service there are elaborate procedures and cost targets, detailed briefs and guidance notes, and for Nucleus hospitals there are fully worked out plans. For a new hospice cost will almost certainly be a major consideration but the formulation of the brief and the design of the building will depend to a far greater extent on the attitudes and experience of the people who are going to run it and on the sympathy, insight and innovative skill of the architect. Each new hospice will be a unique solution. The art of building new hospices is still in its infancy and there is much scope for creative thinking, provided it is generated by an understanding of the needs of the terminally ill.

Twenty-bed plan on the second and third floors of St Christopher's Hospice, Sydenham. The four-bed bays intercommunicate and extend into day space by the windows, from which they can be screened by folding doors. The two-bed rooms can be separated from this space by sliding screens. Architects: Stewart Hendry and Smith

1	day room	6	ward kitchen	10	visitors' room
2	two-bed room	7	patients' bathroom	11	sister's room
3	four-bed room		and toilets	12	treatment room
4	assisted bathroom	8	linen	13	patients' toilets
5	bed lift	9	sluice	14	lift

Eighteen-bed plan at St Gemma's Hospice, Leeds. The four-bed bays are similar to those at St Christopher's with day space by the windows. Bathrooms and toilets are concentrated in one unit. Architects: Stewart Hendry and Smith

1	single-bed room	11	assisted bathroom
2	kitchen	12	toilet
3	drugs	13	bath
4	four-bed room	14	linen
5	interview and night stay	15	staff toilet
6	nurses' station	16	day room
7	sister	17	terrace
8	treatment room	18	chair store
9	sluice room	19	link to Convent
10	equipment store		

Twenty-five bed plan at St Luke's, Sheffield. The five-bed rooms
provide some day space by the windows. Toilets are widely distributed
and there are small washing compartments off the corridor. Architects:
Stewart Hendry and Smith

1   single-bed room
2   toilet
3   bath
4   wash
5   five-bed room
6   nurses' station
7   sister's office
8   sluice room
9   treatment room
10 interview room
11 kitchen
12 cleaner
13 linen
14 trolley bay
15 terrace

As with other buildings for health care the importance
of anticipating growth and change should not be
underestimated. For example there may be no intention
to increase the number of beds beyond those provided
at the outset but it is questionable whether this possibility
should be excluded entirely. Although initially day care
may not be a major element it is unwise to ignore the
implications of its expansion later. The first stage of St
Christopher's consisted in 1967 of the main in-patient
hospice and an old people's home. Since then there
have been additional stages to provide a clinic, a study
centre, nurses' home, crèche, workshops, laundry and
offices. To the original 25-bed unit at St Luke's in
Sheffield was later added a day centre, which was
subsequently expanded by a larger physiotherapy
department and a study centre. In the voluntary sector
success and a high reputation can attract charitable
funds, particularly for enduring capital works.

A hospice should be easily accessible, not only by
motor cars. Some visual contact with passers-by is
appreciated by patients, so integration with a residential
community and proximity to shops can help avoid a
feeling of terminal isolation. In-patients are likely to have
many visitors, at all hours, and day care will attract further
vehicles, so adequate car parking space is important,
not only for staff and home support teams. The entrance
should be welcoming, not self-important and intimidating, and although most people coming in and going out
will do so on foot there needs to be provision for
receiving patients who arrive by ambulance. The
inevitable access to the mortuary for undertakers'
vehicles should be unobtrusive and preferably invisible.

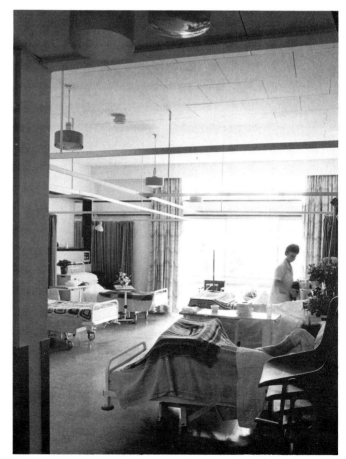

A five-bed room at St Luke's, Sheffield. (Photo: Clive Hicks)

1 entrance hall
2 matron
3 committee room
4 chapel
5 toilet
6 treatment
7 doctor
8 secretary
9 flower bay and volunteers
10 patients' sitting room
11 dispensary
12 overnight/interview room
13 clinical room
14 four-bed room
15 bathroom
16 sluice
17 linen
18 store
19 viewing room
20 dirty linen store
21 single-bed room
22 ward kitchen
23 sister
24 patients' dining room
25 male staff
26 ancillary staff
27 nursing staff
28 nurses' rest room

29 staff dining room
30 kitchen
31 laundry
32 boiler house
33 garage and workshop
34 goods' entrance

St Ann's Hospice, Little Hulton, Worsley, Manchester, provides 30 beds in six four-bed rooms and six single rooms, with the possibility of adding three more four-bed rooms at each end of the building to East and West. There is no specific provision for home support or day care. Each of the four-bed rooms has its own toilet, and all bedrooms open on to a terrace and garden, the four-bed rooms via a day space bay.
Architects: Rod Hackney and Associates

1 reception and day room
2 chapel
3 dining
4 four-bed room and toilet
5 single-bed room and toilet
6 bathroom
7 flowers
8 sister
9 sluice
10 kitchen
11 trolleys
12 chairs
13 linen
14 equipment

15 workshop
16 boiler
17 mortuary
18 viewing room
19 body store
20 laundry
21 kitchen
22 quiet room
23 crèche
24 treatment
25 consulting
26 bath
27 day centre

St Oswald's Hospice, Gosforth, Newcastle upon Tyne has 29 beds, 24 of them in four-bed rooms and the others in single rooms. The four-bed rooms are separated by glazed screens with cupboards below and intercommunicate with one another. All bedrooms have their own toilets. The chapel is off the central day space at the entrance and overlooks a secluded courtyard. There is a 15 place day centre and a crèche, enclosing the entrance forecourt, beyond which there is parking for 40 cars. Upstairs over the day space, dining room and day centre are offices and staff lounge, locker rooms and three bedsitting rooms. All patients' bedrooms open on to terraces and an intimately landscaped garden in which walkways lead to an aviary and a gazebo.
Architects: Jane and David Darbyshire

The ground floor plan of Martin House Children's Hospice, Boston Spa, West Yorkshire. Eight of the ten single bedrooms, where a parent, brother or sister may share the room with the child, open on to a broad terrace. At each end of this range of bedrooms the roofs rise higher, cruciform on plan, and contain at one end the main entrance and communal rooms and at the other the medical treatment rooms and mortuary. On an upper floor within these pyramidal roofs are bedrooms for nurses and the children's familities. Architects: Wildblood MacDonald Partnership

1	lobby		
2	entrance hall		
3	shop		
4	stair		
5	toilet	19	sluice
6	office	20	bathroom
7	lounge	21	assisted bathroom
8	library/quiet room	22	kitchenette
9	activities room	23	dispensary
10	hobbies room	24	bedroom
11	playroom	25	seating area
12	music room	26	nurses' lockers
13	dining room	27	shower
14	kitchen	28	head nurse
15	disabled toilet	29	hydrotherapy room
16	store	30	mortuary
17	dustbin store	31	boiler
18	laundry	32	garage

The mortuary itself will need a viewing room, preferably with a small waiting room and toilet. The means of access to this for the bereaved is important; it is thoughtless to tuck it away amongst stores, disposal rooms and the boiler house.

Garden space with a variety of layout giving opportunities for a sense of intimacy as well as longer prospects is important. It should be easily reached by patients in wheelchairs or with walking difficulties and visible to those who are in bed. Some patients are likely to enjoy tending flowers; raised planters are an advantage to wheelchair users and for those who find it hard to bend down.

Unless the hospice is unusually large it is likely that in a new building all the patients' accommodation, whether for in-patients or day-patients, can be at ground level. This considerably increases the opportunity to create an intimate atmosphere of repose and domesticity, and enables the bedrooms to open directly on to the garden space with easy access. There will, however, be a significant proportion of staff accommodation that can be on an upper floor – offices, meeting rooms and rest rooms, and perhaps one or two bedrooms for visiting relatives. It is also likely that much work will be done by volunteers. They will need office space and somewhere to change. Amongst potential voluntary helpers there will probably be many young mothers; the provision of a crèche can be an important factor in their recruitment.

It should be noted, however, that although the number of in-patients for which the hospice caters may not increase in the future it is the associated accommodation that may need more space if home-based welfare and teaching and study activities expand, which seems to be probable.

Bedrooms are likely to be small, most of the beds probably in bays containing not more than four, perhaps with some sitting space near the window. The opportunity for companionship can be valuable, but it is an advantage in avoiding a feeling of regimentation if each bed can be given a sense of identity, so that the patient can have his or her own territory. Bed curtains will be required, but suspended curtain tracks inevitably give the impression of a hospital ward. Perhaps the possibility should be considered of recessing the tracks in the ceiling or incorporating them in the roof structure if it is exposed.

Some single rooms will be necessary for medical reasons; experience suggests that about 20% of the beds is the right proportion. These single rooms and all toilets need mechanical ventilation to control smells, which can be a nuisance, and it is desirable in the larger bays that the airflow from the windows is controlled to produce a negative pressure.

Wheelchair toilets and a sluice room should be as close to the bedrooms as possible, as should normal and assisted bathrooms. It has been observed that toilets need not be white and clinical but should be warm and cheerful in character, because some patients spend a lot of time in them. Perhaps they should have a bookshelf and some pictures.

Whereas in a hospital the relationship between the beds and the nurses' station can be of some significance

Looking towards the playroom of the Martin House Children's Hospice from the terrace outside the bedrooms

1	reception space
2	chapel
3	courtyard
4	dayroom
5	tea bar
6	dayroom
7	single bedroom with bathroom
8	assisted shower
9	toilet
10	five-bed room

11	bath
12	nurses' station
13	sister
14	ward kitchen
15	treatment
16	sluice
17	family room with bathroom
18	mortuary
19	viewing room
20	interview
21	general office
22	patients' reception
23	home care office
24	pharmacy
25	store
26	office
27	cleaner
28	flowers
29	linen
30	launderette
31	kitchen
32	staff dining
33	boiler room

0   20 m
0   70 ft

The Princess Alice Hospice, Esher, which provides residential care for 26 people suffering from advanced cancer under terminal prognosis, and a home care service. Everyone enters through a large reception space which can be thrown open to the multi-use chapel which has its own private courtyard. The patients' areas enclose a larger courtyard which is overlooked by the main dayroom. There are five single bedrooms, four five-bed rooms and a family room where a married couple or parents with a child can stay. The home care service adjoins the main reception. Medical staff, administrative offices, staff common room and seminar room are on an upper floor over the reception area and the adjoining offices. The hospice is close enough to Esher for the more mobile patients to visit the shops and not feel cut off from the community. *Architects: Hutchison Locke and Monk* in allowing easy observation of most of the ward, and conversely in giving the patients a sense of contact with the nurse, this is unlikely to be thought important in a hospice. Indeed hospices may well dispense with the station altogether. If they have one at all it is more likely to be a room where nursing staff can withdraw for a while for regeneration rather than for observation. A light call system that can lead anyone to the point of origin will probably be thought entirely adequate.

A secure drug store and a treatment room (principally for dressings) will be needed, and a pantry. If the pantry is to be used by patients it may need to be suitable for those in wheelchairs. There will also be a need for a room in which relatives can be interviewed, and a flower room that is preferably more than a small recess in a corridor.

The communal areas will include a lounge and a dining room. The character of these may be open to argument but the atmosphere of a waiting room on the one hand or a commercial cafeteria on the other, so easily produced almost accidentally, is to be avoided. Besides being their main communal spaces the patients will use them for meeting their visitors, and the need for some opportunity of withdrawal and intimacy is desirable. There will also be a chapel, or a 'quiet room' of non-denominational character. All these communal areas must be accessible

The bay window of the main dayroom at the Princess Alice Hospice, overlooking the paved and planted courtyard. (Photo: Graham Challifour)

Ground floor
1 lobby
2 reception
3 information
4 sales
5 dining room
6 quiet room
7 multi-purpose hall
8 toilet
9 lift
10 kitchen
11 laundry
12 goods entrance

0   15m
0   50ft

London Lighthouse at Lancaster Gate, London, completed in 1988, is a 24-bed residential and day care centre for sufferers from AIDS. An old building has been substantially converted internally, two wings have been added at the rear, a lift at the side, and the central part of the frontage has been filled with a projecting bay. The three floors reflect an increasing degree of security: community and public rooms on the ground floor, administration and a variety of counselling rooms on the first, and residential accommodation on the second. A small mezzanine between the ground and first floors includes a mortuary and viewing room, served by the new bed lift and the main stair. The void at the back of the ground floor reception area runs up the whole height of the original façade of the building and is bridged on the floors above for access to the bay on the frontage. Architects: First Architecture

First floor
1 void
2 workshop/group counselling
3 counselling rooms
4 secretarial space
5 office
6 toilet
7 store
8 lift

Second floor
1 void
2 nine-bed room
3 toilet
4 four-bed room
5 three-bed room
6 two-bed room
7 single-bed room
8 day room
9 terrace
10 bath
11 treatment room
12 quiet room
13 staff
14 kitchen
15 clean utility
16 dirty utility
17 lift

by wheelchair and it should be possible to move beds into them easily. They should also have toilets nearby. It is of some importance that throughout the building the clinical character associated with the life-saving hospital should be avoided in every detail, familiar as it will be to many of the patients from their unavailing struggles against illness.

If there is a day centre it is perhaps better seen as a supportive club than as a clinic. Besides giving help with a bath and hairdressing, physiotherapy to relieve aches and improve mobility, and training in home care for relatives, it is likely to offer recreational therapy through which home-based patients can pursue their hobbies and interests and perhaps develop their skills or learn new ones.

AIDS

AIDS has been said to be the major public health issue we have had to face in the world this century.

Although there are now some hospital departments devoted specifically to sufferers there are in Britain as yet few buildings reserved exclusively for this purpose. It may be that in the near future more special hospices will be developed to provide the necessary care. If so they are likely to share the attitudes that characterise the hospice movement generally but to differ somewhat in their planning and accommodation because of the nature of the affliction. Two have now been established in London. Existing hospices are also likely to make provision for AIDS sufferers. By 1989 some 37 were said to be willing to do so.

AIDS (Acquired Immune Deficiency Syndrome) is caused by a virus known as HIV (Human Immune deficiency Virus). The effect of this virus is to impair the patient's immunity to infections and diseases. At present there is no cure. Not all people who are diagnosed HIV positive are affected (in 1987 some 40 000 people were estimated to be HIV positive in Britain) but a proportion will succumb. This proportion has been estimated at about 30%. Most of the maladies that affect those who succumb are fatal. Those who are affected are not predominantly children or the elderly, although these are not immune.

AIDS strikes at the central nervous system and the respiratory and digestive tracts. Some patients will develop severe diarrhoea, or skin lesions and infections of the mucous membrane. They may suffer brain damage leading to confusion, blindness or dementia. Some of these conditions will be infectious and will require the patient's isolation. All conditions, whether terminal or not, will lead to the need for counselling and emotional support for the patients and their families or companions.

It may be premature to assume that independent establishments with distinctive accommodation will become necessary for the victims of AIDS. Perhaps more

general hospitals will make special provision if advances in medical science do not remove the problem itself. In the meantime, however, it seems likely that various organisations, notably voluntary ones, will increasingly respond to the situation.

The requirements for buildings devoted to the needs of AIDS sufferers do not appear to differ fundamentally from those of hospices generally. There may be a greater need for security, but because many victims may be in the prime of life, when acceptance of early death is difficult, the principal difference is likely to be a higher proportion of small rooms for counselling, with somewhat larger ones for seminars and therapy in groups. There will also be a higher proportion of single rooms with toilet, basin and shower *en suite* for reasons of infection control or the seclusion of those suffering from brain damage resulting in disturbed behaviour or dementia. On the other hand, except for those who require isolation, it is argued that communal bedrooms are helpful in encouraging interdependence between patients and avoiding introspection.

London Lighthouse

A pioneer in this new field is the London Lighthouse Centre. It is a support and residential centre which aims to offer an 'integrated range of services to care for people from the initial diagnosis of HIV infection through to providing a loving environment where the terminally ill can die with dignity'. In this building provision is made for counselling, information and training for sufferers from AIDS and their families and friends, and also for statutory and voluntary workers, a home support service, a day centre, and bedroom accommodation with nursing attendance.

Constrained as it was by having to convert and expand premises previously used as a school, but not originally built for that purpose, some of the planning arrangements are perhaps more complicated than would otherwise have been the case, but it has been possible to dispose the accommodation on three floors that reflect an increasing degree of security. Entered past a reception desk the ground floor contains a large multipurpose hall that can be used for exercise, seminars and other gatherings, a quiet room, and a café for up to 100 people which it is hoped to open to people living and working locally. The Community Services team is based on the next floor which contains counselling and training rooms and offices for the administration and supporting personnel. The top floor is the residential unit with 24 beds in rooms containing from one to nine beds and sanitary accommodation *en suite*. The unit also comprises utility and treatment rooms, day rooms and a small kitchen where residents' families and friends can make their own snacks and heat up prepared meals. The aim is to create an atmosphere more like a home than a hospital.

Bibliography

Abel-Smith, B. (1978) *The National Health Service: the first thirty years*, HMSO, London

Allen, R. W. and Karolyi, I. (1976) *Hospital Planning Handbook*, John Wiley and Sons, New York

Baasher, Carstairs, Giel & Hasler (eds) (1975) *Mental Health Services in developing countries* (Papers at a Seminar in Addis Ababa 1973 WHO Offset 22), WHO, Geneva

Baker, Llewelyn-Davies, Sivadon (1959) *Psychiatric service and architecture*, WHO, Geneva

Baynes, K. (ed.) (1971) *Hospital research and briefing problems*, King Edward's Hospital Fund, London

Beales, J. G. (1978) *Sick health centres*, Pitman Medical, London

Bennett, A. E. (ed.) (1974) *Community hospitals: progress in development and evaluation.* Oxford Regional Hospital Board

Bridgman, R. F. (1955) *The rural hospital*, WHO Monograph 22, WHO, Geneva

Calderhead, J. (1975) *Hospitals for people: a look at some new buildings in England*, King Edward's Hospital Fund, London

Carey, D. A. (1986) *Hospice Inpatient Environments*, Van Nostrand Reinhold, New York

Cammock, R. (1973) *Health Centres Handbook*, Borough of Newham and Medical Architecture Research Unit, Northern Polytechnic, London

Cammock, R. (1981) *Primary health care buildings*, Architectural Press, London

Challis, L. and Bartlett, H. (1988) *Old and ill: private nursing homes for elderly people*, Age Concern, London

Chaplin, N. W. (ed.) (1982) *Health Care in the UK*, Kluwer Medical, London

Chaplin, N. W. (ed.) (1988) *Hospital and health services yearbook*, Institute of Health Services Management, London

Conference of Missionary Societies (1975) *A model health centre: working party report by 1972 Medical Committee*, Conference of Missionary Societies in Great Britain and Ireland, London

Culyer and Jonsson (eds) (1986) *Public and private health services*, Blackwell, Oxford

Departments of Health and Social Security. See separate section below

Directory of Hospitals (1988) Churchill Livingstone, Longmans, Harlow

Gainsborough, H. and Gainsborough, J. (1964) *Principles of hospital design*, Architectural Press, London

Gish, O. (1977) *Guidelines for health planners: the planning and management of health services in developing countries*, Tri-Med Books, London

Goldsmith, S. (1984) *Designing for the disabled*, RIBA Publications, London

Ham, C. (1985) *Health Policy in Britain.* Macmillan, London

Heggenhoughen, K. *et al.* (1987) *Community Health workers: the Tanzanian experience*, Oxford University Press, Nairobi

H.M. Government (1989) *Working for patients: the Health Service, caring for the 1990's* (White Paper), HMSO, London

Holroyd, W. H. A. (ed.) (1968) *Hospital traffic and supply problems*, King Edwards's Hospital Fund, London

Home Office (1982) *Draft guide to fire precautions in hospitals*, HMSO, London

Independent Hospitals Association (1988/89) *Directory of Independent hospitals and health services*, Longman, London

James, W. P. and Tatton-Brown, W. (1986) *Hospitals: design and development*, Architectural Press, London

Jamison, T. *et al.* (1984) *China: the Health Sector*, World Bank, Washington DC

Johnson, I. D. A. and Hunter, A. R. (1984) *The Design and utilization of operating theatres* (Royal College of Surgeons symposium), Edward Arnold, London

King, M. (1966) *Medical care in developing countries: a primer on the medicine of poverty*, Oxford University Press, Nairobi

Kleczowski, B. M. and Nilsson, N. O. (1984) *Health care facility projects in developing areas: planning, implementation and operation*, Public Health Paper 79, WHO, Geneva

Kleczowski, B. M. and Piboleau (1976–1985) *Approaches to planning and design of health care facilities in developing areas*, (vols 1–5), WHO, Geneva

Levitt, R. and Wall, A. (1984) The reorganised NHS, 3rd edn, Croom Helm, London

Llewelyn-Davies, R. and Macaulay, H. M. C. (1966) *Hospital planning and administration*, WHO, Geneva

Llewelyn-Davies, R., Weeks *et al.* (1971) *Buildings for mentally handicapped people*, HMSO, London

Medical Architecture Research Unit (1977) *Ward evaluation: St Thomas' Hospital*, MARU, Northern Polytechnic, London

McKeown, S. and Keen, J. (1987) *Impact of Information Technology on the design of future health buildings*, Medical Architecture Research Unit, Northern Polytechnic, London

McLachlan, G. and Maynard, A. (eds) (1982) *The Public/Private Mix for health*, Nuffield Provincial Hospitals Trust

Merrison, A. (1979) *Report of the Royal Commission on the National Health Service*, HMSO, London

Millard, G. (1981) *Commissioning hospital buildings*, 3rd edn, King Edward's Hospital Fund, London

Mills, A. B. (1969) *Functional planning of general hospitals*, McGraw-Hill, New York

National Association of Health Authorities (1987) *Care for the dying: a guide for Health Authorities*, NAHA, Birmingham

National Association of Health Authorities (1985) *Registration and inspection of nursing homes: a handbook for Health Authorities*, NAHA, Birmingham

National Association of Health Authorities/DHSS (1986) *Conference on care for the dying*, HMSO, London

Newell, K. (ed.) (1975) *Health by the people*, WHO, Geneva

Nightingale, F. (1970) *Notes on nursing* (1859 reprinted), Duckworth, London

Norman, A. (1984) *Bricks and Mortals. Design and lifestyle in old peoples' homes*, Centre for Policy on Ageing, London

Nuffield Provincial Hospitals Trust (1955) *Studies in the functions and design of hospitals*, Oxford University Press, London

Nuffield Provincial Hospitals Trust (1963) *Central Sterile supply: principles and practices.* Oxford University Press, London

Oxford Regional Health Board (1970) *The evaluation of a deep ward plan*, Oxford RHB

Paine, L. H. W. and Siem Tjam, F. (1988) *Hospitals and the health care revolution*, WHO, Geneva

Peacock, H. E. A. (1987) *Interstitial space in North American buildings: a research paper*, Building Design Partnership, Preston

Porter, D. R. (1982) *Hospital architecture*, Health Administration Press, Ann Arbor

Pritchard, P. (1981) *Manual of primary health care*, 2nd edn, Oxford University Press, London

Pritchard, P., Low, K. and Whalen, M. (1984) *Management and general practice*, Oxford University Press, London

Pütsep, E. (1973) *Planning of surgical centres*, 2nd edn, Lloyd-Luke, London

Pütsep, E. (1979) *Modern Hospital: International planning practices*, Lloyd-Luke, London

Rawlinson, C. and Mason, G. (1987) *The design implications of caring for people suffering from AIDS*, Medical Architecture Research Unit, Polytechnic of North London, London

Roemer, M. I. (1976) *Health care systems in world perspective*, Health Administration Press, Ann Arbor

Roemer, M. I. (1977) *Comparative national policies on health care.* Marcel Dekker, New York

Royal College of General Practitioners (1983) *General Practitioners' hospitals*, Occasional paper 22, RCGP, London

Saunders, C. *et al.* (eds) (1981) *Hospice: The living idea*, Edward Arnold, London

Smith, H. (1987) *Issues in the registration of private nursing and residential homes*, Project paper 73, King Edward's Hospital Fund, London

Stone, P. (ed.) (1980) *British hospital and health care buildings*, Architectural Press, London

Symons, J. (1987) *Day Care Centres: some developments in England 1970–1980*, Centre on Environment for the handicapped, London

Taylor, H. (1983) *The hospice movement in Britain: its role and its future*, Centre for Policy on Ageing, London

Terry, W. G. and McLaren, J. W. (1973) *Planning a diagnostic radiology department*, W. B. Saunders, London

Thompson, J. D. and Goldin, G. (1975) *The hospital: a social and architectural history*, Yale University Press, New Haven, Ct.

Tucker, H. (1987) *The role and function of Community Hospitals*, King Edward's Hospital Fund, London

University Grants Committee (1987) *University building projects: Notes on control and guidance for medical projects*, UGC, London

Vaisey, J. (1984) *National Health*, Martin Robertson, Oxford
Walt, G. and Melamed, A. (eds) (1984) *Mozambique: towards a people's health service*, Zed Books, London
Willers, J. (ed.) (1980) *Best Buy Hospitals: the MK.1 and MK.2 designs compared*, HMSO, London
Wingate, P. and Wingate, R. (1988) *The Penguin Medical Encyclopedia*, 3rd edn, Penguin, Harmondsworth
World Health Organisation (1975) *Organisation of Mental Health services in developing countries*, Technical report 564, WHO, Geneva
YRM International (1976) *Health buildings in hot climates: a design guide for thermal performance*, DHSS, London
Zeidler, E. H. (1974) *Healing the hospital: McMaster Health Science Centre*, Zeidler Partnership, Toronto

Departments of Health and Social Security

The publications of the Departments of Health and Social Security in Britain are voluminous, but a classified index is published:

Works Guidance Index. An index of current DHSS Building Directorate publications and related information. Revised and reissued annually, about 265 pages. Obtainable from DHSS Leaflets, PO Box 21, Stanmore, Middlesex HA7 1AY

Also available:

Building Law Microfilm. A register of building legislation – design, operations and maintenance. Updated three times a year.

Health Building Notes (formerly *Hospital Building Notes*). Probably most relevant as an introduction. Those still available are listed below, with their HBN number. An asterisk indicates that they are currently in course of revision. All are published by HMSO, London.

1. *Buildings for the health service* (1986)
3.* *The District General Hospital* (1961)
4.* *Ward Units* (1968)
6. *Radiodiagnostic department* (1985)
10. *Catering department* (1986)
12.* *Outpatients department* (1961)
13.* *Central Sterile Supply department* (1961)
15. *Pathology department* (1973)
18. *Administrative department* (1966)
19. *Medical photography and medical illustration* (1966)
20.* *Mortuary and post-mortem room* (1966)
21.* *Maternity department* (1963)
22.* *Accident and Emergency department* (1969)
23. *Hospital accommodation for children* (1984)
25. *Laundry* (1977)
26.* *Operating department* (1967)
27. *Intensive therapy unit* (1974)
28. *Outpatients dental department* (1970)
29. *Pharmaceutical department* (1973)
33. *Rehabilitation centres for psychiatric patients* (1966)
34. *Works departments for district general and teaching hospitals* (1973)
35. *Accommodation for people with acute mental illness* (1988)
36.* *Health centres: interim edition* (1979)
37. *Hospital accommodation for elderly people* (1981)
38. *Accommodation for adult acute day patients* (1982)
39. *Ophthalmic clinic* (1982)
40. *Common activity spaces* (1986) 2 volumes
41. *Accommodation for staff changing and storage of uniforms* (1984)
42. *Accommodation for education* (in preparation)

Articles in British architectural periodicals Dealing with some of the buildings illustrated or mentioned in the text.

A&BN: Architect and Building News
AJ: Architects Journal
AR: Architectural Review
Bldr: Builder
Bldg: Building
RIBAJ: RIBA Journal

Primary care

Bethnal Green Health Centre. *AR*, June 1988
Finsbury Health Centre. *AR*, Jan 1939, June 1988; *A&BN*, 13 Jan 1939; *AJ*, 12 Jan 1939
Highgate Group Practice. *AJ*, 25 March 1987; *AR*, Jan 1984
Lambeth, Community Care Centre. *AJ*, 10 July 1985, 16 Oct 1985; *Bldg*, 13 Sept 1985
Peckham, Pioneer Health Centre. *A&BN*, 29 March 1935; *AJ*, 4 April 1935; *AR*, May 1935; *Bldr*, 12 April 1935
Peckham Surgery. *AJ*, 22/29 Aug 1984
Spitalfields Health Centre. *AJ*, 22/29 Aug 1984
Streatham, Whittington Centre. *AJ*, 23 Oct 1985

Hospitals

Belfast, Musgrave Park. *AJ*, 9 April 1959
Bury St Edmunds (Best Buy). *AJ*, 19 June 1974
Charing Cross (Hammersmith). *AJ*, 28 July 1976
Dundee, Ninewells. *Bldg*, 1 Feb 1974
Ellesmere (Geriatric Day). *AR*, May 1978
Greenock, Larkfield. *A&BN*, 13 Dec 1951; *AJ*, 15 Nov 1951, 21 Feb 1952; *Bldr*, 30 Nov 1951
Greenwich. *AJ*, 26 Nov 1969; *Bldg*, 5 Dec 1969
Harrow, Northwick Park. *AJ*, 2 Feb 1972
High Wycombe. *A&BN*, 12 June 1968; *AJ*, 17 April 1968; *Bldg*, 24 May 1968
London, St Thomas'. *AJ*, 10 Aug 1966, 4 May 1977; *Bldg*, 5 Aug 1966
London, Wellington. *AJ*, 9 Feb 1977; *Bldg*, 26 April 1974, 6 Sept 1974
Maidstone (Nucleus). *AJ*, 21 Sept 1983, 14 Nov 1984; *Bldg*, 9 July 1982
Mold (Community Hospital). *Bldg*, 9 Nov 1974
Newcastle upon Tyne, Royal Victoria. *AR*, June 1965
Nottingham. *Bldg*, 30 March 1979
Slough, Wexham Park. *A&BN*, 4 Dec 1957; *AJ*, 1 Feb, 8 Feb 1967
York. *AJ*, 1 June 1977
Ystradgynlais (Community hospital). *Bldg*, 25 July 1986

Psychiatric

Beckenham and Bexley (Medium secure units). *AJ*, 8 June 1988

Hospices

Gosforth, St Oswald's. *AJ*, 10 March 1982, 25 Feb 1987; *RIBAJ*, Jan 1989
London Lighthouse. *AJ*, 23 Sept 1987; *Bldg*, 19 Aug 1988
Manchester, St Ann's. *AJ*, 10 March 1982

Index

163